65944

SHAW, LADY GREGORY AND THE ABBEY
AND THE ABBEY
A Correspondence and a Record

SHAW, LADY GREGORY AND THE ABBEY

A Correspondence and a Record

edited by
Dan H. Laurence
and
Nicholas Grene

COLIN SMYTHE
Gerrards Cross, 1993

First published in **1993** by Colin Smythe Limited,
Gerrards Cross, Buckinghamshire

British Library Cataloguing in Publication Data
Shaw, Bernard *1856–1950*
Shaw, Lady Gregory and the Abbey : a correspondence
and a record.
1. Drama in English. Shaw, Bernard 1856–1950
I. Title   II. Gregory, *Lady 1852–1932*
III. Laurence, Dan H. *1920–*   IV. Grene, Nicholas *1947–*
822.912

ISBN 0-86140-278-2

Printed and bound in Great Britain by The Cromwell Press

CONTENTS

ILLUSTRATIONS

INTRODUCTION

On 26th March 1897, Lady Gregory attended a meeting of the Irish Literary Society in London to hear a lecture by a young journalist, Frederic Whyte, on 'Irish actors of the century'. The lecture was apparently very bad but, as Lady Gregory noted in her journal, 'the afternoon was redeemed by Bernard Shaw'. Shaw demolished the unfortunate Whyte, pointing out that the actors he had talked about were not Irish:

> As to what an Irishman is, he said, is a complex question; for wherever he may have been born, if he has been brought up in Ireland, that is quite sufficient to make him an Irishman. It is a mistake to think an Irishman has not common sense: it is the Englishman who is devoid of common sense, or at least has so small a portion of it that he can only apply it to the task immediately before him to do. That is why he is obliged to fill the rest of his horizon with the humbugs and hypocrisy that fill so large a part of English life. The Irishman has a better grasp of facts and sees them more clearly; only, he fails in putting them into practice and has a great objection to doing anything that will lead to any practical result. It is also a mistake to think the Irishman has feelings—he has not, but the Englishman is full of feeling. What the Irishman has is imagination; he can imagine himself in the situation of others. But the Irish language is an effete language, and the Irish nation is effete, and as to saying there are good Irish actors, there are not, and there won't be until the conditions in Ireland are favourable for the production of drama—'and when that day comes I hope I may be dead'.[1]

We can see here that what were to become the central ideas of *John Bull's Other Island* were already in Shaw's mind seven full years before it was written. The passage also illustrates his exaggerated hostility at this time towards his own country and its cultural revival. Though Shaw's speech may have enlivened an otherwise unsatisfactory afternoon for Lady Gregory, she can hardly have agreed with the views he expressed. Widowed in 1892, after a twelve-year marriage to the much older Sir William Gregory, a former Governor of Ceylon, Lady Gregory had met Yeats in 1894 and was already enlisted in the service of the revival. She was to visit the Aran islands in May 1898, a visit overlapping that of J.M.Synge, partly to collect folklore for

Yeats, partly to develop her knowledge of the 'effete' Irish language. In 1897, the very year Lady Gregory recorded Shaw's speech in her journal, she, Yeats and Edward Martyn were to draft the manifesto proposing an Irish Literary Theatre, with the aim of creating just those conditions 'favourable for the production of drama' in Ireland that Shaw had hoped would not come until after his death. He was to live another fifty-three years, become a close friend of Lady Gregory and an active if intermittent collaborator with her in the Abbey Theatre. This book is the record both of the friendship and of the collaboration.

What most people recall as Shaw's main connection with the Irish National Theatre was a non-connection—he wrote *John Bull's Other Island* for them and they turned it down. It was Shaw's own account of the rejection of *John Bull* in the preface to the play published in 1907 that conditioned all later views of the incident:

> John Bull's Other Island was written in 1904 at the request of Mr William Butler Yeats, as a patriotic contribution to the repertory of the Irish Literary Theatre. Like most people who have asked me to write plays, Mr Yeats got rather more than he bargained for. ... [The play] was uncongenial to the whole spirit of the neo-Gaelic movement, which is bent on creating a new Ireland after its own ideal, whereas my play is a very uncompromising presentment of the real old Ireland.[2]

There is here, as so often in Shavian rhetoric, a degree of misrepresentation beneath the appearance of the bluntly matter-of-fact. The facts are rather more complicated than Shaw makes them appear. Yeats and Shaw had known one another since 1888, had both been involved with Florence Farr and with Florence Farr's season at the Avenue Theatre in 1894, subsidised by Annie Horniman, the future patroness of the Abbey. It was at the Avenue that Yeats had had his London theatrical début with *The Land of Heart's Desire* and Shaw his first public performance with *Arms and the Man*. Yeats did not, however, initially commission *John Bull*, as Shaw implies; a letter of Yeats to Lady Gregory of 12th March 1900 makes clear that the play was not written at his request: 'I saw Shaw to-day. He talks of a play on the contrast between Irish and English character which sounds amusing'.[3] Shaw by this stage, it seems, was already considering turning the ideas he had expressed at the 1897 Irish Literary Society meeting into dramatic form, but the casualness of Yeats's reference would indicate that there was no question of his commissioning the play. In October 1901, when Yeats was in Dublin preparing for the third season of the Irish Literary Theatre, he did write to Shaw urging him to come over and 'help to stir things up',[4] but there was still no mention of a play to be written specially for the Theatre. Although by December 1902 the possibility had been mooted—'Bernard Shaw talks again of writing a play for us', Yeats wrote to Frank Fay[5]—a letter from Shaw to Yeats of June 1903 includes no suggestion that the projected play was to be written for what had by then become the Irish National Theatre: 'I have it quite seriously in my head to write an Irish play (frightfully modern—no banshees nor leprechauns) when I have finished a book I now have in hand on the succulent subject of Municipal Trading'.[6] *John Bull* was certainly never intended exclusively for Dublin. A production by the Vedrenne-Barker partnership at the London Royal Court Theatre had been planned from the beginning as at least simultaneous with a Dublin performance, and it was Shaw's main consideration through the summer of 1904 when he was writing the play.

If *John Bull* failed to become the inaugural performance of the newly founded Abbey Theatre, as it notionally might have been—the Abbey opened in December 1904—it was not, as Shaw implies in the preface, because the play proved unacceptable to the 'neo-Gaelic movement' in its 'presentment of the real old Ireland'. Although Yeats did not particularly like *John Bull*, calling it 'fundamentally ugly and shapeless' when he finally saw it produced in London,[7] the play was quite genuinely beyond the resources of the company, at that stage composed of a mix of amateur and professional actors accustomed to no more than simple one-act plays. Even so, the Directors did not give up hope of producing it and hung on to their option until May 1905.

Shaw, while acknowledging in his preface that *John Bull* was beyond the practical capacity of the infant Abbey, suggested that the theatre rejected the play as unsympathetic, as too tough-minded and clear-sighted about Ireland to suit the theatre's revivalist notions. Yet in some ways the play can be construed as a genuinely 'patriotic contribution' without the topspin of irony that Shaw seems to intend in the preface. He gave to Larry Doyle many of his own ideas on the differences between English and Irish character, on Irish imagination, on Irish political issues. Moreover, in Larry Doyle also he confronted the ambiguities of his own feelings as an Irish exile (Larry has been away for eighteen years to Shaw's twenty-eight) and produced a deeply incisive analysis of the destructiveness and self-hatred involved, the emotions glimpsed in the outburst against the 'effete' Irish nation witnessed by Lady Gregory in 1897.

Larry, however, is not the only Shavian persona in *John Bull*; in Peter Keegan Shaw created a character to transcend the limitations of Doyle that were the limitations of one part of himself, the Irish exile's conviction of inadequacy and provincialism. What Keegan voices is an ideal of Ireland that is not so far, after all, from the ideals of Yeats and the revival. His talk of Ireland as 'holy ground' is endorsed by Shaw at one point in the preface: ' "The island of the saints" is no idle phrase. Religious genius is one of our national products; and Ireland is no bad rock to build a Church on'.[8] Shaw was not altogether immune from the Messianic belief of the Irish literary revival in Ireland's special spiritual and cultural destiny. Keegan's final 'dream of a madman' is of a 'country where the State is the Church and the Church the people: three in one and one in three'. Though this is an integral part of Shaw's vision, it can also be read as a Shavian version of Yeats's most cherished ideal of the early revival period, the ideal of Unity of Culture.

John Bull is not as unidealistic, as anti-nationalist an Irish play as Shaw would in the preface have us believe, but at the time of writing he remained estranged from Ireland and distanced from the theatre movement. It was not until 1905, the year after *John Bull*, that he paid his first return visit to Ireland—largely at the insistence of his wife Charlotte, who was always more devoted to Ireland than he was—and it was not until 1908 that he overcame his Dublin phobia sufficiently to go back to the city where he was born. His description of that return, recorded by Lady Gregory in *Seventy Years*, is very suggestive of his feelings:

> He spoke of Dublin and the dislike he had had to re-visiting it, and how at last he had come in a motor, and hadn't minded coming in, as it were, by the back door. It looked to him just as before, the houses had never been painted since, and the little shops had eggs in the windows, with mice and rats running over them, and rubbish that looked as if on its way to the dust heap.

In 1908 only the very wealthy had their own 'motor', and driving into Dublin was evidently some sort of reassurance for Shaw of the success he had achieved since his departure. Still, the sordidness, the poverty, the provincial slovenliness which he had been escaping in moving to London were still there. For a Protestant Dubliner of the 'downstart', the shabby-genteel class, the acting of the Irish National Theatre was unlikely to have any of the charm or glamour that so attracted English audiences and critics. He saw the company perform, almost certainly for the first time, when they brought over *The Playboy* to London in the year of the riots, 1907. Ben Iden Payne, the Englishman who was at that time briefly manager at the Abbey, described Shaw's reaction:

> He shrugged his shoulders about the play and did not admire the acting. For some reason I spoke of the players' 'Irish brogue'. Shaw interjected contemptuously, 'It is not a brogue, it's a Dublin accent; it would do them good to be told so'.[9]

Shaw was always insistent on preserving the precise meaning of 'brogue' as an Irish country accent, but the snort here is for the English who were incapable of detecting the inauthenticity of the Dublin actors playing Synge's western peasants.

Yet Shaw's sceptical and dismissive attitude towards the theatre company was to change in 1909, the year which saw the beginning of his working relationship with Lady Gregory. It is not clear when the two first met socially, though certainly before 1908, for on 19th January of that year Shaw wrote to Conal O'Riordan, who worked under the name of Norreys Connell and was about to have a play put on for the first time at the Abbey: 'Lady Gregory seems to me a very sensible nice sort of woman: I dont think you need have any trouble with her. However, I have met her in private life only'.[10] All Shaw's previous contacts with the Abbey over *John Bull* had been with Yeats.

The easy degree of acquaintance with Lady Gregory, together with Shaw's changed attitude towards the Abbey company (which he had seen act again in Dublin on his 1908 visit), are registered in Lady Gregory's journal record of his reaction to the Abbey's performance in London in June 1909:

> *Playboy* went very well. *Cathleen ni Houlihan* went beautifully, and afterwards I went round to the Shaws' box, and G.B.S. said his wife had 'howled' all through, and he said, 'When I see that play I feel it might lead a man to do something foolish' (I was as much surprised as if I had seen one of the Nelson lions scratch himself).[11]

As late as 1940, Shaw was to remember this incident himself:

> The Abbey Players were enormously interesting ... At Kathleen ni Houlihan my wife filled the box with her tears; and though I was by that time a hardened professional in the theatre I was quite touched by it.[12]

Yeats's play would not send Shaw out to fight the British—

> Did that play of mine send out
> Certain men the English shot?[13]

—but it clearly made him more sympathetic to the cause of the Irish National Theatre.

Significantly, it was Lady Gregory who now took on the task of translating this new sympathy into active involvement with the Abbey. Following closely on the appreciative reaction to *Kathleen Ni Houlihan*, Lady Gregory made her first visit to Shaw's country home in Ayot St Lawrence to try to persuade him to join herself and Yeats as one of the Theatre's directors. As Synge had died in March of that year, there would obviously have been enormous value in replacing him with a playwright of Shaw's international standing and experience. Shaw, already relatively well-off himself and with an independently wealthy wife, might also have offered much needed financial support to the Theatre at a moment when Miss Horniman, whose relations with the directors had become increasingly strained, seemed likely to withdraw her backing. Shaw, however, was unable to contribute because of the losses sustained in the later Vedrenne-Barker seasons and, as Lady Gregory reported:

> he won't come as Director, for he never will do that unless he can work at a thing, and [she quotes Shaw] 'the irony of it is, I am engaged in trying to build up a theatre in England'. But he will think it over, and help us if a means should arise.

Shaw was not about to shift his theatrical base to Ireland from England, where, besides his support of the repertory movement represented by the Vedrenne-Barker partnership, he was currently working towards the establishment of a Shakespeare Memorial National Theatre. What he was able to do immediately for the Abbey directors was to offer them the play the English Censor had turned down on grounds of blasphemy and immorality, *The Shewing-up of Blanco Posnet*.

The offer and the Abbey's acceptance of it had self-interest on both sides. Shaw was in the thick of a war against the Lord Chamberlain's office, which had just banned, not only *Blanco Posnet*, but also the topical satiric sketch written for the suffragettes, *Press Cuttings*. He was girding his loins to play his part as star witness in a Parliamentary enquiry to be set up on the censorship of stage plays. He saw the opportunity of getting round the Censor's ban by the historical accident that the Lord Chamberlain's writ did not run in Ireland. There were as well considerable political advantages in it for the Abbey, which still suffered in Ireland from the odium of the *Playboy* riots. Clearly Yeats and Lady Gregory hoped that in being seen to be defying the British censorship they might win a respite from the continuing violent hostility of the nationalist press.

In *Our Irish Theatre* Lady Gregory was to take pains to 'balance' the chapter on 'The Fight over "The Playboy" ' with one on 'The Fight with the Castle'. When the news of possible interference by Dublin Castle first broke, the comments of both Shaw and Lady Gregory in their letters show how alert they were to the public relations potential. Lady Gregory wrote on August 9th, 'One of the Belfast papers in its notice that Blanco was to be performed put as a heading "Probable interference of the Lord Lieutenant" but that is too good to be true—we could raise a great cry of injustice to an ill treated son of Erin if this were done'. And the 'son of Erin' wrote back in similar vein: 'If the Lord Lieutenant would only forbid an Irish play without reading it ... forbid it at the command of an official of the King's household in London, then the green flag would indeed wave over Abbey St'. In the event, although the nationalist papers continued to be basically hostile to the Abbey and its Directors, they did support the theatre in its resistance to censorship and warned their followers not to disrupt the performance of *Blanco Posnet*.

The time and situation were such as to make for maximum publicity. The play was announced for the opening week of the Abbey's new season, the week when the Dublin Horse Show crowded the city with visitors and with Ireland's horse-riding upper-classes. The Parliamentary Commission on censorship, which was by then sitting in London, had made *Blanco Posnet* news. The Irish authorities had no wish to get involved, but when the newspapers pointed out that the Lord Lieutenant had effective responsibility for censorship in Ireland, Dublin Castle could not afford to ignore the situation.

The story of the negotiations with the Castle, which Lady Gregory tells in her journal account and her letters to Shaw, is a wonderful social and political comedy. The Under Secretary, Sir James Dougherty, and the Liberal Lord Lieutenant, the well-meaning but ineffective Lord Aberdeen, both tried a mixture of coaxing and threats on the assumption that Lady Gregory would respond like a well-bred lady of her class. They were in no way prepared for the toughly intransigent negotiator they found; Sir James Dougherty can hardly have expected Lady Gregory to quote Parnell to him—'No man has the right to set a bound to the march of a nation'. The Abbey was dependent for support on largely nationalist Dublin audiences, but they had important allies and backers among the Anglo-Irish Ascendancy class as well. The argument that Society, with a capital S, might object to *Blanco Posnet* was easily countered with the revelation that Lord Iveagh had booked tickets for a large party.

Beyond Ireland, Shaw was able to mobilise other upper-class

influences in the play's favour, writing to his friend Gilbert Murray, the son-in-law of the Earl of Carlisle, to intervene with Lord Crewe, a former Lord Lieutenant of Ireland, who was then serving in the Liberal Government as Secretary of State for the Colonies and Lord Privy Seal. 'Whatever may be the right policy about the Censorship', Murray wrote to Crewe on 17th August:

> I think the prohibition of *Blanco Posnet* was one of the most grossly unintelligent of Mr Redford's actions. ... I do not defend the taste of the writing throughout; but I do think, first, that the actual theme of the play is both grand and tragic, in spite of its ugly and grotesque setting; and secondly, that this is the play in which Shaw has quite directly and without any subterfuge or nervous laughter expressed his religious faith—or a fragment of it. ... I do not believe that even Mr Redford could have condemned it had he not been blinded by some preconceived imagination of Shaw's 'immorality'. As a matter of fact Shaw is intensely in earnest about his religious preaching, though it is possible that all he has done is to discover the Ten Commandments over again.[14]

Crewe responded reassuringly to Murray on 21st August, and the adroit use of a second letter, from Murray to Shaw, materially helped to convince Dublin Society of the respectability of *Blanco Posnet*.

In the end *Blanco Posnet* was played without objection, to tumultuous applause: the Abbey had gained a famous victory, as well as a play that was to be a valuable part of its permanent repertory for the next quarter of a century. Shaw, throughout all the controversy in daily, at times hourly, contact with Lady Gregory and Yeats, resolutely stayed away from Dublin. This was the more striking because he was in Ireland at the time, on holiday in Parknasilla, Co. Kerry. Lady Gregory and Yeats, nervous at producing a Shaw play for the first time, were most anxious to have him attend rehearsals. As Yeats said, 'I doubt if any of us have the experience to do Posnett properly—it is a sort of play the English have a monopoly of us'. Lady Gregory, in fact, took over the direction, her first solo effort, and was sufficiently confident to suggest cuts to Shaw, which he, normally so recalcitrant to directorial alterations, accepted, and improved upon.

The motives Shaw gave for staying away from the production are significant. In a letter to Lady Gregory intended for publication after the production, he said: 'I kept away from Dublin in order that our national theatre might have the entire credit of handling and producing a new play without assistance from the author or from any other person trained in the English theatres. Nobody who has not lived, as I have to live, in London, can possibly understand the impression the Irish players made there this year, or appreciate the artistic value of their performances, their spirit, and their methods'. This no doubt was slanted for public consumption—there is surely some disingenuousness in the phrase about *having* to live in London—but it is an authentic tribute to the achievement of the Abbey, including a recognition of Shaw's own quite different 'training' in the English theatrical tradition. It was backed up in a private note to Lady Gregory as well: 'You and W.B.Y. handled the campaign nobly. You have made the Abbey Theatre the real centre of capacity and character in the Irish movement: let Sinn Fein and the rest look to it'. *Blanco Posnet* confirmed Shaw as a friend of Lady Gregory and a friend of the Abbey.

From the beginning Lady Gregory, relying on Shaw's greater experience in business matters, had turned to him for advice, whether in the project for a collected edition of Synge's works after his death, in the thorny problem of handling Miss Horniman, or on an offer for her own plays. Over the years she was to invoke his aid on any number of theatrical and other issues in which his knowledge, his influence, and his skills as publicist could be put to use. He was a forceful ally. When, for example, on the Abbey tour of 1911–12, the company faced violent opposition from Irish-American nationalists over *The Playboy*, Shaw weighed in with a long self-drafted interview, published in the New York *Evening Sun*, ridiculing the Clan na Gael protesters and proclaiming Lady Gregory 'the greatest living Irishwoman'. During the row following the mass arrest of the actors in Philadelphia Lady Gregory was told 'there is no one Americans *feel* but Bernard Shaw'. Although for the most part Shaw's assistance to the Abbey came in the form of advice, public backing, and moral support, rather than money, he did return his royalties for *Blanco Posnet*, which had been one of the plays performed on the 1911–12 tour, as a donation.

Visiting Coole for the first time in 1910, Shaw carved his initials on the famous autograph tree, an honour reserved for Lady Gregory's most distinguished guests, and came to appreciate Yeats, who was also there. Earlier, Shaw had been impatient with Yeats's posturing, seeing him as the incarnation of Gilbert and Sullivan's pseudo-Wilde, the poet Bunthorne in *Patience*; but at Lady Gregory's, Shaw learned 'what a penetrating critic and good talker he was; for he played none of his Bunthorne games, and saw no green elephants, at Coole'.[15]

Shaw's longest and most productive visit to Coole came in April 1915, one that brought about an even warmer friendship between Lady Gregory and both the Shaws: from this point on in the correspondence he becomes 'G.B.S.' and Mrs Shaw 'dear Charlotte'. It provided Shaw with the setting for his two remaining dramatic pieces with an Irish background. The desolate landscape around Robert Gregory's house in nearby Burren supplied the backdrop for *The Tragedy of an Elderly Gentleman*, Part IV of *Back to Methuselah*. In *O'Flaherty V.C.*, as Shaw wrote to Lady Gregory, 'the scene is quite simply before the porch of your house ... Properties: a garden seat and an iron chair as at Coole'. (Among the photographs of Shaw taken at Coole by his fellow-guest and Abbey Theatre mentor, W. F. Bailey, is one of him sitting on the garden seat; in another of him, on a pier, he looked very much like the Elderly Gentleman in the opening stage direction of the *Tragedy*.)

O'Flaherty V.C. was written in September 1915 as a pick-me-up for the ailing Abbey, which was experiencing hard times, partly because the war made impossible the lucrative tours to America that had helped to support it in the pre-war years, partly due to troubles with actors and managers and a dearth of new plays. Shaw, by the time he came to write his one-act comedy, knew the Abbey actors sufficiently well to be able to pre-cast the play, as he always tried to do with his plays for the London theatre. Visiting the Abbey before he went to Coole in the spring, he was particularly impressed with the acting of the comedian Arthur Sinclair in a play by Lady Gregory, *Shanwalla*, which nobody but he (and Lady Gregory) liked. He wrote the part of O'Flaherty especially for Sinclair, with the comic character part of O'Flaherty's mother designed for Sara Allgood. (Both of them did play those roles when the work was finally performed in London in 1920, but not under the auspices of the Abbey company.)

Though Shaw was eventually (1930) to subtitle *O'Flaherty V.C.* 'A Recruiting Pamphlet', it is hard to tell just how seriously he may have intended it as such at the time. Concerned with recruiting for the British army in Ireland from as early as 1914, Shaw was later to offer the draft of a possible recruiting poster and, later again, his pamphlet *War Issues for Irishmen*, which encouraged support for the war. But *O'Flaherty V.C.* represents an argument for recruiting such as only Shaw could have devised: Irishmen should join up in order to escape from their mothers and motherland. Shaw had left Ireland originally in 1876 to rejoin rather than to escape from his mother, who had departed for London three years previously; but his belief in the beneficial effects of emigration for Irishmen was no doubt based on his own experience. England had made a man of him, as it had of his earlier dramatic counterpart, Larry Doyle.

Shaw intended *O'Flaherty V.C.* to be as provocative as possible, as he made clear to Lady Gregory when describing it to her:

The picture of the Irish character will make the Playboy seem a patriotic rhapsody by comparison. The ending is cynical to the last possible degree. The idea is that O'Flaherty's experience in the trenches has induced in him a terrible realism and an unbearable candor. He sees Ireland as it is, his mother as she is, his sweetheart as she is; and he goes back to the dreaded trenches joyfully for the sake of peace and quietness. Sinclair must prepare for brickbats.

The play is hardly as terrible as Shaw makes out, if only because of the even-handedness with which all its targets are satirised: the complacently feudal assumptions of the Anglo-Irish general Sir Pearce Madigan; the British patriotic rhetoric; the insular and self-interested nationalism of Mrs O'Flaherty. Shaw contrives to subvert all forms of jingoism, the Irish as well as the English. As O'Flaherty says, speaking for the Shaw who had written the wildly unpopular pamphlet *Common Sense about the War*, 'Youll never have a quiet world til you knock the patriotism out of the human race'.[16] The only hope Shaw can see emerging out of the war is that those who survive it may have a truer sense of reality, an awareness of the wider world which may enable them to escape from the distorting perspectives both of class and nation. And it is to this final end that he wants Irishmen to go to fight for the British.

Not surprisingly, the military authorities failed to see it in quite this light. Though the play was duly announced for production at the Abbey, there followed something like a re-run of the situation over *Blanco Posnet*, with disapproving noises coming from the Castle. This time, however, there was much more to be said against the play being produced and much less possibility of defence. To start with, there was the real-life Lieutenant Michael O'Leary V.C., whose decoration early in 1915 had given Shaw the idea for the play, and who might be thought to be slighted by the association. A number of people normally sympathetic to Shaw and to the Abbey, including Sir Horace Plunkett, thought it might provoke a riot. In the end, Sir Matthew Nathan, the Under Secretary at the Castle, wrote Shaw a very sympathetic letter in which he said that in the light of likely demonstrations in which 'the fine lesson of the play would be smothered', 'the production of the play should be postponed till a time when it will be recording some of the humour and pathos of a past rather than of a present national crisis'. And so Shaw's second play written for the Abbey failed to get its première there.

Ironically, it was to be the following year, 1916, that *John Bull's Other Island* was at last given its first Abbey production. The immediate occasion was the appointment of J. Augustus Keogh as manager of the Abbey. Keogh, a Shaw enthusiast, had just mounted a production of *Widowers' Houses* in Dublin as his own venture. This gave Lady Gregory an idea, as she wrote to Shaw:

> a brilliant thought struck me ... to do an autumn season of G.B.S.—our Irish Shakespeare—I hope for an annual festival of him! ... I would like to put on John Bull (written for us and never acted by us); Devil's Disciple which should appeal to the romantic side of our audience; Doctor's Dilemma, not my favourite but which I am inclined to think acts best of all ... and I should like much to put on Androcles, if we could borrow the lion.

Shaw's initial response was not very encouraging. The Abbey was welcome to *John Bull*, but Shaw feared that it was 'rather hackneyed in Dublin by this time'. (Since its first highly successful production there in 1907 by the Vedrenne-Barker company, it had in fact frequently been played in Dublin.) He vetoed *The Devil's Disciple*, a play he would not allow to be performed during the war lest it be construed as anti-British propaganda, and which in any case he said was well beyond the Abbey's technical resources. *The Doctor's Dilemma* was also vetoed: 'it required', said Shaw, '*polished* acting by a cast of cockney stars'. And as for *Androcles*, 'how on earth could Keogh get it on to the Abbey Street stage? There is hardly room for the lion: one spring would carry him half way to the G.P.O.'. Although he suggested *Widowers' Houses* and *Candida* as the safest bets among his own plays, he enthusiastically urged a proposal of Charlotte's, that the Abbey should turn to Ibsen instead.

The resulting exchange with Lady Gregory (though we have only Shaw's side of the correspondence at this point) is of considerable interest in terms of Shaw's view of the theatre movement. Lady Gregory evidently responded negatively to Shaw's Ibsen suggestion, referring to Synge's view that the Abbey should concentrate on native work to the exclusion of modern European drama. Shaw agreed: 'I am with Synge in thinking that the Irish should do their own Ibsenising', but the problem at the time was that new Irish plays were not being written. If the theatre were forced to introduce foreign work (and it is significant that Shaw included his own in this category) then there was much more to be said for Ibsen than for the classic drama of Sophocles or Molière that Lady Gregory was proposing instead. Ibsen, Shaw argued, 'is a great modern poet and teacher whom the Irish especially need, and whom they have a right to know as a part of their culture'. Though the point of view represented in the letter is partly familiar from *The Quintessence of Ibsenism*, it is significant to see it transferred to a specifically Irish context. Shaw is arguing, as George Moore and Edward Martyn had in the very early stages of the Irish Literary Theatre, and indeed as the young Joyce felt so strongly, that Ireland desperately required the astringent realism of Ibsen. But Shaw had no more luck than Moore and Martyn in breaking down the anti-Ibsenist prejudices of Yeats and Lady Gregory.

The Abbey got its Shaw season. Over the winter of 1916–17 it produced no fewer than six of his plays, opening with *John Bull*, *Widowers' Houses* and *Arms and the Man*, in succession, and then offering in the spring of 1917 *Man and Superman*, the one-act war skit *The Inca of Perusalem*, and, in spite of Shaw's doubts, *The Doctor's Dilemma*. All these were produced by Keogh: when he left the Abbey at the end of the season a good deal of the positive commitment to Shaw went with him. When Keogh sought permission to produce Shaw plays in Ireland under his own management, Shaw used the occasion to put a little pressure on the Abbey. He was, he said, prepared to keep Dublin rights of performance for the Abbey while conceding provincial rights to Keogh but, as he wrote to Lady Gregory, 'I foresee a rather awkward situation':

> Keogh's trump card, which he has already thrown down boldly, is that when he leaves the Abbey Theatre there will be no more of my plays there as they do not 'meet with the approval of Mr Yeats for production at the Abbey'. I understand exactly what this means; so you need not soothe my unwounded feelings... But ... if it should prove possible to keep the Abbey going by fresh native work and by what I call the quartier Latin cum Bedford Park cum Gaelic League School (to distinguish them from the Irish School, which so far buzzes apart as a bee from your own bonnet), then it will inevitably happen that Keogh, if he can keep going, will be exploiting my plays vigorously all over Ireland, and asking me whether I seriously mean to impoverish myself and break his back by keeping them out of Dublin for the sake of a rival theatre which never performs them at all, and never did except as stopgap in a desperate emergency.

Much can be read between the lines here. For all Shaw's denial that his feelings were wounded, it is obvious he noticed that Lady Gregory had conceived of the Shaw season only because the normal repertory of peasant plays was temporarily unavailable. Clearly he was not pleased at Yeats's opposition to his work, retaliating with the malicious description of Yeats's poetic drama as the 'quartier Latin cum Bedford Park cum Gaelic League School'. (Bedford Park, where Yeats lived in London when Shaw first knew him in the 1880s and 90s, had been the centre for much early Irish literary revival activity.) There is an attempt to prise Lady Gregory apart from Yeats with the flattering reference to her plays as belonging to a uniquely authentic Irish school: never an admirer of Yeats's plays or poems, he consistently praised Lady Gregory's work throughout the years of their association. Moreover, though Shaw in this letter is declaring his continued loyalty to the Abbey—he *will* go on giving them first Irish rights in his plays—he is issuing a warning that there is a limit to such loyalty.

The Abbey was never to undertake another Shaw season like that of 1916–17, but from this period Shaw plays were to become an important part of the company's stock-in-trade. *John Bull*, so long left unperformed, became a mainstay of the Abbey's repertoire. After the initial production in 1916, the play was revived for at least a week's run every year until 1931, playing a total of some 135 performances. The original problem of casting Broadbent was triumphantly solved with the Abbey comic actor Barry Fitzgerald apparently playing a brilliant Broadbent opposite the Larry Doyle of F.J. McCormick. By 1937, although the politics of *John Bull* might have dated, Lennox Robinson could still describe it as remaining 'the most profound statement of the Englishman in his relation to the Irishman'.[17] Besides the six plays staged in the 1916–17 Keogh season, the Abbey between 1919 and 1932, the year of Lady Gregory's death, performed six more Shaw plays for the first time, including some that Shaw himself thought totally unsuitable for it, like *Androcles and the Lion* and *Caesar and Cleopatra*. With many of the individual works often revived, particularly *Arms and the Man*, *The Doctor's Dilemma*, *Fanny's First Play*, and *The Man of Destiny*, Shaw was actually one of the most frequently produced dramatists at the Abbey in the period, with over 360 play performances to his credit. Shaw may never have been a part of the Irish dramatic movement as such, but his plays, as a staple of the Abbey repertory, must be considered as an important part of the theatrical tradition, the tradition that produced O'Casey, on whom Shaw was a major influence.

While Shaw continued to support the Abbey in a variety of ways and to give Lady Gregory reluctant permission to produce the works she wanted, he was sceptical of the theatre's capacity to perform his plays adequately. He reported very unfavourably to Lady Gregory on a visit to a 1920 matinée performance of *The Devil's Disciple*, the only time he saw one of his own plays performed at the Abbey:

> an execrable performance, not improved by the hideous nervousness my presence set up. I can imagine that in the evening, with

a less depressing audience and in finer weather, it goes better; but they are not up to my stage tricks anyhow, poor lambs! ... The gallows scene was ... frankly impossible on that tiny stage without a crowd, an army, and a street. And the omission of a great deal of my stage business (as I produce it) made a difference; but nobody can do all that but myself.

Shaw, trained in the huge auditoria and on the scenic stages of London, accustomed to the technical assurance of London acting, could only see the Abbey version of his play as amateurish and hopelessly reduced in scale. At times the wider context of events made him impatient with Lady Gregory's endless soliciting of support for the Abbey. He turned down her request for a lecture in aid of the Theatre in 1921:

I feel provoked to say that if the child needs so much nursing it had better die. Why should it survive when so many other children are being killed? The war ... [has] destroyed my susceptibility to any calamity involving less than the death of ten million babies. When they discussed the best means of protecting St Pauls against fire, Dean Inge's sole contribution to the debate was 'Let it burn'. I feel like that about the Abbey. Let it go smash.

Lady Gregory's journal entry recording this letter notes only Shaw's excuse that he is overworked: 'I am afraid it is true', she comments, 'but I wish some of his work could be given to Ireland'.

They could never really agree about Ireland. The disagreement was to become deeper over the years, but it did not diminish their friendship. In the pre-war period they both looked forward to the coming of Home Rule, feeling that some form of independence for Ireland was both inevitable and, more or less, desirable. Both stood opposed to the nationalist separatism of Sinn Féin, its racialist opposition to the British, its sentimental pieties of harp and shamrock, though Shaw was to defend bravely and eloquently the leaders of the 1916 Rising, whose cause he heartily disliked. His fits of violent reaction against his native country tended, however, to become more extreme under the pressure of his anguished awareness of the Great War going on beyond Ireland. In 1917 he refused an invitation from Lady Gregory to lecture on behalf of the Irish National Theatre with a vociferous 'NO':

The very words nation, nationality, our country, patriotism, fill me with loathing. Why do you want to stimulate a self-consciousness which is already morbidly excessive in our wretched island, and is

deluging Europe with blood? ... Since my recent visit [to Dublin] I
feel like putting up a statue to Cromwell.

Again, during the so-called Anglo-Irish war, when the Black and Tan
troops were terrorising the neighbourhood around Coole and Lady
Gregory urged Shaw to come over and publicise their atrocities, he
replied that it would be futile. The horrors of the situation were
well-known already; he had done everything he could but, 'as usual, I
cannot get the Irish question out of the old grooves'.

The Civil War of 1922–3 made him even more despairing of
Ireland. In an interview with the *Irish Times*, just before he went back
to England after a holiday in Rosslare, he invoked a plague on both the
warring houses, Free Staters and Republicans:

> I am returning to England because I can do no good here, and
> because the postage is a halfpenny cheaper. ... I cannot stand the
> stale romance that passes for politics in Ireland. I cannot imagine
> why people bother so much about us: I am sure we dont deserve it.
> ... The bottom has fallen out of the centre of Europe, and England
> is on the brink of the abyss. But what matter if for Ireland dear we
> fall! It is too silly: I must hurry back to London. The lunatics there
> are comparatively harmless.[18]

He came back one more time, in 1923, the summer he finished *Saint
Joan* at Parknasilla, but never again after that. Though he did not
explicitly state his intention of never returning to Ireland and continued to mention the possibility of revisiting Coole, it seems probable
that the events of the Troubles, including the burning of Charlotte
Shaw's childhood home in Co. Cork, and that of his friend Sir Horace
Plunkett, where the Shaws had frequently stayed, made the prospect
of going back too painful.

Through his letters to Lady Gregory in the 1920s can be seen
Shaw's efforts to disentangle his warm feelings for her personally from
his bitterness and antagonism towards the Ireland she continued to
love, and its national causes that she continued to espouse. Writing in
1925 from Scotland, where he and his wife had taken to holidaying
instead of Ireland, he described the contrast between the two in
something between playfulness and real hostility:

> The [Scottish] people are goodlooking, civil, and free from obtru-
> sive virtues and heroic traditions: in short quite likable. Sell Coole
> and settle here: you will find all the beauties of Ireland without the
> drawback of Irish inhabitants.

Though Shaw sympathised with and supported Lady Gregory in her struggle to have the Lane pictures returned to Ireland from the London National Gallery, in the controversy over the disputed will that was to take up so much of her energy from 1915 on, he was inclined to see the failure of the campaign as a well-deserved punishment on Dublin for its Philistinism. Lady Gregory's opposing point of view, defending her continued work for Ireland, was well put in answer to Shaw's argument that the Lane pictures would be more appreciated in London than in Dublin: 'I am more appreciated in London than in Dublin, but I spend more time in Dublin because I think I am more useful there'. This loyalty to Ireland and determined refusal even in adverse circumstances to abandon her work there, which Shaw could not share, he enormously admired in Lady Gregory.

As a workaholic himself, Shaw warmed to Lady Gregory's capacity for work and her unstinting willingness to do whatever was necessary for the task in hand. It was he who called her 'the charwoman of the Abbey', a soubriquet that was to stick with her and be quoted in her obituaries. The phrase was apparently used in a February 1910 lecture, which Shaw did not repeat in the version prepared for publication, perhaps feeling that it sounded derogatory. Lady Gregory, however, took it to herself with pride, quoting it to American journalists in 1911. She felt it as the compliment Shaw intended it to be: a tribute to someone who, besides her own literary gifts, was content to be the Abbey's maid-of-all-work, someone whose dignity was bound up with the idea of service.

Lady Gregory dedicated her play *The Golden Apple* to Shaw as 'the gentlest of my friends'. Gentleness being rarely thought of as one of Shaw's outstanding attributes, at least as far as his public reputation went, no doubt the wording of the dedication was chosen to startle those who knew him only as the ferocious and irascible polemicist. As *The Golden Apple* was prepared for publication after Shaw's extended visit to Coole in 1915, when he had first come to know the three Gregory grandchildren, it may well have been his relations with them that helped to make Lady Gregory aware of this gentleness. She would, in fact, have included in the dedication a reference to the impression he had made on the children, if Shaw had not objected. Evidently Shaw had the capacity for that spontaneous and unselfconscious playfulness that makes adults popular with children. One of the 'nicest visitors to Coole' from a child's point of view, Anne Gregory recalls him, in her delightful childhood memoir, *Me and Nu*, even if he did disillusion the children terribly by cheating at 'Hunt the

Thimble'.[19] For Lady Gregory who looked after the children at Coole for much of their childhood, Shaw's capacity to get on with the 'chicks', as she called them, strengthened the bond between them, making him a family friend rather than a personal or professional one.

Again and again, Lady Gregory spoke of Shaw's kindness, 'a sort of kindly joyousness about him'. She had experience of the joyousness in his play with her grandchildren, and she had occasion to rely on his kindness in a number of times of trouble. He was at Coole in 1915 when the news arrived of the sinking of the *Lusitania*, in which Lady Gregory's nephew Hugh Lane was lost. His letter of condolence in 1918 when her son Robert was killed struck just the right note: 'I was hoping for a letter from you. I knew it would be helpful'. As it happened, Lady Gregory was again with Shaw in 1921, staying at Ayot, when she heard of what was very nearly another family tragedy, the IRA ambush where her daughter-in-law was the only one out of a party of five to survive. Friendship takes on a different sort of depth and intimacy when shock and sorrow have been shared in this way.

In the relationship between them as it is shown in the letters and the journal entries, Lady Gregory characteristically appears to be the dependent one: it is she who looks for help, advice, support, who argues defensively for her causes, the Abbey or the Lane pictures. Shaw responds often generously, but on his own terms and, at times, with an element of perverse aggression, saying the Lane pictures are better off in London anyway, or that the Abbey might be as well converted into a cinema. The aggression is always held in check and never directed at Lady Gregory personally, but it appears that occasionally Shaw may have been wearied by Lady Gregory's belief in him as all but omniscient and omnipotent in public matters. Yet it is noticeable that in issues where they differed, Lady Gregory was rarely the one to alter course. He did *not* convince her of the merits of Ibsen, for all the eloquence of his pleading. *Androcles* he thought totally unsuitable for the Abbey, yet he was persuaded by Lady Gregory to let the company produce it: 'there is no use talking to you: you are simply the most obstinate and unscrupulous devil on earth: and I well know the vanity of remonstrance'. Requests for a lecture on behalf of the Abbey might elicit streams of Shavian invective, but a lecture would eventually be delivered. On the subject of Richard Gregory's schooling, Shaw was especially assertive, haranguing Richard's grandmother on the horrors of Harrow and the advantages of the modernised Oundle: 'I really cannot have Richard sent to that obsolete and thrice accursed boy farm which is an evil tradition in the family'. Nonetheless, Richard went to Harrow as his father and grandfather had before him. Shaw may have only been half joking when he commented on Lady Gregory's praise of his wise advice: 'I always find out what she wants and then advise it—that's an easy way to get a reputation'.

Apart from their personal feeling for one another, it was an attractive and valuable social relation for both of them. Lady Gregory enjoyed the comforts of her weekends at Ayot, particularly in the 1920s when life at Coole had become bleak and beleaguered. She got on extremely well with Charlotte Shaw, who liked very few of Shaw's female companions and friends; it is clear from the evidence of Charlotte's engagement diaries that she and Lady Gregory met quite frequently, even when Shaw himself was away, and they carried on a separate correspondence. Lady Gregory's journals show how much it meant to her to be with sympathetic friends for whom money was not a problem. On his side, Shaw was no snob, but had good reason to appreciate the friendship of Lady Gregory of Coole Park. When he married Charlotte Payne-Townshend, from a well-to-do Anglo-Irish family, he was identified initially by such as Charlotte's cousin, Edith Somerville (of Somerville and Ross) as an adventurer, remembered as a junior clerk in the Townshend land-agent's office. Though he overcame such hostility, he was never easy with Irish county society, and was all the more grateful for the attentions of someone of that class, like Lady Gregory, who valued him for the important person he had become, rather than thinking of him as the former nobody he had once been. His sense of the class difference between them emerges in his recommendation of Lady Gregory as play critic to his boyhood friend, Edward McNulty, who came from a background similar to his own: 'being a lady who knows the great world, she can correct social solecisms and rub out little vulgarities: things that are sure to crop up because everybody has weaknesses of that kind of which he is not conscious. After a time they all get pointed out; but a critic is useful at first'. Shaw liked the idea of Lady Gregory as aristocrat and urged her in *Our Irish Theatre* to cultivate the impression of the fight with Dublin Castle as a gallant but honourable duel with Lord Aberdeen. 'The grand manner becomes us in Ireland: we are the only people in these islands who can still do it'. Shaw never cultivated anything like Yeats's myth of the Anglo-Irish ascendancy or the poetic idealisation of Coole; yet one can detect as a dimension in his relationship with Lady Gregory a slight weakness for the airs and graces of landed gentry.

The warmth, depth and duration of the friendship with Lady Gregory stands out in contrast with Shaw's relations with Yeats. Shaw and Yeats were never antagonists: they had a real mutual respect and could work together for a common cause; but there was little sympathy there and not much appreciation of each other's writing. Asked for an evaluation of Yeats after his death, Shaw replied that '[I] did not read enough of him to pontificate about his work'.[20] Yeats, unlike Lady Gregory, did not care for *Saint Joan* or *The Apple Cart*, any more than he had liked *John Bull*. He did not trust Shaw or depend upon him as an ally to nearly the extent that Lady Gregory did, fulminating, for instance, against Shaw's conduct as 'utterly inexcusable',[21] when in 1910 he tried to mediate between Miss Horniman and the Abbey directors. Where Lady Gregory became a regular visitor with the Shaws from 1909 on, Yeats seems to have lunched only occasionally at their London flat and once at Shaw's Corner; he was never invited to spend a weekend at Ayot.

Given this comparative lack of sympathy between Yeats and Shaw, it seems clear that without the relationship with Lady Gregory, Shaw would never have become involved with the Abbey Theatre to the extent that he did. It was Lady Gregory who was appointed emissary in 1909 to invite Shaw to become one of the Theatre's directors, only to be offered *Blanco Posnet* instead. It was Lady Gregory who had the idea for the Shaw season in 1916, and it was almost certainly through her initiative that further Shaw plays were performed at the Abbey in succeeding years. Shaw, perhaps, could never have taken a full part in the national theatre movement. Dublin was too deeply associated with the provincial and the second-rate, with poverty and failure, for it to be possible for him to settle down to work with a theatre there. Both the poetic and the nationalist strain within the movement were antipathetic to him, though he could be moved by the patriotic rhetoric of *Kathleen Ni Houlihan*. London remained the fulcrum point from which he believed he could shift the world. And yet he was capable of responding to the ideals of the theatre movement and could recognise and respect the independent artistic principles and practice of the Abbey, however unlike his own they might be. The very warm and human relationship between two such different people as Shaw and Lady Gregory is of interest in itself; the full record of that relationship, here assembled for the first time, also shows that Shaw had a much more important role in the Abbey than has previously been recognised. But even the limitation as to how far he could allow himself to become involved is significant. If for Shaw the Abbey represented 'the path not taken', then his awareness of that path, the play of attitudes and emotions surrounding his decision not to take it, can illuminate both the playwright and the theatre movement that he did not choose to join.

Notes to Introduction

1. Lady Gregory, Manuscript diary: Berg, NYPL. Frederic Whyte, a journalist and translator, recalled this, his maiden address, and his rough treatment at the hands of Shaw, in *A Bachelor's London* (London, 1931), misdating the incident as 1898.
2. Shaw, *Collected Plays with their Prefaces* (London, 1970), II, p. 808.
3. *The Letters of W.B. Yeats*, ed. Allan Wade, (London, 1954), p. 335.
4. ALS: BL.
5. Yeats, *Letters*, p. 387.
6. Shaw to Yeats, 23rd June 1903, APCS: Burgunder, Cornell.
7. Yeats, *Letters*, p. 442.
8. *Collected Plays with their Prefaces*, II, p. 837.
9. Ben Iden Payne, *A Life in a Wooden O: Memories of the Theatre* (New Haven, 1977), pp. 76–7.
10. APCS: Robert H. Taylor Collection, Princeton University.
11. Lady Gregory, *Seventy Years*, ed. Colin Smythe (Gerrards Cross, 1973), p. 444. Although we have retained Lady Gregory's spelling *Cathleen ni Houlihan* here, elsewhere in the text we have consistently used *Kathleen Ni Houlihan*, which was the title as it appeared in the early Abbey productions of the play.
12. Shaw to Stephen Gwynn, 28th August 1940, TLS: Ellen Clarke Bertrand Library, Bucknell University.
13. 'The Man and the Echo', *Collected Poems of W.B. Yeats* (London, 1950), p. 393.
14. TT/p: BTA.
15. Shaw to Stephen Gwynn, as cited above.
16. Shaw, *Collected Plays with their Prefaces*, IV, p. 1000.
17. Lennox Robinson to Shaw, 26th May 1937, TLS: BL. This letter is actually the citation by Robinson, on behalf of the Council of the Irish Academy of Letters, on the occasion of the award by the Academy to Shaw of the Gregory Medal, its greatest honour established in memory of Lady Gregory.
18. 'G.B.S. on Ireland', 21st August 1922: collected as 'The Eve of Civil War' in *The Matter with Ireland*, eds. Dan H. Laurence and David H. Greene (New York, 1962), pp. 255–7.
19. Anne Gregory, *Me and Nu: Childhood at Coole* (Gerrards Cross, 1970), pp. 26–7.
20. Shaw to Stephen Gwynn, as cited above.
21. Yeats to Lady Gregory, postmarked 30th January 1910, ALS/p: NLI.

EDITORS' NOTE

This edition contains all of the surviving correspondence of Bernard Shaw and Lady Gregory known to us, reproduced from original texts except in the case of four pieces of Shaw correspondence stolen from the home of Colin Smythe and a letter preserved only in a transcription by Lady Gregory. The texts are reproduced in their entirety.

We have cast our nets wide to seek incidents and conversations that would illuminate the public and private relationship between GBS and Augusta Gregory. Drawing upon letters to and from other correspondents, diaries and engagement books, private memoranda, newspaper reports, and press releases, we have revealed as fully as possible their theatre involvements, works in progress, travels, social and political interests and activities, and such humanising elements as Shaw's rapport with the Gregory grandchildren. As more of Shaw's letters are extant than are those of Lady Gregory, her side of the picture has been fleshed out by recourse to her diary and letter-journal memoirs.

These largely sporadic and often disjointed and non-chronological memoirs create problems, for some survive, not in holograph, but in corrected typescript only; and when she drew upon them as source material for her books Lady Gregory often retyped and re-edited earlier typescripts. Much of this material is now published in *Seventy Years* (1973), and in the two volume edition of *Journals* (1978–88). We have reproduced relevant portions of the published texts, with a few emendations of editors' misreadings, but have also gone to unpublished holograph manuscripts and to revised typescript versions later published, with further revision and abridgment, in *Our Irish Theatre* (1913).

In our editing of the texts of the correspondence we have retained Shaw's designed eccentricities of spelling and punctuation, but have otherwise corrected carelessnesses of spelling and grammar and regularised the punctuation by use of single quotation marks, placement of full stops outside the quotation marks, insertion of omitted commas where the sentence construction demands them, and elimination of most of the dashes habitually employed by Lady Gregory as substitutes for virtually every other form of punctuation. As it was the custom of both correspondents to write titles of works without quotation marks or underlining, we have confined an italicised setting to our own headnotes and narrative bridges, regularising titles in the few instances in the texts where they varied from the norm.

As both correspondents also had a propensity for misspelling proper names, we have left these unaltered in the letters, with the corrected spelling reserved for editorial notes and bridges. Words accidentally omitted from correspondence under the pressure of deadlines for posting have been inserted in square brackets, as have editorial insertions of related factual information. Uniformity has been given to place and date of writing and to salutations and valedictions. Except for a few words characteristically shortened by Lady Gregory in her letters and memoirs, abbreviations have been spelled out.

To the following individuals and institutions we acknowledge with gratitude permission to publish correspondence and related material.

For Shaw and Lady Gregory: Library Board of the Cornell University Library (Bernard F. Burgunder Collection); New York Public Library, Astor, Lenox, and Tilden Foundations (Henry W. and Albert A. Berg Collection); Harry Ransom Humanities Research Center, University of Texas at Austin (T.E. Hanley Collection); British Library (Shaw Archive); Mugar Library, University of Boston (Special Collections); Wellesley College Library (English Poetry Collection); Rutgers University Libraries (Special Collections and Archives); Princeton University (Robert H. Taylor Collection).

For John Campbell Gordon, Lord Aberdeen: the Most Hon. the sixth Marquess of Aberdeen and Temair; for Joseph Holloway's manuscript theatre diaries: Council of the Trustees of the National Library of Ireland; for Gilbert Murray: Mr Alexander Murray; for Sir Matthew Nathan: Bodleian Library and Mrs Joan I. Longden; for Sir Horace Plunkett: Plunkett Foundation for Co-operative Studies, Oxford; for unpublished correspondence of W.B. Yeats: John S. Kelly and Oxford University Press; for published letters of W.B. Yeats and two lines from 'The Man and the Echo' by W.B. Yeats: A.P. Watt & Son for the Macmillan Press and Michael B. Yeats, and Macmillan and Co, New York. We have reproduced without permission a letter written by the Rt. Hon. W.F. Bailey, for whom we have been unable to trace a surviving executor or heir, on the assumption that permission would in the normal course of events have been accorded to us.

For unstinted and valuable assistance we are indebted to Dr Jacques Barzun, Ernest Bates, Michael Collins, Vincent Dowling, Father Ignatius Fennessy (O.F.M.), Christopher Fitz-Simon, the late Major Richard Gregory, Ken Hannigan, Cathy Henderson, Vivien

Jenkins, Dr Edward Connery Lathem, Geraldine Mangan, Walter Noel Morrison, Dr Christopher Murray, Matthew O'Mahony, Daphne Plessner, Michael Purcell, Dr Hugh Shields, Colin Smythe, the late Dr Lola L. Szladits, Dr James Tyler, Patsy Twomey; Steven J. Mayover, Chief, Central Public Services Division, and staff of the Free Library of Philadelphia and the staffs of the Abbey Theatre, British Library of Political and Economic Science, British Theatre Association, Ellen Clarke Bertrand Library of Bucknell University, the National Library of Ireland, Theatre Museum (London), and the Library of Trinity College Dublin, to all of whom we express our warmest thanks.

DHL
NG

ABBREVIATIONS

ACCS	Autograph correspondence card signed (in full or initials)
AccS	Autograph 'compliments' card signed
ALS	Autograph letter signed
TLS	Typewritten letter signed
TMS	Typewritten manuscript
TT	Typewritten transcription
d	draft, unsigned
p	photocopy
ts	typewritten signature or initials
Berg	New York Public Library (Henry W. and Albert A. Berg Collection)
BL	British Library
BTA	British Theatre Association (formerly British Drama League)
Burgunder	Cornell University Library (Bernard F. Burgunder Collection)
HRC	Harry Ransom Humanities Research Center, University of Texas, Austin
NLI	National Library of Ireland
SPO	State Paper Office, Dublin

BIOGRAPHICAL NOTES

Allgood, Sara (1883–1950): Dublin-born actress known to all as Sally, sister of Molly Allgood, made her first stage appearance in February 1904 in the Irish National Theatre Society production of Lady Gregory's *Twenty-Five*. She was in the cast of *Spreading the News* on the opening night of the Abbey Theatre the following December, subsequently appearing in almost all of the Abbey's principal productions, her roles including Molly Byrne in *The Well of the Saints* (1905), Widow Quin in *The Playboy of the Western World* (1907), and Feemy Evans in *The Shewing-up of Blanco Posnet* (1909). In 1914 she left the company, but returned in 1920, 1924, and 1926, creating the roles of Juno Boyle in *Juno and the Paycock* and Bessie Burgess in *The Plough and the Stars*. She settled in Hollywood in 1940, appearing in many films; in 1945 she became a U.S. citizen.

Campbell, Beatrice Stella (Mrs Patrick) (1865–1940): one of the great ladies of the British stage, former leading lady of Johnston Forbes-Robertson, noted for her appearances in *The Second Mrs Tanqueray*, *The Notorious Mrs Ebbsmith*, *Magda*, *Pelléas et Mélisande* (opposite Sarah Bernhardt), and *Hedda Gabler*, and, in 1914, Shaw's *Pygmalion*, which had been written for her. She performed with the Irish National Theatre Society at the Abbey in Yeats's *Deirdre*, 1906, repeating the role under other auspices in London two years later.

Dougherty, the Rt. Hon. Sir James (1844–1934): Under-Secretary to the Lord Lieutenant of Ireland in 1909. A civil servant whose appointments ranged from Clerk to Her Majesty's Privy Council to Commissioner of Education (1890–95) in Ireland, he subsequently was Liberal M.P. for Londonderry city from 1914 to 1918.

Ervine, St John (1883–1971): Belfast-born playwright, biographer, and theatre critic (he wrote for *The Observer* 1919–23 and 1925–39), whose plays performed at the Abbey included *Mixed Marriage* (1911), *The Magnanimous Lover* (1912), *John Ferguson* (1915), and *The Island of Saints* (1920). He briefly served as manager of the Abbey Theatre in 1915–16. Thoroughly disliked in the literary world, he was elected to membership in the Irish Academy of Letters in 1932 at the insistence of Shaw (his neighbour at Whitehall Court, London) and by the strategic manoeuvring of Yeats. He published in 1956 a very opinionated biography, *Bernard Shaw: His Life, Work and Friends*.

Gordon, John Campbell (1847–1934), **seventh Earl of Aberdeen**: a Liberal who served as Lord Lieutenant of Ireland for six months in 1886, during which troubled times (after the Phoenix Park murders) he renewed relations with the Lord Mayor of Dublin and the Dublin Corporation and bravely travelled with his wife through the troubled southern counties. In 1906 (having served in the interim as Governor General of Canada), he was reappointed to the Lord Lieutenancy of Ireland, serving for nine years, the longest term of any appointee and among the most popular with the Irish.

Gregory, Lady (1852–1932): born Isabella Augusta Persse, one of a large landowning family in Co Galway, she married in 1880 Sir William Gregory, a former Governor of Ceylon and the owner of Coole Park, a substantial Galway estate. Sir William, who was more than thirty years older than his wife, died in 1892 and Lady Gregory wore widow's weeds for the rest of her life. Having met Yeats in 1894, she became associated with him in the Irish literary revival, helping him with her knowledge of Irish and in collecting folklore; in 1897 they founded the Irish Literary Theatre (together with Edward Martyn). Although she had done some literary work before, including the editing of her husband's memoirs, her real career as a writer began with the publication in 1902 of *Cuchulain of Muirthemne*, her collection of translations from the Irish sagas, a seminal work for both Synge and Yeats, and her first one-act plays for the Irish Literary Theatre, written in 1901–2. Appointed, with Yeats and J.M. Synge, as one of the three directors of the Abbey Theatre in 1905 and acting initially as its patentee in trust for Annie Horniman, its English benefactress, she was to be continuously involved in the active management of the Abbey for the rest of her life: as play director (beginning with *The Shewing-up of Blanco Posnet* in 1909), as a prolific dramatist, writing more than twenty-five original plays and many adaptations and translations for the company, and even once as substitute actress in *Kathleen Ni Houlihan* which she had written in collaboration with Yeats. She made four visits to the United States, three times accompanying the Abbey players on their American tours (1911–12, 1912–13, 1915), and once on a lecture tour by herself (1915–16). In Ireland she continued to live permanently at Coole Park, making a home there for her three grandchildren for a great deal of their childhood. Much of the Coole estate had already been sold before the death of her only son Robert in the war in 1918; although she struggled to retain the property for her grandson, financial and political pressures made this difficult, and in 1927 she sold the property to the Irish Free State government, though retaining the right to live in the house. Through the 1920s she suffered from bad health, undergoing two operations for cancer; she died at Coole on 23rd May 1932. In 1941 her beloved Coole House was demolished, an event Shaw described as 'an unforgivable vandalism'.

Gregory, Robert (1881–1918): only child of Lady Gregory, was an artist, who assisted his mother in the early years of the Irish National Theatre Society by designing or painting scenery for its productions, notably *Deirdre* in 1906. In 1907 he married Margaret Parry (1884–1979); they had three children, Richard (1909–81), Augusta Anne (b. 1911), and Catherine (b. 1913). Enlisting in the British Army in 1915, Robert Gregory eventually served as a pilot in the 40th Squadron of the Royal Flying Corps. On 21st February 1917 he performed at the front in the first production of *O'Flaherty V.C.*, in the role of O'Flaherty's fiancée Teresa Driscoll. Major Gregory's plane was accidentally shot down in 1918 by an Italian pilot; he was buried in Padua. Ten years later his widow became Mrs Guy Gough.

Horniman, Annie Elizabeth Fredericka (1860–1937): a pioneer, often called the founder, of the repertory movement in the modern theatre. She served as Yeats's secretary for five years, during which time she underwrote publication of his *Collected Poems* by Maunsel in Dublin. She also provided the financial support that enabled the Irish National Theatre Society in December 1904 to commence operations in the Abbey Theatre. In 1910, after founding a repertory company at the Gaiety Theatre, Manchester, she withdrew support from the Abbey.

Keogh, J. Augustus (d. 1942): began his stage career in England at seventeen, allegedly specialising eventually in Shaw roles, presumably in the provinces. On his return to Dublin in 1916 he was invited to assume the managerial post at the Abbey, succeeding Ervine. On his initiative six Shaw plays were produced, staged by himself, in the 1916–17 season, to Yeats's displeasure. When this 'commercialisation' of the theatre failed to bring boxoffice improvement, he was hastily supplanted by Fred O'Donovan. For a brief period he toured Ireland with his own Shaw company, then emigrated to the United States, where he headed the Boston Repertory Theatre and New York's Irish Repertory Theatre. While touring with the USO in Arkansas in 1942 he was struck and killed by a car.

Lane, Sir Hugh (1875–1915): art connoisseur, collector, and critic, was the son of Lady Gregory's sister Frances. Under the influence of Yeats and the Irish Literary Revival movement, he founded and fostered a modern-art municipal gallery in Dublin, commissioning John B. Yeats to paint a series of portraits of distinguished countrymen and making many gifts of modern art to the city. After controversy, however, over the design for the new gallery, Lane withdrew his personal loan collection of paintings from the temporary gallery and transferred it to the National Gallery in London, bequeathing the collection to that institution in 1913. Following his death in the sinking of the Lusitania in 1915, an unwitnessed handwritten codicil to his will was found, in which he restored the pictures to Dublin. Lady Gregory gave much of her energy for the remainder of her life to an unsuccessful battle to wrest the pictures from London and to restore them to Dublin.

O'Casey, Sean (1880–1964): in his earlier life a manual labourer, an activist in the Gaelic League and the Irish Citizen Army, who became the most celebrated dramatist of his generation in Ireland. The Abbey successfully presented his first three plays, *The Shadow of a Gunman* (1923), *Juno and the Paycock* (1924), and *The Plough and the Stars* (1926), though the latter play, which dealt with the Easter Rising, provoked a riot in the theatre. The Abbey's rejection of his next (more experimental) play *The Silver Tassie* angered O'Casey, confirming him in his decision to make England his permanent home. *The Silver Tassie* was eventually produced at the Abbey (1935), but O'Casey never wrote specifically for the Abbey again and never returned to live in Ireland.

Plunkett, Sir Horace (1854–1932): author and public servant, was the pioneer promoter of agricultural co-operation in Ireland, who founded the Irish Agricultural Organisation Society in 1894, and served as Commissioner of the Irish Congested Districts Board from 1891 to 1918. An M.P. for Dublin County South (1892–1900), he was elected to the Irish Free State Senate in 1922.

Robinson, (Esmé Stuart) Lennox (1886–1958): playwright, director, actor, critic, teacher, and sometime librarian, born in County Cork, whose first play *The Clancy Name* was produced at the Abbey in 1908. A sound craftsman, equally adept at tragic treatment of political and nationalist themes and at satiric comedy, his best-known play is *The White-Headed Boy* (1916). Manager of the Abbey from 1910 to

1914, he was re-appointed in 1919, eventually becoming one of the directors in 1924, a position he held until his death.

Shaw, G. Bernard (1856–1950): born in Dublin, third and youngest child and only son of Lucinda Elizabeth Gurly, daughter of a country gentleman, and George Carr Shaw, a poor relation of Sir Robert Shaw, Baronet, of Bushy Park, near Dublin. George Carr Shaw was a civil servant in the Four Courts, who mortgaged his pension to enter the wholesale grain business. Unsuccessful, he became a reclusive drunk, while his wife immersed herself in Dublin's amateur musical life as a singer. Her association with a music teacher and conductor, George John (later Vandeleur) Lee, led to a domestic arrangement whereby the Shaws and Lee shared a house in Hatch Street and a cottage in Dalkey, where Shaw spent the happiest years of an otherwise unhappy boyhood. Shuttling from school to school (five in all), finding little affection at home, Shaw as a lonely adolescent haunted the art gallery, bought cheap pit seats to the theatre, and wrote stories and plays in a compact with a school friend, Edward McNulty. At fifteen he abandoned formal education for a clerkship in an estate agent's office, whose proprietor Charles Uniacke Townshend was a relation of Shaw's future wife. Though promoted to the post of cashier he found the work—and Dublin—uncongenial, uninspiring, and unprofitable. At the end of March 1876, following his mother (who had deserted her husband and son three years earlier), he abandoned Ireland for England, and did not set foot on his native soil again for 29 years.

During the first years of his emigration Shaw sought employment desultorily, living off his mother while he wrote five unpublishable novels. Hitherto 'flatly Fenian' in his political leanings, he immersed himself in the international Socialist movement. Joining the newly created Fabian Society in 1884 he became its driving force, helping to raise it to political prominence as a middle-class Socialist organisation. He also began to make inroads as a journalist, becoming in rapid succession an accomplished reviewer of books, art, music and drama. His interest in Ireland in these years manifested itself only slightly, in a few book reviews, membership in the fledgling Celtic League (attending only one meeting), and acquaintanceship with Oscar Wilde, George Moore, and W.B. Yeats, to whom he was introduced at the home of William Morris on 12th February 1888.

In December 1892 the Independent Theatre privately presented his first completed play *Widowers' Houses*. Two years later his *Arms and the Man* had a West End production, underwritten by an anonymous benefactor later identified as Annie Horniman. Seven of Shaw's plays were published as *Plays Pleasant and Unpleasant* in 1898, two months before his marriage to the wealthy Charlotte Payne-Townshend of Derry, Rosscarbery, Co. Cork. With his sponsorship in 1904 (the same year in which the Abbey Theatre opened) of the Vedrenne-Barker repertory experiment at the Court Theatre, London, with more than seven hundred performances of sixteen of his plays presented over a three year period, Shaw became the recognised leader in the new English theatre of ideas. One of the most successful of the Court productions was *John Bull's Other Island* (1904), intended for but declined by the Abbey.

The next year Charlotte Shaw prevailed upon her husband to return to Ireland for the first of fourteen visits; the last of these was in 1923, during which he completed *Saint Joan*. From his first return, as though to compensate for years of neglect, Shaw concerned himself polemically with all the important issues of Ireland's political and social life: Home Rule, nationalism, religious dissension, partition, language, censorship, and wartime neutrality. From 1905, as well, he took an interest in the activity of the Irish National Theatre, developing a close personal and working relationship with Lady Gregory.

In his late years Shaw became First Citizen of the World, celebrated internationally, visiting five continents, honoured by the award of the Nobel Prize for Literature, and published in more than two dozen languages and dialects. He outlived Charlotte by seven years, his death occurring at Ayot St Lawrence on 2nd November 1950. When his executor, in response to his testamentary wishes, declined the suggestion of the Dean of St Patrick's that Shaw should be buried in Dublin beside Swift, his ashes, mingled with those of Charlotte, were strewn over the lawns and garden at Ayot.

Synge, (Edmund) John Millington (1871–1909): Ireland's first modern playwright and, with Yeats and Lady Gregory, one of the Abbey's first directors. Although he lived only long enough to complete six plays, these rapidly established him as one of the great dramatists of the twentieth century. His satiric comedy *The Playboy of the Western World* (1907) outraged the Irish at home and abroad by its realism and bitter irony, triggering riotous demonstrations in Dublin when first produced and again in the United States during the Abbey Players' first tour of that country in 1911.

Yeats, William Butler (1865–1939): the eldest child of the portrait-painter John B. Yeats, grew up between England and Ireland. An admired poet from the appearance of his first volume *The Wanderings of Oisin* (1889), he spent his early career working as a literary journalist. The driving-force of the Irish literary revival, he helped to found the Irish Literary Society (London) in 1891, the National Literary Society (Dublin) in 1892, and the Irish Literary Theatre in 1897. He made his theatrical début in 1894 with the production of his *The Land of Heart's Desire* in the London season of plays at the Avenue Theatre that included Shaw's *Arms and the Man*, and was a prolific poetic playwright all his life. In 1904 he solicited *John Bull's Other Island* for the Irish National Theatre (about to become the Abbey), but the play proved too demanding for the company. A very close friend and life-long associate of Lady Gregory, he spent a large part of most summers at Coole Park from 1897 on. In 1917 he married Georgiana Hyde-Lees; they had two children. He served as a Senator in the newly-established Irish Free State from 1922 to 1926, was awarded the Nobel Prize for Literature in 1923, and with Shaw established the Irish Academy of Letters in 1932. He died in the south of France in 1939.

PLATES

FORBIDDEN IN ENGLAND, PRODUCED IN IRELAND.

BERNARD SHAW'S "THE SHOWING UP OF BLANCO POSNET," AT THE ABBEY THEATRE, DUBLIN.

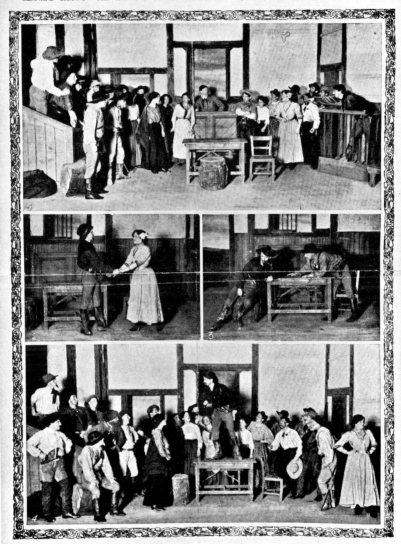

1. THE TRIAL OF BLANCO POSNET FOR HORSE-STEALING: THE SCENE IN THE PRIMITIVE COURT-HOUSE.

2. MR. FRED O'DONOVAN AS BLANCO POSNET, AND MISS SARAH ALLGOOD AS FEEMY EVANS.

3. MR. FRED O'DONOVAN AS BLANCO POSNET, AND MR. ARTHUR SINCLAIR AS ELDER DANIELS.

4. BLANCO ADDRESSING THE CROWD IN THE COURT-HOUSE: "I'M FOR THE GREAT GAME EVERY TIME."

In the first picture the chief figures (reading from left to right) are Mr. Arthur Sinclair as Elder Daniels; Miss Maire O'Neill as the Woman, Mr. S. J. Morgan as the Sheriff; Mr. J. M. Kerrigan as Strapper Kemp; Miss Sarah Allgood as Feemy Evans; and Mr. Fred O'Donovan as Blanco Posnet. In the fourth photograph Mr. Fred O'Donovan is seen on the table; Miss Sarah Allgood is on the extreme right. Mr. Shaw's "sermon in crude melodrama," "The Showing Up of Blanco Posnet," received magnificent advertisement from the action of Mr. Redford, who refused to license it for production. Thereupon it was decided to give it at the Abbey Theatre, Dublin, the jurisdiction of the Censor not extending to Ireland. It was found, however, that the Lord Lieutenant had power of veto. For a time, Lord Aberdeen showed signs of using this power to the full, but, in view of a slight rewriting of certain sentences in the play, did not do so, with the result that it was duly produced on Wednesday last.—[*Photographs by Lafayette.*]

Plate 1
(Photo by Lafayette; Dan H. Laurence Collection, University of Guelph)

Plate 2
Coole Park, 1915
(Photo by Bernard Shaw; Colin Smythe Collection)

Plate 3
Shaw at Coole, 1915
(Photo by the Hon. W. F. Bailey; Bernard F. Burgunder Collection, Cornell University)

Plate 4
Lady Gregory on the front lawn of Coole, *c.*1915
(Photo by Bernard Shaw; Colin Smythe Collection)

Plate 5
Coole, 1915.
Lady Gregory's grandson Richard is at the wheel of
the car, her granddaughters Anne and Catherine
with their nurse watch from the window above.
(Photo by W. F. Bailey;
Bernard F. Burgunder Collection, Cornell University)

Plate 6

Plate 7
Ireland, *c.*1908, with Charlotte F. Shaw.
(Photographer unidentified;
Dan H. Laurence Collection, University of Guelph)

Plate 8
Shaw at Burren Pier.
(Bernard F. Burgunder Collection, Cornell University)

Plate 9
Coole, 1915, with grandson Richard Gregory.
(Photo by Bernard Shaw; originally published in,
and reproduced from, F. E. Lowenstein's
Bernard Shaw through the Camera, 1948, p.91)

Plate 10
Ayot St Lawrence, (undated).
(Photo by Bernard Shaw; Shaw Photographic Archive,
British Library of Political and Economic Science)

Plate 11
Hall-doorknob from Coole: presented to
Shaw by Frank Curran of Galway in 1947
after the demolition of Coole House;
preserved in the study at Shaw's Corner.
(Photo by Gerald James; courtesy of
the National Trust)

Plate 12
Lithograph reproduction of pastel
portrait of Lady Gregory, 1893,
by Lisa Stillman (Mrs Jopling);
a similar reproduction hung
in the study at Shaw's Corner.
(Colin Smythe Collection)

Plate 13
Lady Gregory as Kathleen Ni Houlihan,
at the Abbey Theatre, 20 March 1919.
"When I see that play I feel it might lead a man
to do something foolish" GBS
(Photographer unidentified; Colin Smythe Collection)

Two ladies of Galway named Cathrine and Anna
Whom some called acushla and some called alanna
On finding the gate of the fruit garden undone
Stole grandmamma's apples and sent them to London

And grandmamma said that the poor village schoolchildren
Were better behaved than the well-brought-up Coole children
And threatened them with the most merciless whippings
If ever again they laid hands on her pippins

In vain they explained that the man who was battening
On grandmamma's apples would die without fattening
    She seized the piano
    And threw it at Anna
Then shrieking at Cathrine "Just let me catch you"
She walloped her hard with the drawingroom statue.

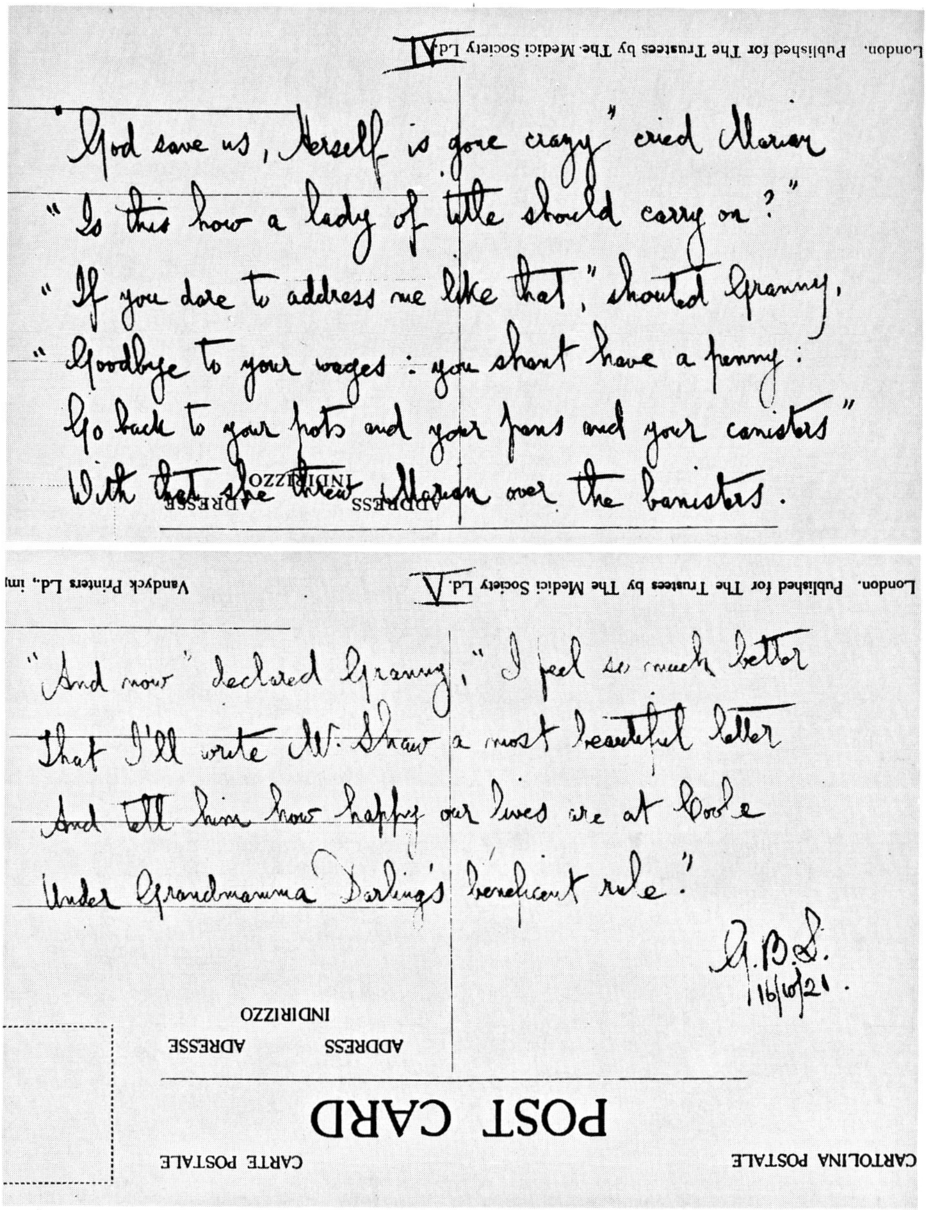
London. Published for The Trustees by The Medici Society Ld. IV

"God save us, Herself is gone crazy" cried Marian
"Is this how a lady of title should carry on?"
"If you dare to address me like that," shouted Granny,
"Goodbye to your wages: you shan't have a penny:
Go back to your pots and your pans and your canisters"
With that she threw Marian over the banisters.

ADDRESS INDIRIZZO ADRESSE

London. Published for The Trustees by The Medici Society Ld. V Vandyck Printers Ld., im

"And now" declared Granny, "I feel so much better
That I'll write Mr. Shaw a most beautiful letter
And tell him how happy our lives are at Coole
Under Grandmamma Darling's beneficent rule."

G.B.S.
16/10/21.

ADDRESS INDIRIZZO ADRESSE

POST CARD

CARTOLINA POSTALE CARTE POSTALE

Plate 14

A series of five postcards comprising Shaw's verses for the Gregory Granddaughters, 1921 (see pp.160-1).
(Stolen from Sotheby's, present location unknown)

Plate 15
Embroidered picture of the Abbey Theatre
by Susan Mary (Lily) Yeats
(Cuala Industries, date unknown; Anne Yeats Collection)

SHAW TO LADY GREGORY
[TLS: Burgunder, Cornell]

10 Adelphi Terrace. London
12th June 1909

[Lady Gregory was in London for performances by the Abbey company at the Royal Court, where she joined the Shaws in their box during the production of *The Playboy* and *Kathleen Ni Houlihan*. Following the death of Synge in March, Yeats and Lady Gregory had been going through his papers with a view to publishing a collection of his work. The mooted subscribers' de luxe edition by Elizabeth Yeats's Cuala Press never materialised, but Maunsel did include a de luxe issue of Synge's *Works* when it was published in four volumes the following year. Lady Gregory's first collection, *Seven Short Plays*, was published by Maunsel in June 1909.]

Dear Lady Gregory

I think the best thing to do is to collect Synge's work first; so that you may know exactly how big a book it would make. Then, if no alternative method of publication had presented itself in the meantime, you could send the stuff to Miss Yeats and ask her for an estimate of the cost of what I call a first folio, which, as folios are so unwieldy, had better be a first quarto; but which, anyhow, should be a masterpiece of printing, able to rank with the books of Ashendene, the Doves, or the Kelmscott presses. I think it is possible that with an artistic prospectus and sample page, judiciously circulated, we might get sufficient subscriptions at, say, two guineas a copy to make the enterprise feasible. By this I do not mean completely covering the cost. If the loss could be reduced to a bearable point, then you might ask me and any others whom you have reason to regard as squeezable in the matter, to make up the difference.

I think we should also guarantee whatever sum might be necessary to pay Miss Yeats for experimental pages, the prospectus, postage, and so forth, in case the thing fell through. Also, as people are not accustomed to pay for books of this kind until they are ready for delivery, and as Miss Yeats might not be in a position to advance the necessary capital, it may be necessary to advance money to her on the security of the subscriptions. Within reason, I am prepared to help in this way; and I daresay my wife would also lend a hand.

The alternative would be to print and publish a collected edition in the ordinary way. I should not hawk it about to publishers asking them to speculate and pay a royalty. It would be better to scrape together enough money—say £130—to print and bind an edition and publish on commission. I think it quite probable that the edition would sell out, in which case it would repay the cost twice over. Those who advanced the money could be paid with interest if necessary. The editors could also be paid a little if they cannot afford to do it for nothing (I do not know how Yeats is situated in this respect); and the rest could be handed with the plates to Synge's executors, who could then take the matter over, and if the market was not exhausted, order fresh editions at their own expense, or make an arrangement with the publisher as seemed best to them. Our work in the matter would be finished, as Synge would have been effectually rescued from oblivion.

There is no reason why both plans should not be carried out if sufficient support were forthcoming. The edition by Miss Yeats at two guineas would not interfere with an ordinary edition. It would help if it got talked about; but probably it would have no perceptible effect at all, as the two things appeal to quite different markets, and there is still extraordinarily little public notice taken of artistic bookmaking.

Are your own plays published? I should like very much to read them, because I shall have no opportunity of seeing them. They are quite out-of-the-way good even from a mere professional point of view; and I should like to know where they can be got on occasion. Dont give them to me: never give people books: I never read books that people give me; but when I buy them I feel I have thrown my money away unless I read them. Let this sordid truth be your golden rule through life. The real superiority of the English to the Irish lies in the fact that an Englishman will do anything for money and an Irishman will do nothing for it.

Yours sincerely
G. Bernard Shaw

The original patent for the Abbey Theatre, which had been granted in 1904, was due to expire in 1910, and it already seemed unlikely that Miss Horniman, who had been on bad terms with the company for some time past, would renew her subsidy to the Abbey. Lady Gregory, looking to Shaw for support, clearly hoped that he might even join Yeats and herself as one of the theatre's Directors. Although Shaw was unwilling to go so far, he did agree to help; on 24th June, when Lady Gregory was already back at Coole, Yeats reported to her: 'I have just seen Shaw. He advises a statement asking for funds and promises a guarantee and that his name can go on the circular' [ALS/p: NLI].

After the great success of the partnership between J.E. Vedrenne and Harley Granville Barker in their seasons at the Royal Court (1904-7), a West End season at the Savoy in 1907-8 had been a disastrous financial failure. *The Shewing-up of Blanco Posnet*, subtitled 'a Sermon in crude Melodrama', was written between 16th February and 8th March 1909 for Herbert Beerbohm Tree's After Noon Theatre. It was already in rehearsal when, on 13th May, the theatre management was notified that the play had been denied a licence by the Lord Chamberlain's reader on the grounds that it was blasphemous. By an historical accident, however, the Lord Chamberlain had no powers over the production of plays in Ireland, so that, by having it performed in the Abbey, Shaw could evade the Censor.

A year earlier, from 28th September to 3rd October 1908, after a motoring tour of other parts of Ireland, Shaw had made his first return to Dublin since his departure in 1876, visiting both the Abbey Theatre and the Municipal Gallery that Hugh Lane had helped to establish earlier that year.

LADY GREGORY: *SEVENTY YEARS*

[June 1909]

... on my last day in London I went down to Wheathampstead Herts to see Bernard Shaw. He met me at the station and we went to his house, a rather uninteresting little villa (it is a rectory), in the sort of country I hate, all green hedges and red villages and parish churches and no horizon. We talked the theatre matter out. He is very sympathetic, says we have done wonders, and the players have come on very much, and agrees that Synge's plays could not be given by any English players, and it is unlikely they will want to give them. But he calculates we ought to have £5,000 to our back to apply for a new patent, and says he can't take it on himself, for he had to pay £6,000 for the Granville Barker Vedrenne experiment that failed. ... And he won't come as Director, for he never will do that unless he can work at a thing, 'and the irony of it is, I am engaged in trying to build up a theatre in England'. But he will think it over, and help us if a means should arise.

He thought we would get help from the Corporation, but I said we should lose our independence doing that, the first thing they would do would be to forbid *Playboy*.

He gave me *Blanco Posnet* and says the Censor objects to the sentence, 'I accuse Feemy of immoral relations with Strapper', not to the so-called blasphemy. He spoke of Dublin and the dislike he had had to re-visiting it, and how at last he had come in a motor, and hadn't minded coming in, as it were, by the back door. It looked to him just as before, the houses had never been painted since, and the little shops had eggs in the windows, with mice and rats running over them, and rubbish that looked as if on its way to the dust heap. I said there were at least two bright spots now, our theatre and Hugh Lane's gallery, and he cordially agreed, and said the gallery was wonderful. ...

When Yeats came to Coole I asked if we couldn't put on *Blanco Posnet* as the Censor has refused leave for it in London...

LADY GREGORY TO SHAW
[TLS: BL]

Coole Park. Gort. Co. Galway
6th July [1909]

Dear Mr Shaw
W.B. Yeats arrived today, and I said 'Couldn't we do Blanco Posnet?' and he said 'I want to and Shaw has offered it'. I think we could do it well, and I don't think anything could show up

the hypocrisy of the British Censor more than a performance in Dublin where the audience is known to be so sensitive. Mr Yeats spoke to Miss Allgood in London and she also was very much excited at the idea. It would be a great advantage if you could come over and rehearse it yourself. Norreys Connell who might have rehearsed it has resigned (in consequence avowedly of 'an incomprehensible letter from Miss Horniman from which I gather that she commands me to apologise to her because you (Yeats) did not restrain Sara Allgood from abetting Mrs Lyttelton in a political demonstration').

Miss Allgood is very anxious to produce it, but she has only produced peasant plays, and Mr Yeats cant get to Dublin before Horse Show.

Yours sincerely
A Gregory

The Horse Show comes on last week of August.

Norreys Connell was the pen-name of Conal O'Riordan, the Irish author and playwright, who was an acquaintance of Shaw, and who had taken over as managing director of the Abbey after the death of Synge. The incident over which he resigned his directorship involved Sara Allgood, one of the Abbey's leading actresses, who, while in London with the company, had at the suggestion of Mrs Patrick Campbell given a reading at a meeting organised by Mrs Edith Lyttelton, a friend of Mrs Campbell and the author of several plays. Miss Horniman, interpreting this as a breach of the principle she had laid down that politics should be avoided in connection with the Abbey Theatre, angrily reacted with a threat to withdraw the subsidy to the Abbey due on September 1st and to find a new tenant for the theatre. This further sign of her worsening relations with the Abbey came at a time when much of her interest, as well as a good deal of her money, was being diverted to the Gaiety Theatre, Manchester, for the repertory company she had established there in 1907.

LADY GREGORY TO SHAW
[TLS: BL]

Coole Park. Gort
8th July [1909]

[The letters enclosed were the correspondence over the incident of
Sara Allgood's recitation: Miss Horniman's letter of 1st July 1909 to
Lady Gregory with her reply of 6th July, and Mrs Patrick Campbell's
letter of apology to Miss Horniman of 5th July with Miss Horniman's
response of the same date, in which she repeated her threat to
discontinue her subsidy for the Abbey.]

Dear Mr Shaw
    Would you be so kind as to look at enclosed letters, and to ask
Mr Barker or some professional (if you don't know yourself) if
Miss Horniman is right in saying that we can control Miss
Allgood's liberty of taking engagements at concerts etc during
her vacation? We are ready to go as far as we can towards
complying with Miss Horniman's demands, but we don't want
to make a demand of Miss Allgood which we have no right to
do, and we cannot be sure of this. Miss Horniman may
probably raise some other point if we give in, for she told Yeats
'it was time for our theatre to end', and I think from various
indications it is the money she wants, for her other enterprise.
However we must hold on as long as we can, and I daresay we
could get Mrs Lyttelton to make some sort of apology. It may
end in law, for Miss Horniman made no definite stipulation
with us as she says, but only talked a great deal about Irish
politics and her dislike of them. A break up on September 1
would be too sudden to allow us fair time to make an appeal for
capital, or to provide for the future of our actors. Anyhow we
want to walk circumspectly, and so it will be a great help if we
can get correct information on this point of meddling with Miss
Allgood. It was I believe an 'At Home' given by the Women's
Conservative association she gave her recitation at.

Yours sincerely
A Gregory

SHAW TO LADY GREGORY
[TLS: Berg, NYPL]

10 Adelphi Terrace. London
9th July 1909

My dear Lady Gregory

Your power over Miss Allgood depends altogether on the terms of your contract with her. If she has signed an agreement giving you her professional services *exclusively* for a definite period, then she has no right to take an engagement without your permission. Though of course her ordinary rights as a citizen would remain unimpaired; for instance, she could speak at a Home Rule or any other meeting if she pleased, if this also were not provided for by a clause in your agreement.

But agreement or no agreement, all this talk about apologies is utter nonsense. No doubt Miss Allgood can and should apologize if she has broken her agreement or even if she has violated the spirit of an honorable understanding with Miss Horniman. But why on earth should Mrs Lyttelton apologize? Of course she might be amiable enough to do so just as she might do any absurd and harmless thing to humour a lunatic. But as Miss Horniman is not a lunatic, or at least not a certified one: that is, she is as sane as you or I or Yeats (which is perhaps not saying much), there is no mortal reason that I can see why Mrs Lyttelton should take any other ground except the obvious one of seeing Miss Horniman very considerably dashed first.

The real crux of the situation is the contract of the theatre with Miss Horniman. If the subsidy depends absolutely on Miss Horniman's personal caprice—if by simply opening her hand she can let the theatre sink into the sea—then of course the theatre must perish unless by any chance Mrs Lyttelton attaches such importance to it as to be willing to humiliate herself in the way demanded by Miss Horniman. But surely there must be something behind all this. I know Miss Horniman. She is a strange creature, a quarrelsome devil as ever walked, a crank of the first order; but she has genuine artistic enthusiasm and public spirit, and she is a woman of honor, incapable of carrying one of her tantrums to the point of breaking her engagements and wrecking a national enterprise merely to gratify her temper. I do not believe she cares two-pence about Mrs Lyttelton:

she only wants to stand the theatre on its head for a day or two for the fun of it.

Still, though I do not think her letter to Mrs Patrick Campbell can be considered official, it is necessary to take some formal and serious decision on the letter to you dated the 1st July. In that she says formally that she will stop the subsidy and take the theatre out of your hands, unless you can induce Mrs Lyttelton to do something which you not only cannot compel her to do, but which you obviously have no right even to ask her to do. Under these circumstances, you can do nothing except write to Miss Horniman with equal formality to say that since one of the conditions she proposes is obviously beyond your powers, she has left no course open to you except to announce that the theatre must suspend its operations in consequence of her action, and to ask her if her resolution to let the Abbey Theatre to a permanent tenant excludes the possibility of your becoming that tenant if you can procure the capital for a reconstructed enterprise.

You can see by Mrs Patrick Campbell's letter that she regards Miss Horniman as a baby who must be petted back into good humor; and I do not think anybody can blame Mrs Campbell for it. It serves Miss Horniman right. But Miss Horniman, as you can see by the degree of success she has achieved, is not fundamentally an incapable woman. If a straight and dignified line is taken with her, she will respond to it. I know that that is the line which would be natural and congenial to you. Fight it out with Miss Horniman yourself. She loves a row; but she knows a lady when she meets one, and is even capable of doing a little in that way herself, in spite of her perverse delight in assuring the world that she is nothing but a commercial traveller. It often happens that in these matters qui s'accuse s'excuse.

Yours sincerely
G. Bernard Shaw

LADY GREGORY TO SHAW
[TLS: BL]

Coole Park. Gort
11th July [1909]

[The 'friend from America' who supported the Abbey was John Quinn, the New York lawyer and patron of the arts, who as early as 1903 had given money to the theatre movement and continued to help in many ways, including the American copyrighting of plays. Lady Gregory's son Robert had worked as scene designer on a number of plays both of his mother and of Yeats at the Abbey from 1903 on. Edward Martyn, co-founder of the Irish Literary Theatre in 1897 and financial backer for its first season in 1899, had doubts about the religious orthodoxy of Yeats's *The Countess Cathleen* and as a devout Catholic considered that he might have to withdraw his support.]

My dear Mr Shaw

A great many thanks indeed for your letter. It is a very valuable one, and may come in useful if we have further trouble. For the moment things have been settled by the quite unexpected action of Mrs Lyttelton (who probably heard of the difficulty through Mrs Campbell). She writes to Miss Horniman: Dear Madam, I understand that I should not have engaged Miss Allgood to give a recitation without managerial permission. I was not aware that this was necessary or would certainly have applied for it. I am sorry the mistake should have arisen. Yours truly, Edith Lyttelton.

Whether Miss Horniman thinks this formal and very stiff epistle worth all her outbreak I don't know, but we can now make the other concession she asks for, and all will be quiet till there is another full moon. I see in Moore's Almanac there was one just then! Her conduct was really very bad, for Yeats went to see her in London and showed such indignation at her demand for these apologies, especially Mrs Lyttelton's, that she promised to withdraw it, and be satisfied with a note in the programme about permission for actors. Then as soon as he had started for Ireland she wrote the letter to Mrs Campbell reiterating the demand. We should not have given in to her right to stop the work without legal opinion. There is no formal bond, but there are many letters in none of which can we remember a clause of the kind she infers. Also though she has given so

much, there has been a good deal of actual money outside hers
put into the business, mine and some from a friend from
America chiefly, and even some of Yeats, besides all our work,
for we have done the actual work of secretary and manager, and
my son of scene painter, to carry it on. Then the plays; at the
very opening of the Abbey Theatre I had an offer for my first
comedy 'Spreading the News' and refused it that I might keep it
exclusively for the Theatre, as I did all my comedies [until] the
other day. (I have never had a penny out of the Theatre nor has
Yeats.) We engaged actors and made engagements on the
strength of lasting till 1910, and we should have to pay for
broken contracts if it came to an end now, and I don't think the
law of contracts would allow her to break her engagement for a
moment's caprice. However it's a blessing we haven't got to try.
As to a motive behind, Yeats hears from an old friend of hers
that she was snubbed in her youth, and wants to avenge herself
now by snubbing any of the 'classes' she can get at, but I think
also she has spent more than she intended in Manchester, and
grudges what she promised us. But we think from old experience we shall have a peace for a while after this exhibition.

What about Blanco? Our players have holidays now, and go
to Belfast first week in August, so they must begin rehearsals
there. Then they will have a clear fortnight in Dublin with
nothing to do but rehearse Blanco and run through some old
work for the Horse Show week, which begins 23rd. I have been
going carefully through it and think we can cast it well. They
could begin learning their parts at any time, while on their
holiday, if they had the script. Shall we have it typed or will you
give copies?

Thank you very much for your opinion on Miss Allgood's
freedom. Her contract has been a very loose one, but we must
tighten it up now in deference to our capitalist. Our first
capitalist Ed. Martyn, tried to throw us over at a moment's
notice, but that was an affair of saving his soul, which he
thought was risked by being 'accessory after the fact' to the
Countess Cathleen saving hers—so deserved more sympathy!

Yours sincerely
A. Gregory

SHAW TO LADY GREGORY
[TLS: Berg, NYPL]

10 Adelphi Terrace. London
7th August 1909

[*Press Cuttings*, a topical sketch on suffragism written between March
and May 1909 for performance in aid of the London Society for
Women's Suffrage, had been refused a licence on 24th June, but
would be passed on 17th August with the names altered. In the event,
the Abbey company did not take up Shaw's suggestion of performing
Blanco Posnet in 'broad Irish', instead attempting American accents,
with only moderate success.]

Dear Lady Gregory
    It has just occurred to me that as Blanco Posnet is not long
enough to make a complete play bill, and as you may not have a
fresh brace of short plays ready, it might be worth while to try
the effect of an all-Shaw program, and follow up Blanco Posnet
with Press Cuttings. Press Cuttings has also been forbidden by
the Censor; and though I understand he is now going to license
it on condition of my changing the names Mitchener and
Balsquith to Bones and Johnson, still you could retain the
original names in Dublin and thus keep up the air of defying the
Saxon tyrant.
    I enclose a copy of the play for your consideration.
    I have been asked whether I want Blanco Posnet done with an
American accent. I reply that I do not care with what accent it is
done, provided it is made effective. I should play it in broad
Irish, especially as that language will lend itself very congenially
to the blasphemies with which the dialogue bristles.
    If this suggestion of Press Cuttings is at all inconvenient, do
not give it a second thought. It was suggested to me by an
application from Miss Horniman's people to be allowed to do
Press Cuttings in Manchester; and it immediately occurred to
me why not Dublin also?

Yours sincerely
G. Bernard Shaw

LADY GREGORY TO SHAW
[TLS: BL]

Coole Park. Gort
9th August [1909]

[Her worries about the lack of an adequate producer for *Blanco* in a company that had previously been limited largely to peasant plays brought Lady Gregory to Dublin on the 12th August, sooner than she had planned. At that stage she was hoping to get the help of an (unidentified) London actor friend on the production. In a letter to her from Coole, postmarked the 12th August, Yeats wrote 'I doubt if any of us have the experience to do Posnett properly—it is a sort of play the English have a monopoly of us and besides I had just as soon we had not the responsibilities of it at this moment—Shaw is so important' (ALS/p: NLI). In the event, however, Lady Gregory took over rehearsals herself.]

Dear Mr Shaw

Thank you very much indeed for Press Cuttings, and for giving us the chance, or the offer of doing it. We have been considering possibilities however and have decided that it would not be possible for our company to get it up in time, as they are only just back from Belfast, and it will take them all their time to get up Posnett, with other work they have to get up for the week of Horse Show. In fact we had decided not to put Posnett on until Wednesday 25th, to give an extra couple of days, as W.B. Yeats and I will only be able to get to Dublin 20th to see to last rehearsals. It is its being just outside their usual line of peasant work that makes a little more time necessary. I think they should give a very good show. Press Cuttings is extraordinarily amusing, we have all been delighting in it, but on the whole Blanco is our best cheval de bataille, and I am glad we had it first. It is great fun the respectable Lord Aberdeen being responsible, especially as he can't come to see it, as vice-royalty doesn't like the colour of our carpets. We have never put down red ones, I always suggest their wearing red slippers.

We have just had a victory in taking the Playboy to Belfast, and playing it two or three times. This is its first Irish provincial appearance, and we were a little anxious, but it was very well received, just a little booing but nothing that mattered, and the Press notices good. One of the Belfast papers [*Northern Whig*,

5th August 1909] in its notice that Blanco was to be performed put as a heading 'Probable interference of the Lord Lieutenant' but that is too good to be true—we could raise a great cry of injustice to an ill treated son of Erin if this were done.

Yours sincerely
Augusta Gregory

LADY GREGORY TO SHAW
[Telegram: HRC]

Dublin
12th August 1909
1.55 p.m.

HAVE PRIVATE INFORMATION CASTLE STOPS PER-
FORMANCE WOULD PRIVATE PERFORMANCE OR
FORMING SOCIETY BE BEST ALTERNATIVE

GREGORY ABBEY THEATRE

A very important factor in the circumstances surrounding the production of *Blanco Posnet* was the Joint Committee on Dramatic Censorship, which had been set up by the British Parliament and which had met for the first time in London on 29th July 1909. The Committee had heard evidence from Shaw and many other eminent men of the theatre opposed to censorship; the issue was thus very much in the news. After the announcement of the intended production of *Blanco Posnet* by the Abbey during the week of the Royal Dublin Society's Horse Show, Dublin's busiest social week of the year, a paragraph appeared in the *Irish Times* on 5th August headed 'Mr Shaw's Prohibited Play. Is there an Irish Censorship?', maintaining that there was 'a separate Irish Censorship, the duty devolving on the Lord Lieutenant of the day'. At this, Dublin Castle took alarm and a note went from the Metropolitan Police Office on 6th August to the Under Secretary, Sir James Dougherty, drawing his attention to the *Irish Times* piece and other press notices of the 'proposed production' of 'Bernard Shaw's play the performance of which in England has been prohibited by the Censor of plays'[SPO]. As the jurisdiction of the Lord Chamberlain on dramatic censorship did not extend to Ireland, the only weapon the Irish authorities had was the power of the Lord Lieutenant, which was limited to Dublin, to revoke a theatre's patent on grounds of infringing the terms under which it had been granted. At first the Castle tried to exert pressure by an indirect approach to the Abbey's solicitors, Whitney and Moore, who had handled the original patent application.

LADY GREGORY'S JOURNAL
[TMS with holograph revisions: HRC]

Thursday 12th August [1909]
7.30

[Parts of Lady Gregory's journal were published in her account of the 'fight with the Castle' in *Our Irish Theatre* in 1913, but she had to suppress some of the names and the substance of her interviews with Dublin Castle, and she misrepresented the chronology of events.

It was Miss Horniman who put up the money for the establishment of the Abbey theatre; when, however, it came to the patent application it was discovered that the patentee had to be an Irish resident, so Lady Gregory applied for the patent on Miss Horniman's behalf. The *Irish Times* article of 5th August had incorrectly said that the patent had been transferred from Miss Horniman 'to Lady Gregory, Mr Yeats and the Irish National Theatre Company'. The philanthropist, Edward Cecil Guinness, 1st Viscount (later Earl of) Iveagh, though a Unionist in politics, was highly regarded by the nationalist community and was to be presented with an address of thanks by the Dublin Corporation for his many and lavish gifts to the city in September 1909. His support for *Blanco Posnet* was therefore a very strong card for Lady Gregory to play. *The Merry Widow*, the immensely popular musical comedy, produced in Dublin in the same week as *Blanco Posnet* by the London theatrical entrepreneur, George Edwardes, and *The Devil*, Henry Hamilton's adaptation of Ferenc Molnár's *Az Ördög*, presented in London in April-May 1909, had both been cited in the controversy over censorship as examples of

plays of dubious merit passed by the Censor. William Joseph Walsh
had been Roman Catholic Archbishop of Dublin since 1885. G.A.
Redford, the Lord Chamberlain's examiner of plays, was previously a
bank manager.]

At the theatre this morning [W.A.] Henderson [secretary of the
Abbey] told me Whitney and Moore had telephoned that they
had a hint there would be interference with the production of
Blanco Posnett by the Castle and would like to see me.

I went to see Dr Moore. He said a Castle official, whose name
he would not give, had called the day before yesterday and said
'as a friend of Sir Benjamin's (Whitney) I have come to tell you
that if this play is produced it will be a very expensive thing for
Miss Horniman'. Dr Moore took this to mean the patent would
be forfeited. I talked the matter over with him, and asked if he
would get further information from his friend as to what
method they meant to adopt, for I would not risk the immediate
forfeiture of the patent, but would not mind a threat of refusal
to give a new patent, as by that time Dec 1910 it is not likely
either the present Lord Lieutenant or the present Censor would
be in office.

Dr Moore said he would go and see his friend, and at a
quarter past two I had a message on the telephone from him that
I had better see the Under Secretary, or that he wished to see me
(I didn't hear very well) before 3 o'c. I went to the Castle and
saw Sir James Dougherty. He said 'Well'. I said 'are you going
to cut off our heads?' He said, 'This is a very serious business, I
think you are very ill-advised to think of putting on this play.
May I ask how it came about?' I said, 'Mr Shaw offered it and
we accepted it'. He said, 'you have put us in a most difficult and
disagreeable position by putting on a play which the English
Censor objected to'. I said 'we do not take his view of it, and we
think it hypocrisy objecting to a fallen woman in homespun on
the stage, when a fallen woman in satin has been the theme of
such a great number of plays passed'. He said 'It is not that the
Censor objected to, it is the use of certain expressions which
may be considered blasphemy. Could not they be left out?' I
said 'then there would be no play. The subject of the play is a
man, a horse-thief, shaking his fist at Heaven, and finding
afterwards that Heaven is too strong for him. If there were no

defiance there could be no victory. It is the same theme that
Milton has taken in Satan's defiance in "Paradise Lost". I
consider it a deeply religious play, and one that could hurt no
man, woman or child. If it had been written by some religious
leader, or even a dramatist considered safe, nonconformists
would admire and approve of it'. He said 'We have nothing to
do with that, the fact for us is that the Censor has banned it'. I
said, 'yes, and passed "The Merry Widow", which is to be
performed here the same week, and which I have heard is
objectionable and "The Devil" which I saw in London'. He said
'We would not have interfered but what can we do when we see
such paragraphs as these', handing me a cutting from the 'Irish
Times' headed 'Have we a Censor?'. I said 'we had not written
or authorised it, as you might see by its being incorrect. I am
sole Patentee of the theatre'. He said 'Dublin society will call
out against us if we let it go on'. I said 'Lord Iveagh has taken six
places'. He said 'For that play?' I said 'Yes, for that play, and I
believe Dublin society is likely to follow Lord Iveagh'. He said
'and Archbishop Walsh may object'. I was silent. He said 'It is
very hard on the Lord Lieutenant, you should have had more
consideration for him'. I said 'we did not know or remember
that the power rested with him, but it *is* hard on him, for he
can't please everybody'. He said 'Will you not give it up?' I said
'what will you do if we go on?' He said 'Either take no notice or
take the patent from you at once'. I said 'If you decide to forfeit
our patent we will not give a public performance: but if we give
no performance to be judged by, we shall rest under the slur of
having tried to produce something bad and injurious'. He said
'We must not provoke public opinion'. I said 'We provoked
Nationalist public opinion in the "Playboy" and you did not
interfere'. He said 'Aye, exactly so, that was quite different,
that had not been banned by the Censor'. I said 'time has
justified us for we have since produced Playboy in Dublin and
on tour with success, and it will justify us in the case of this
play'. He said 'Blanco Posnett is very inferior to "The Playboy"'. I said 'Even so, Bernard Shaw has an intellectual
position above that of Mr Synge, though he is not above him in
imaginative power; he is recognised as an intellectual force, and
his work cannot be despised'. He said 'Lord Aberdeen will have
to decide'. I said 'I should like him to know that from a business

point of view the refusal to allow this play already announced would do us serious injury'. He said 'No advertisements have been published'. I said 'Yes, the posters have been out some days, and there is a good deal of booking already from England as well as here. We are just beginning to pay our way as a theatre. We should be able to do so if we get about a dozen more stalls regularly. The people who would take stalls will be frightened off by your action. The continuance of our theatre may depend on what you do now. We are giving a great deal of employment, spending in Dublin over £1500 a year, and our Company bears the highest possible character'. He said 'I know that well'. I said 'I know Lord Aberdeen is friendly to our theatre, though he does not come to it, not liking the colour of our carpets'. He said 'He is a supporter of the drama. He was one of Sir Henry Irving's pall bearers'. I said 'When shall we know the decision?' He said 'In a day or two, perhaps tomorrow'. He said 'You can produce it in Cork, Galway or Waterford, it is only in Dublin the Lord Lieutenant has power'. He read from time to time a few lines from the patent or Act of Parliament before him 'just to get them into your head'. The last he read were 'There must be no profane representation of sacred personages and that', he said, 'applies to Blanco Posnett's representations of the Deity'. I told him of the Censor's note on the 'Playboy' ['The expression "Khaki cut-throats" must be cut out, together with any others that may be considered derogatory to His Majesty's forces'], and he laughed, and I said 'how can we think much of the opinion of a man like that?' He said 'I believe he was a Bank Manager'. We then said goodbye.

LADY GREGORY TO SHAW
[Telegram: HRC]

Dublin
12th August 1909
4.00 p.m.

HAVE INTERVIEWED CASTLE DECISION IN DAY OR TWO KEEP MATTER PRIVATE

GREGORY

LADY GREGORY TO SHAW
[ALS: BL]

Abbey Theatre. Dublin
Thursday [12th August 1909]

Dear Mr Shaw

A Castle official called 'in a friendly way' on our solicitors a day or two ago—and warned them that if we put on Blanco 'it would be an expensive business for Miss Horniman'. I only heard this today, and I sent the solicitor to find out, also 'in a friendly way', what they were going to do. Then I had a message asking me to go and see [the] Under Secretary, Sir J. Dougherty at the Castle. He was very threatening and says the English Censor having reported the play as profane, and the Irish papers having drawn attention to the Lord Lieutenant as responsible, they will probably be forced to stop it as 'Archbishop Walsh might object, or Dublin Society'. I told him Lord Iveagh had taken six places which is committing him, and I rejected the idea of having the dialogue altered. The L. L. is in Scotland, and the matter is being referred to him, and we shall know in a day or two. I am anxious to decide what to do if it is prohibited, whether to give an invitation performance or to form a sort of Stage Society—or to produce it in Cork where we go September 6, and where [the] L. L. has no dramatic authority. We are not saying a word about it to anyone. I am here to see rehearsals etc, and will stay till the matter is settled.

Yours
A Gregory

SHAW TO LADY GREGORY
[ALS: Berg, NYPL]

12 Adelphi Terrace. London
12th August 1909

[Shaw was here replying to Lady Gregory's letter of 9th August and her two telegrams of the 12th.]

My dear Lady Gregory

Your news is almost too good to be true. If the Lord Lieutenant would only forbid an Irish play, without reading it, and after it had been declared entirely guiltless and admirable by the leading high class journal on the side of his own party (The Nation)—forbid it at the command of an official of the King's household in London, then the green flag would indeed wave over Abbey St, and we should have questions in parliament and all manner of reverberating advertisement and nationalist sympathy for the theatre.

I gather from your second telegram that the play has perhaps been submitted for approval. If so, that will be the worse for us, as the Castle can then say they forbade it on its demerits without the slightest reference to the Lord Chamberlain.

In any case, do not threaten them with a contraband performance. Threaten that we shall be suppressed; that we shall be made martyrs of; that we shall suffer as much and as publicly as possible. Tell them that they can depend on me to burn with a brighter blaze and louder yells than all Fox's martyrs.

On Saturday I start on a motoring tour. I expect to land in Waterford on Tuesday morning, and to reach Parknasilla Hotel, Sneem, Co Kerry, a couple of days later.

Yours sincerely
G. Bernard Shaw

LADY GREGORY'S JOURNAL
[TMS with holograph revisions: HRC]

Friday [13th August 1909]
5 o'c

[The Abbey had been considering a production of Sophocles' *Oedipus Rex*, either in a translation by John Eglinton or in a version being developed by Yeats. Though it was still at this time a censored play, a translation by Gilbert Murray was licensed without difficulty by the Lord Chamberlain's office and performed the following year.]

Dr Moore sent for me at 4 o'c. I went with W.B. Yeats, who had arrived. Mr Malachy Kelly, Crown Solicitor at the Castle, Sir B. Whitney's 'friend', had called and told him the Lord Lieutenant was 'entirely opposed to the play being proceeded with and would use every power the law gave him to stop it'. Mr Kelly 'thought it would be much better for us to lay the play aside'.

We decided to go on with our performance and let the patent
be forfeited, and if we must die, die gloriously. Yeats was for
this course, and I agreed. Then I thought it right to let Sir J.
Dougherty know my change of intentions, and after some
unsuccessful attempts on the telephone, W.B.Y. and I went to
see him at the Castle. He was most smiling and amiable this
time, and implored us, as we had understood him to do through
the telephone, to 'save the L. L. from this delicate position'.
'You defy us, you advertise it under our very nose, at the time
everyone is making a fight with the Censor'. He threatened to
take away our patent before the play came on at all, if we
persisted in the intention. I said that would give us a fine case.
Yeats said we intended to do *Edipus* and that this was also a
censored play, and we should be prevented if we gave in now.
He said 'leave that till the time comes, and you needn't draw our
attention to it'. We said the Irish Times might again draw his
attention to it. He proposed our having a private performance
only. I said I had a letter from Mr Shaw objecting to that course.
He moaned, and said, 'it is very hard upon us. Can you suggest
no way out of it?' We said, 'none, except our being left alone'.
He said, 'oh, Lady Gregory, appeal to your own common
sense'. When I mentioned Shaw's letter he said, 'all Shaw wants
is to use the Lord Lieutenant as a whip to lay upon the Censor'.
Yeats said he would use him in that way whatever happens. 'I
know he will', said Sir James. At last he asked if we could get
Mr Shaw to take out the passages he had already offered to take
out for the Censor. We agreed to ask him to do this, as we felt
the Castle was beaten, as the play even then would still be the
one forbidden by the English Censor.

LADY GREGORY TO SHAW
[ALS: HRC]

Dublin
Friday [13th August 1909]

[Enclosed with this letter must have been Lady Gregory's journal
notes of the day's meeting with Sir James Dougherty. The '£5
pamphlet' was the *Statement of the evidence in chief of George Bernard
Shaw before the Joint-Committee on Stage Plays*, which Shaw had had

privately printed for the members of the committee, the press and fellow dramatists. The committee refused to accept it in evidence but, Shaw complained in a letter to the *Times* of 2nd August, the demand for copies was such that 'my statement in its present form, printed for the convenience of the 12 members of the committee, will presently be worth about five guineas as a curiosity'.]

Dear Mr Shaw

The enclosed 'explains itself' and I think qualifies us for one of those valuable £5 pamphlets as a reward! We look on it as a victory, and hope you will delete as asked, for we have gained the point, that the Castle differentiates itself from the English Censor. Please keep us informed of your address in case of new complications.

Yours
A Gregory

SHAW TO LADY GREGORY
[Telegram: Berg, NYPL]

West Strand. [London]
[13th August 1909]

[Lady Gregory had wired to Shaw saying the Castle asked him to cut out the passages he had offered to delete for the English Censor. This telegram was his response.]

WHAT PASSAGES PLAY AS PRINTED IS AS ALTERED TO MAKE MEANING CLEAR TO CENSOR SPECIFY PAGE AND LINE AND WILL REPLY AT ONCE

SHAW

SHAW TO LADY GREGORY
[Telegram: Berg, NYPL]

West Strand. [London]
14th August 1909

[H.W. Massingham, in an unsigned article 'The Incorrigible Censor', in *The Nation* on 28th May, had enumerated the censor's suggested deletions in the *Blanco Posnet* text.]

THE NATION ARTICLE GIVES PARTICULARS OF
CUTS DEMANDED WHICH I REFUSED AS THEY
WOULD HAVE DESTROYED THE RELIGIOUS SIGNI-
FICANCE OF THE PLAY THE LINE ABOUT IMMORAL
RELATIONS IS DISPENSABLE AS THEY ARE MEN-
TIONED IN SEVERAL OTHER PLACES SO IT CAN BE
CUT IF THE CASTLE IS SILLY ENOUGH TO OBJECT
TO SUCH RELATIONS BEING CALLED IMMORAL
BUT I WILL CUT NOTHING ELSE IT IS AN INSULT TO
THE LORD LIEUTENANT TO IGNORE HIM AND
REFER ME TO THE REQUIREMENTS OF A SUBOR-
DINATE ENGLISH OFFICIAL I WILL BE NO PARTY
TO ANY SUCH INDELICACY PLEASE SAY I SAID SO IF
NECESSARY

BERNARD SHAW

LADY GREGORY'S JOURNAL
[TMS with holograph revisions: HRC]
Saturday 14th [August 1909]
8.30

[Having received] telegrams from Shaw and the *Nation* article
... we went to the Castle to see Sir James, but only found his
Secretary who offered to speak for us through the telephone,
but the telephone was wheezy, and after long trying all we could
arrive at was that Sir J. wanted to know, if we had seen Sir H.
Beerbohm Tree's evidence [before the censorship committee]
in which he said there were passages in Blanco that would be
better out. Then he proposed our going to see him at the lodge
as he has gout and rheumatism and couldn't come to us.
    We drove to the Under Secretary's lodge. He began on Tree,
but Yeats told him, Tree was the chief representative of the
commercial theatre we are opposed to. He then proposed our
giving a private performance, and we again told him Shaw had
forbidden that. I read him the telegram refusing cuts and saying
'it is an insult to the Lord Lieutenant to ignore him and refer me
to the requirements of a subordinate English official. I will be
no party to any such indelicacy. Please say I said so if neces-

sary'. He seemed to have forgotten he had asked for cuts. We told him we were asking Mr Shaw's leave to make one the Censor had not asked for, for practical reasons. [He] repeated his appeal to spare the L. L. I showed him the Nation article, and he read it and said 'but the Book of Job is not by the same author, as Blanco Posnett'. Yeats said 'Then if you could you would Censor the Deity'. 'Just so', said Sir James. He asked if we could make no concession. We said no, but if they decided to take the patent, we should put off the production until the beginning of our season, end of September, and produce it with Edipus, and they would have to suppress both together. He brightened up and said if we could put it off things would be much easier, as the Commission would not be sitting then or the Public so much interested in the question. I said 'Of course we should have to announce at once that it was in consequence of the threatened action of the Castle we had postponed it'. He said 'Oh you really don't mean that, you would let all the bulls loose, it would be much better not to say anything at all or to say the rehearsals took longer than you expected, it would be better'. I said 'the public announcement will be more to our own advantage'. 'Oh that is dreadful', he said. I said also 'we did not give in one quarter of an inch to Nationalist Ireland at the Playboy time, and we certainly cannot give in one quarter of an inch to the Castle'. He again said 'We must think of Archbishop Walsh'. I said he would be slow to move, for if he ordered his flock to keep away from our play he can't let them attend many of the Censor's plays, and the same thing applies to the L. L. He said 'I know that'. We said we did not give into the Church when Cardinal Logue [Roman Catholic Archbishop of Armagh] denounced the Countess Kathleen; we played it under police protection. He said 'I never heard of that, why did he object?' Yeats said 'For exactly the same objection as to [the] present one, speeches made by demons in the play'. Yeats spoke very seriously then about the principle involved; that we are trying to create a model on which a great National Theatre may be founded in the future, that if we give into the English Censor's Law running in Ireland he may forbid a play like Wills's Robert Emmett which Irving was about to act, and was made to give up for political reasons. He said 'you want in fact to have liberty to produce all plays refused by the

Censor'. I said 'we have produced none in the past and not only that we have refused plays that we thought would hurt Catholic religious feeling. We refused for instance to produce Synge's Tinkers much as we uphold his work, because a drunken Priest made ridiculous appears in it. That very play was asked for by Tree who you have been holding up to us, directly after Synge's death for production in London'. He said 'I am very sorry attention was drawn to the play; if no attention had been drawn to it by the papers, we should be all right. It is so wrong to produce it while the Commission is actually sitting and the whole question is sub judice'. He said 'we are in close official relation with the English officials of whom the Lord Chamberlain is one, that is the whole question'. We said 'we see no way out of it, we are determined to produce the play. We cannot accept the Censor's decision as applying to Ireland and you must make up your mind what course to take, but we ask to be let know as soon as possible if we are to be suppressed. We must find places for our players who will be thrown out of work'. He threw up his hands and said 'oh my dear lady, but do not speak of such a thing as possible'. I said 'why what else have you been threatening all the time'. He said 'well the L. L. will be here on Tuesday and will decide. He has not given his attention to the matter up to this' (this does not bear out Malachy Kelly's story). 'Perhaps you had better to see him'. I said I wanted to get home but would stay if absolutely necessary. He said 'O yes stay and you will probably see Lady Aberdeen also'. We have decided to go home.

LADY GREGORY TO SHAW
[Telegram: HRC]

Dublin
14th August 1909

DECISION DEFERRED TILL ABERDEENS RETURN TUESDAY.

GREGORY

LADY GREGORY TO SHAW
[ALS: HRC]

Dublin
Sunday [15th August 1909]

[Shaw, taking literally Lady Gregory's remark about the '£5 pamphlet' in her previous letter, had evidently sent her a copy of his *Statement* on censorship. Dervorgilla, the twelfth-century mistress of Diarmuid, King of Leinster, and the subject of a play by Lady Gregory in 1907, was the *casus belli* for the Norman invasion. It was one of the charges the nationalist press were to bring against the Abbey Theatre directors that, by their mishandling of the *Blanco Posnet* affair, they were giving the English authorities an opportunity to extend censorship to Ireland. The lines that Lady Gregory proposed cutting appeared in Blanco's dialogue with his hypocritical preacher brother, Elder Daniels, after Blanco's 'conversion'. The first passage ran:

> Either He killed the child a purpose or else He was beat by the croup. He cant have wanted to kill the child.

The second was longer:

> ...I lost the rotten feel all the same.
> ELDER DANIELS. It was the Lord speaking to your soul, Blanco.
> BLANCO. Oh yes: you know all about it, dont you? Youre in the Lord's confidence. He wouldnt for the world do anything to shock you, would He, Boozy? Yah! What about the croup? I guess He made the croup when He was thinking of one thing; and then He made the child when He was thinking of something else; and the croup got past Him and killed the child. Some of us will have to find out how to kill the croup, I guess. I think I'll turn doctor, just on the chance of getting back on Him by doing something He couldnt do. Anyhow, I'll do something different.

On 22nd August Shaw was to make his own alterations, cutting the first sentence from the first passage and substantially re-writing the second passage. The changes can be seen in successive states of the rough proofs of the play.]

Dear Mr Shaw

A great many thanks for the 'Statement'. You made out a tremendous case and it is very useful to us, tho' it is not the did I go soft myself? Why did the Sheriff go soft? Why did Feemy go soft? Whats this game that upsets our game? For seems to me theres two games bein played. Our game is a rotten game that makes me feel I'm dirt and that youre all as rotten dirt as me. T'other game may be a silly game; but it aint rotten. When the Sheriff played it he stopped being rotten. When Feemy played it the paint nearly dropped off her face. When I played it I cursed myself for a fool; but I lost the rotten feel all the same.

ELDER DANIELS. It was the Lord speaking to your soul, Blanco.

BLANCO. Oh yes: you know all about it, dont you? Youre in the Lord's confidence. He wouldnt for the world do anything to shock you, would He, Boozy? Yah! What about the croup? I guess He made the croup when He was thinking of one thing; and then He made the child when He was thinking of something else; and the croup got past Him and killed the child. Some of us will have to find out how to kill the croup, I guess. I think I'll turn doctor, just on the chance of getting back on Him by doing something He couldnt do. Anyhow, I'll do something different. I got the rotten feel off me for a minute of my life; and I'll go through fire to get it off me again. Look here! which of you will marry Feemy Evans.

THE BOYS [*uproariously*] Who speaks first? Who'll marry Feemy? Come along, Jack. Nows your chance, Peter. Pass along a husband for Feemy. Oh my, Feemy!

FEEMY [*shortly*] Keep your tongue off me, will you?

BLANCO. Feemy was a rose of the broad path, wasnt she? You all thought her the champion bad woman of this district. Well, she's a failure as a bad woman; and I'm a failure as a bad man. So let Brother Daniels marry us to keep all the rottenness in the family. What do you say, Feemy?

FEEMY. Thank you; but when I marry I'll marry a man that could do a decent action without surprising himself out of his senses. Youre like a child with a new toy, you and your bit of human kindness.

Blanco Posnet
Rough proof/rehearsal copy, second state, 1909.
(Dan H. Laurence Collection, University of Guelph)

Feemy go soft? Whats this game that upsets our game? For seems to me theres two games bein played. Our game is a rotten game that makes me feel I'm dirt and that youre all as rotten dirt as me. T'other game may be a silly game; but it aint rotten. When the Sheriff played it he stopped being rotten. When Feemy played it the paint nearly dropped off her face. When I played it I cursed myself for a fool; but I lost the rotten feel all the same.

ELDER DANIELS. It was the Lord speaking to your soul, Blanco.

BLANCO. Oh yes: you know all about it, dont you? Youre in the Lord's confidence. He wouldnt for the world do anything to shock you, would He, Boozy? Yah! What about the croup? It was early days when He made the croup, I guess. It was the best He could think of then; but when it turned out wrong on His hands He made you and me to fight the croup for him. You bet He didnt make us for nothing; and He wouldnt have made us at all if he could have done His work without us. By Gum, that must be what we're for! He'd never have made us to be rotten drunken blackguards like me, and good-for-nothing rips like Feemy. He made me because he had a job for me. He let me run loose until the job was ready, and then I had to come along and do it, hanging or no hanging. And I tell you it didnt feel rotten: it felt bully, just bully. Anyhow, I got the rotten feel off me for a minute of my life; and I'll go through fire to get it off me again. Look here! which of you will marry Feemy Evans.

THE BOYS [*uproariously*] Who speaks first? Who'll marry Feemy? Come along, Jack. Nows your chance, Peter. Pass along a husband for Feemy. Oh my, Feemy!

FEEMY [*shortly*] Keep your tongue off me, will you?

BLANCO. Feemy was a rose of the broad path, wasnt she? You all thought her the champion bad woman of this district. Well, she's a failure as a bad woman; and I'm a failure as a bad man. So let Brother Daniels marry us to keep all the rottenness in the family. What do you say, Feemy?

Blanco Posnet
Rough proof/rehearsal copy, fourth state, 1909.
(Dan H. Laurence Collection, University of Guelph)

English censorship that is our fight, but his being put upon our necks here. I don't want to be like Dervorgilla, who 'first brought the English (Censor) into Ireland!' I enclose notes of our last conversation with Sir J Dougherty.

Now to a technical and practical question. Would you object to our cutting some sentences on p 31 and 32? On p 31 from 'Either he killed' to 'Kill the child' (inclusive); page 32 from 'rotten feel all the same' to 'I'll do something different'. Or if this is too much, from 'Lord's confidence' to 'Anyhow'.

The reason is, that I had a feeling at every rehearsal that it was a dangerous bit, not in itself, or if it had come earlier in the play, but that it comes after the crisis, when there is more time to criticise. Up to Blanco's leaving the bar, the audience will be too interested and excited about him to take much notice of his words. And I noticed at the first Playboy row, the rioters took care to wait till the play was nearly over, and they had little to lose by interrupting it. I said nothing of this to Mr Yeats, but when he had seen a full rehearsal he said 'that croup passage is the dangerous one, and tho' it is a good point, it is not necessary, as it can be gathered from the earlier part'.

The worst thing that could happen to you, indeed the only real danger I see, is that there would be any demonstration against the play. This would justify Redford, and enable the L.L to warn us not to repeat it, so I hope you will allow us to take it out. There need be no public announcement of this, not that it much matters, as it doesn't seem to have been noticed by the Censor. We make no offer of withdrawing 'immoral relations' as the Castle now puts the whole difficulty on their being bound by the Censor. I wish they would forbid it, we have such a strong hand and the publicity might bring us capital to start again, but I don't think they have enough backbone.

Yours affectionately
A Gregory

Lady Gregory, deciding to return to Coole, wrote to Sir James Dougherty to tell him so on Sunday 15th: 'We are, as you know,

arranging to produce "Blanco" on Wednesday 25th as advertised and booked for, unless you serve us with a "threatening
notice", in which case we probably will postpone it till September 30, and produce it with the already promised "Oedipus" '
[AL/d.: Berg, NYPL]. Plans for a production of *Oedipus* were
to continue until January 1910 and beyond, but the Abbey did
not finally produce the play until Yeats's version was staged in
the 1920s.

Sinn Féin and *The Leader*, two of the most aggressively
Nationalist papers of the time, were vociferously opposed to the
Abbey because of its production of *The Playboy*. On 21st
August *Sinn Féin* published an article and an editorial on
Blanco, both of them hostile to Shaw and the Abbey, but
strongly advising its readers to avoid any demonstration against
the play for fear of giving the Castle a pretext for introducing
censorship: 'any person who takes any part in disturbing this
play is simply playing the Castle game, consciously or uncon-
sciously'. In the week of the production itself, however, *Sinn
Féin*, which had just started to appear in a daily issue, adopted a
more sympathetic attitude, including a special interview with
Yeats on 25th August. *An Claidheamh Soluis*, the organ of the
Gaelic League, took a line similar to *Sinn Féin*, proclaiming
loudly its lack of any interest in 'the literary fate of Mr George
Bernard Shaw', yet arguing that 'we are bound to stand by the
Theatre in its fight against the imposition of a British
Censorship'. *The Leader* alone among the nationalist papers
appears to have remained unremittingly hostile.

LADY GREGORY TO SHAW
[ALS: HRC]

Coole Park. Gort
Tuesday, 17th [August 1909]

We came home last night, thinking it better to have no more
personal interviews, but to write our intentions and put in our
advertisements and leave the L. L. to face the situation. Yeats
sent an emissary to 'Sinn Fein' and I gave a hint to the Editor of

the 'Leader' [D.P. Moran], asking them not to attack the play, as it is the question of bringing Ireland under the English Censor that is involved. We also made the 'croup' cuts, you being out of reach.

We had actually written a telegraph message to you on Saturday morning to ask leave, when yours came, and we were afraid if we sent it then you would think it was part of the Castle negotiation, which it was not.

Yeats goes back to Dublin Monday, but I don't think I will go up again, unless it is necessary. Can I persuade you and Mrs Shaw to come here for a couple of days—any days that suit you? It would be a very great pleasure to me and my son and his wife—and I don't think we can be very far out of your road. Do come.

A. G.

SHAW TO LADY GREGORY
[ALS: Berg, NYPL]

Lake Hotel. Killarney Lakes
17th August 1909

[The Shaws crossed by boat from Fishguard to Waterford the preceding night.]

Dear Lady Gregory

I am here on my way to Parknasilla. On Thursday I shall, I expect, arrive there. The address is The Southern Hotel, Parknasilla, Sneem, Co. Kerry. I forget whether I gave it to you before.

I saw an Irish Times today with Blanco announced for production; so I presume the Castle has not put its foot down. The officials made an appalling technical blunder in acting as agents of the Lord Chamberlain in Ireland; and I worded my telegram in such a way as to make it clear that I knew the value of that indiscretion.

I daresay the telegram reached the Castle before it reached you.

What is the leading Dublin paper, irrespective of politics? In my time the Irish Times and the Daily Express disputed pre-eminence. I want to know, in case I should have to say something about Blanco.

I am almost asleep after motoring 140 miles today.

Yours sincerely
G. Bernard Shaw

P.S. I have had no letters nor telegrams since I left London on Saturday morning. Probably I shall find plenty waiting for me at Parknasilla.

LORD ABERDEEN TO LADY GREGORY
[ALS: Berg, NYPL]

Private

Vice Regal Lodge. Dublin
17th August 1909

[The passages of this letter quoted by Lady Gregory in her letter to Shaw of 18th August are here set in italics. Lord Aberdeen's quotations from memory are from Lady Gregory's first play, the one-act *Twenty-Five*, performed in London at the Queen's Gate Hall, South Kensington, on 2nd May 1903.]

Dear Lady Gregory

I arrived here today from Scotland, and I regret to learn that you have had occasion to leave Dublin, as I would have liked to have the pleasure of a conversation with you.

It seems to me a curious and rather unkind fate that I should find myself called upon to act as the instrument for preventing the performance of any piece at the Abbey Street Theatre, for I have always been an appreciative admirer of the Dramatic work with which it is associated: i.e. ever since I witnessed some of the plays given by the Company in London. And I need scarcely add that these included, naturally, some of your own productions.

Another, which I thought very effective, was one, the title of which, curiously, I forget, but you would doubtless recognize it if I quote one or two phrases—such as 'Do you like Michael?' and 'Woman of the house', and again (a pathetic tirade) 'Probably some labouring man's ticket'.

I make these preliminary, and as it might seem, rather irrelevant remarks, simply in order to indicate that I have not approached the question which has unexpectedly been submitted to me, in a spirit which would be liable to any unfavourable bias, with reference to the National Theatre, but rather the reverse.

Now as to the actual subject of dissension. It really comes to be a question of the interpretation and application of an official document, under which the Abbey Street Theatre carries on business. I refer of course to the Patent.

And in order to make the more sure of the ground, and also as to whether I am called upon to intervene, I have obtained the opinion of the official legal adviser of the Irish Government; and this is entirely in support of the views and purpose already indicated to yourself and Mr Yeats by Sir James Dougherty on my behalf.

An official communication will, in due course and as soon as possible, be forwarded to you; but meanwhile I write this informally, partly in order that you may have the earliest intimation of what is impending, and also, as already indicated, to explain something of the spirit and the methods in accordance with which the subject has been dealt with here.

I of course regret any inconvenience that has been, or may be, occasioned to yourself or colleagues.

And perhaps I may be forgiven for expressing the belief that when, at the first interview with Sir James Dougherty, you indicated a disposition to change the piece, it was an instance of that 'woman's wit', or *instinct*★, which somehow seems often the guide to the best course more surely than some of the *processes*★ which are supposed to be more *regular*★, and more characteristic of the other sex.

In view of the importance of the question which has been raised, it would seem that one further personal conference might be very desirable, and therefore I hope that it may be possible for you to revisit Dublin on the earliest available day.

I should of course be most happy to have an opportunity for a talk with Mr Yeats.

I remain
very truly yours
Aberdeen

P.S. It may possibly occur to you as somewhat singular, in view of what I have said regarding appreciation of the National Theatre, that neither Lady Aberdeen nor I have been present at performances at *Abbey Street*★. But that is solely because of a technically official obstacle for which we are not responsible.

And I would much like to confer with you as to the possibility of evading that hindrance.

Aberdeen

★ underlined in the original

LADY GREGORY TO SHAW
[TLS: HRC]

Coole Park. Gort
Wednesday 18th [August 1909]

Dear Mr Shaw

A long holograph letter from the L.L. this morning, very flattering and friendly, but going on: [here Lady Gregory quotes the substance of Aberdeen's letter, as indicated above.]

Sir J Dougherty also wrote asking me to go up tomorrow, so though it is very troublesome, Yeats and I are going in the morning, will arrive at Broadstone [railway station] at 2–15, and go straight to the interview. We do not intend to give in one inch, and are only going because it would seem discourteous not to. If he keeps to his threat, we mean to go to the newspaper offices in the evening, and have our statement in as a surprise for Aberdeen's breakfast. We say in short that we will not give up Blanco, but will postpone it till we can get up Edipus to put on with it, and have the fight over both plays. We should of course very much like to see you, in fact it is entirely necessary, as we must not take different lines in our campaign. I hope you may be able to come here, as we expect to be back here in a day or two. If that is not possible, we must meet elsewhere. Please wire your address to us at the Abbey.

Yours sincerely
A Gregory

LADY GREGORY'S JOURNAL
[TMS with holograph revisions: HRC]

Dublin
Friday 20th [August 1909]

We arrived Broadstone yesterday at 2.15 and were met by Sir J. Dougherty's Secretary, who asked us to go to the Vice Regal Lodge. Arrived there, a secretary came and asked me to go and see the L. L. alone, and Mr Yeats could join us later.

Lord A. began by stating 'you must not think I am a sour faced Puritan, I am very much interested in the drama. In fact at Oxford it was often said that that would be my line. My Grandfather also, though considered so strict, went so far as to take a part in plays under a pseudonym. So you see I have a great deal of sympathy with you'.

I said 'May I be told on what clause of the Patent we are to be suppressed?' He said 'Here is the Patent'; he read several passages which were not relevant and then passages against indecency, blasphemy and disorder, but could not say on which count we were charged, except that there was one against riot being stirred up, and he thought there might be a riot. I said 'we have no reason to think so, *Sinn Fein* to-day [but dated 21st August] calls on its members not to raise one, and it was Sinn Fein that raised the Playboy riots so I think we are safe'. He said 'But religious people might make a disturbance'. I said 'they do not usually go to theatres here, and in any case we, as responsible Managers, have watched the play very carefully in rehearsal, and have taken out some passages which might have given offence, and are not integral to the play. The play is a religious one, and its argument must be left untouched. We are not accepting the Censor's cuts because they would, as Mr Shaw wired to us, have "destroyed the religious significance of the play" '.

He said 'I am in a very painful position. I admire the work you have been doing. I am in entire sympathy with it, but the fact is, in my position I am expected not to go against the Lord Chamberlain, and this especially because the King is in favour of the retention of the Censorship, in fact he has seen some of the Actors and has told them so. Could you not therefore help me, by publishing in your own name this notice?' I am not sure

of the words, but it was to the effect that as the question of the
Censorship was not quite defined and some difficulty had arisen
the production of Blanco Posnet has been deferred. I said 'till
when?' He shook his head. I said 'if we put it off till autumn are
you prepared to allow it then?' He said, 'oh no, I don't say that'.
I said 'then I cannot agree to put it off'. I said our secretary had
reported to us 'There is very heavy booking. First class people,
a great many from the Castle!' He said, 'Has it not struck you
that an actress of good character might object to take the part of
Feemy?' I said 'We left the casting of the women to our leading
actress [Sara Allgood], and she chose that part for herself'. At
this point Yeats who had been sent for arrived. Lord A.
repeated some of what he had said to me. Yeats asked the same
question 'on what clause of the Patent are you going?' He read
out various sentences in one of which the word blasphemy
occurred, and said he was bound by the opinion of his legal
advisors. Yeats said, 'are your legal advisors consulted on
particular passages, or on the whole tendency of the play?' He
said, 'well there are passages that might be thought objectionable'. Yeats said it was so in many great works, the Bible among
them, as the *Nation* has pointed out. He said 'Yes, yes,' and
began to read bits from the Nation article. We told him Blanco
was brought to a better frame of mind at the end of the play. He
said, 'where he shakes hands with Feemy?' I read out to him the
passage in which he says 'there is a great game and a rotten
game, and I am for the great game every time'; this surprised
him, he did not seem to have read it. Yeats said, 'We think it
sufficient if the main tendency of the play is righteous'. He said
'I wish other playwrights thought that'. I warned him, that if he
took the responsibility of stopping this play he would be made
responsible for every bad play that is imported from England,
putrid meat cans labelled safe by the Censor. He said 'I am in a
great difficulty; I have nothing to do with the Censor. I have
only to do with the Lord Chamberlain because of the courtesies
of officials towards one another; and I as the King's representative cannot go against the King'. Yeats said, 'are not the
conditions totally different in England and Ireland?' He said,
'they are, and I wish the King could understand it'. We then
went through the play, told him what we had cut. He made an
objection to the immoral relations phrase and we said we had

Mr Shaw's leave to cut that and would do so at his wish. He asked if we would cut 'dearly beloved brethren', as it might offend the susceptibilities of the Church of Ireland. I said, 'no, we must have some respect for our audience and not treat them as babies'. I asked to be let know his decision as soon as possible. He said, 'at the first possible moment, but I shall have to write to the King'. He asked us to go on to the Castle and see Sir J. D., a very experienced official. We apologised for taking so much of his time and he said 'There cannot be too many conversations on this subject'.

We found Sir J. D. rather in a temper; he had been trying to hear Lord A's account of the interview through a telephone, and couldn't. We gave our account; he was rather threatening in tone very much repeating what he had said before. He said 'we would be as much attacked as they would whatever happened, and that men connected with two newspapers had told him, they were only waiting an opportunity of attacking not only the L. L. but the Abbey, if the play is allowed, so we should also catch it'. I said, 'après vous'; he said Mr Yeats said at the Patent enquiry the Abbey was for the production of romantic work. I quoted Parnell, 'who shall set bounds to the march of a Nation?'

We told him Lord A. had promised to let us know the decision as soon as possible, but that he had to write to the King.

He said he would go, and see the Lord Lieutenant on his way home. We went to Dame Street post office and wired to Shaw.

LADY GREGORY TO SHAW

[Telegram: TMS journal, HRC]

[Dublin]
[Thursday 19th August 1909]

HAVE SEEN ABERDEEN DELETED IMMORAL RELATIONS REFUSED OTHER CUTS HE IS WRITING TO KING WHO SUPPORTS CENSOR

SHAW TO LADY GREGORY
[Telegram: Berg, NYPL]

Sneem. [Co. Kerry]
[19th August 1909]

THEN IT IS REALLY THE KING AFTER ALL SO MUCH
THE BETTER ANNOUNCE THE FACT AND GIVE UP
THE PERFORMANCE

SHAW

SHAW TO LADY GREGORY
[ALS: Berg, NYPL]

[Great] Southern Hotel. Parknasilla
19th August 1909

[Agnes Lady Grove, a writer active in the women's suffrage
movement and other socio-political matters, had crossed pens with
Shaw in letters to *The Academy* in June 1907, over his lecture 'The
New Theology', delivered on 16th May.]

Dear Lady Gregory

I have just arrived and found all your letters waiting for me.

I am naturally much entertained by your encounters and
Yeats', with the Castle. I leave that building cheerfully in your
hands.

But observe the final irony of the situation. The English
censorship being too stupid to see the real blasphemy, makes a
fool of itself. But you, being clever enough to put your finger on
it at once, immediately proceed to delete what Redford's
blindness spared.

To me, of course, the whole purpose of the play lies in the
problem 'What about the croup?' When Lady Grove, in her
most superior manner, told me 'He is the God of Love', I said
'He is also the God of Cancer and Epilepsy'. That does not
present any difficulty to me. All this problem of the origin of
evil, the mystery of pain, and so forth, does not puzzle me. My
doctrine is that God proceeds by the method of 'trial and error',
just like a workman perfecting an aeroplane. He has to make
hands for himself and brains for himself in order that his will

may be done. He has tried lots of machines—the diphtheria bacillus, the tiger, the cockroach; and he cannot extirpate them except by making something that can shoot them or walk on them, or, cleverer still, devise vaccines and anti toxins to prey on them. To me the sole hope of human salvation lies in teaching Man to regard himself as an experiment in the realization of God, to regard his hands as God's hand, his brain as God's brain, his purpose as God's purpose. He must regard God as a helpless Longing, which *longed* him into existence by its desperate need for an executive organ. You will find it all in Man and Superman, as you will find it all behind Blanco Posnet. Take it out of my play, and the play becomes nothing but the old cry of despair—Shakespear's 'As flies to wanton boys so we are to the gods: they kill us for their sport' [*King Lear*]—the most frightful blasphemy ever uttered, and the one from which it is my mission to deliver the world.

Frankly, I dont think the excision will save the play. If the actor cannot take the audience by storm with his desperate perplexity of soul, they will probably stop him long before he reaches that line. If he does reach it they will either miss its meaning or swallow it with a gasp. However, the matter is in your hands. Only, I must play fair with Redford. If it be really true that the play is less possible in Ireland than in England, you must not ask me to conceal the fact.

But the practical moral of all this is that we had better ride for a fall. Between the last two sentences your telegram of today (Thursday) arrived. If we can only fix the suppression of the play on the King, then 'if the color we must wear be England's cruel red' ['The Wearing of the Green'] we perish gloriously. You say it is necessary to see me; but it really isnt. I can say nothing in Dublin that I cannot say here; and spoil the second half of my holiday for Redford as I have already spoilt the first, I flatly will not. I must close this hastily on the chance of catching tonight's post, if there is such a thing here.

Yours sincerely
G. Bernard Shaw

PS I hope to see you at Coole Park later on, when all this is over.

At about this time Shaw drafted the following letter for Lady Gregory to send to Lord Aberdeen [AL/d: Berg, NYPL], indicating in a circled note that she was to incorporate the first paragraph of a letter of 18th August from Gilbert Murray, which he enclosed. The suggested passage is here inserted in square brackets.

[*c*. 19th August 1909]

My dear Lord Aberdeen
     I feel rather uneasy lest you should think that in the matter of Mr Shaw's play I am a mere *frondeuse*, acting 'agin the Government' for the fun of the thing. May I tell you privately that I am acting on opinions which I think you will admit (unofficially) to be of much greater weight than that of Mr Redford, whose judgment has been condemned by every witness before the commission, including the strongest supporters of the censorship as an institution.
     The following is part of a letter written to Mr Shaw by Gilbert Murray, who is, as you know, the Earl of Carlisle's son-in-law, and Regius Professor of Greek at Oxford, besides being famous for his translations of the Greek drama. I select him as the most unquestionable authority I could rely on. He says:
     ['This is perfectly monstrous about the Dublin Castle officials: flagrantly unjust to you and insulting to the intelligence of those who have any serious interest in Literature or Drama. I think, and my wife [Lady Mary Murray], whose tastes are severe, agrees with me, that the condemnation of Blanco Posnet is one of the most utterly unintelligent things in Redford's record' (TLts: Edward Connery Lathem).]
     I could easily get further testimony for you; but I think this is enough to convince you that we are not acting without grave justification in disregarding Mr Redford's notions of what is fitting for us to produce.

Yours sincerely

It does not appear that Lady Gregory made use of the draft, but Murray's letter was strategically employed in convincing Lady Lyttelton, wife of the commander-in-chief of British forces in

Ireland, to attend the play with her party, as Shaw reported to Murray in a letter of 29th August [ALS/p: BTA]: 'I sent the letter to Lady Gregory; Lady Gregory planked it down confidentially on Lady L's dressing table; and Lady L. took her Bible and hymnbook and brought her whole flock to the play with military honors. Down came the Castle flag; Charlotte was overwhelmed with invitations to the Vice Regal Lodge'.

LADY GREGORY TO SHAW
[ALS: Berg, NYPL]

Dublin
Thursday [19th August 1909]
5.00

[Thomas Philip LeFanu, chief clerk at the Irish Office, had been asked to appear before the Committee on Censorship to testify as to the law in Ireland. On 14th August he had telegraphed to the Chief Secretary's office for briefing on how to respond to questions about *Blanco Posnet* and instructions had been issued by Sir James Dougherty for him as far as possible to 'steer clear of it'(ALS: SPO). However, when he gave his testimony on 19th August, he was pressed on the issue by one of the Committee, as reported in *The Times* on 20th August:

> LORD NEWTON.—In the case of the play *Press Cuttings* [*sic*], which it is intended to produce during Horse Show Week, there is nothing to prevent that play being produced, whether the Lord Lieutenant approves of it or not? — I think no legal steps could be taken. Unless it is done in a friendly way I think there would be no power to stop production.]

Dear Mr Shaw

We are disappointed by your saying you won't come and speak. It would be a splendid chance to state the case—there is the greatest curiosity about you in Dublin and there would be a greater crowd to hear you speak than even to see a play of yours. The excitement over this whole business is so great in Dublin that if there is no play and no you, we shall have to hide our heads. Of course we don't know yet if we are going to be stopped. The evidence in today's papers, given by LeFanu the Castle representative, is in our favour. I have just had a message from Sir J. Dougherty asking where a letter will find me tomorrow. I will stay here for it, and I suppose it will bring the decision. There is great doubt still whether it is just all bluff. But in case we cannot produce the play, because of fine (£300 my counsel says, and forfeiture of patent) please let us have a letter we can publish, withdrawing the play—or the public will never believe we weren't frightened by the Castle.

Yours sincerely
A. Gregory

SHAW TO YEATS AND LADY GREGORY
[Telegram: Berg, NYPL]

Sneem
[20th August 1909]

[Yeats and Lady Gregory may have sent Shaw another telegram, once more urging him to come to Dublin to speak at the first night, and this was his response. The promised letter was delayed until August 27th, too late for the first performance.]

NO WILL SEND LETTER FOR PUBLICATION AND READING TO AUDIENCE

SHAW

SIR JAMES DOUGHERTY TO LADY GREGORY
Dublin Castle
20th August 1909

[This, the long-awaited official letter, was released to the press by the Castle together with the following two letters. It was published by the Dublin *Evening Telegraph* and many other of the English and Irish papers, including the *Freeman's Journal* and the London *Times*, on 24th August.]

Dear Lady Gregory

I am directed by the Lord Lieutenant to state that His Excellency's attention has been called to an announcement in the public Press that a play entitled 'The Showing up of Blanco Posnet', is about to be performed in the Abbey Theatre.

This play was written for production in a London Theatre, but its performance was disallowed by the authority which in England is charged with the censorship of stage plays. The play does not deal with an Irish subject, and it is not an Irish play in any other sense than that its author was born in Ireland. It is now proposed to produce this play in the Abbey Theatre which was founded for the express purpose of encouraging dramatic art in Ireland and of fostering a dramatic school growing out of the life of the country.

The play in question does not seem well adapted to promote these laudable objects or to belong to the class of plays originally intended to be performed in the Abbey Theatre, as described in the evidence on the hearing of the application for the Patent.

However this may be, the fact of the proposed performance having been brought to the notice of the Lord Lieutenant, His Excellency cannot evade the responsibility cast upon him of considering whether the play conforms in other respects to the conditions of the Patent.

His Excellency, after the most careful consideration, has arrived at the conclusion that in its original form the play is not in accordance either with the assurances given by those interested when the Patent was applied for, or with the conditions and restrictions contained in the Patent as granted by the Crown.

As you are the holder of the Patent in trust for the generous founder of the Theatre [Miss Horniman], His Excellency feels bound to call your attention, and also the attention of those with whom you are associated, to the terms of the Patent, and to the serious consequences which the production of the play in its original form might entail.

I am to add that the Lord Lieutenant would deeply regret should it become necessary to take any action which might inflict loss upon the public-spirited lady who founded a home for the Irish National Theatre, or which might result in depriving the Society, that has already done good work for Irish dramatic art, of the means of prosecuting a worthy enterprise with which His Excellency is in entire sympathy, and which, if judiciously pursued, may do much to refine and elevate the literary taste of the community.

I am
yours most truly
J.B. Dougherty

LADY GREGORY TO SIR JAMES DOUGHERTY

Nassau Hotel. [Dublin]
20th August 1909

Dear Sir James

Thank you for your letter. Please explain to His Excellency that the play is not in its original form as refused by the Censor. The printed version is not in that form, our modified stage version is still less in that form, and we are now taking out another passage in deference to His Excellency's opinion expressed to us yesterday.

I will not write at greater length, as I have just (11 o'clock) come back from a full rehearsal.

Believe me,
sincerely yours
Augusta Gregory

SIR JAMES DOUGHERTY TO LADY GREGORY

Dear Lady Gregory

I have received your letter, which I shall duly submit to the Lord Lieutenant.

I am,
yours truly
J.B. Dougherty

The action taken by the Lord Lieutenant, according to the *Times* article on 'Mr Shaw's Play in Dublin' of 21st August, was intended as a 'precautionary notice' which 'puts upon the Abbey Theatre Company the entire responsibility for the production of Mr Shaw's play. If its first performance on Wednesday leads to an immediate disturbance, or is followed by any public complaints of a representative character, the Lord Lieutenant will be in the position of having forewarned the company of any action which he may think it necessary to take'. The Abbey directors, however, interpreted it as a stronger threat than this and issued a public statement [*Dublin Evening Mail* 21st August]:

> If our Patent is in danger it is because the English censorship is being extended to Ireland, or because the Lord Lieutenant is about to revive, on what we consider a frivolous pretext, a right not exercised for 150 years, to forbid at his pleasure any play produced in any Dublin theatre, all these theatres holding their Patent from him.
>
> We are not concerned with the question of English censorship, but we are very certain that the conditions of the two countries are different, and that we must not by accepting the English censor's ruling, give away anything of the liberty of the Irish theatre of the future. Neither can we accept, without protest, the exercise of the Lord Lieutenant's claim at the bidding of the censor or otherwise. The Lord Lieutenant is definitely a political personage, holding office from the party in power, and what would sooner or later grow into a political censorship cannot be lightly accepted.
>
> We have ourselves, considering the special circumstances of Ireland, cut out some passages which we thought might give offence at a hasty hearing, but these are not the passages because of which the English censor refused his license.

> W.B. YEATS, Managing Director.
> A. GREGORY, Director and
> Patentee.
> Abbey Theatre, 21st August 1909.

The paper war continued over the weekend, with a further statement from the Abbey on Sunday night, August 22nd [*Irish Times* 23rd August]:

During the last week we have been vehemently urged to withdraw Mr Shaw's play, which has already been advertised and rehearsed, and have refused to do so. We would have listened with attention to any substantial argument; but we found, as we were referred from one well-meaning personage to another, that no one would say that the play was hurtful to man, woman, or child. Each said that someone else had thought so, or might think so. We were told that Mr Redford had objected, that the Lord Chamberlain had objected, and that, if produced, it will certainly offend excited officials in London, and might offend officials in Dublin, or the Law Officers of the Crown, or the Lord Lieutenant, or Dublin Society, or Archbishop Walsh, or the Church of Ireland, or rowdies up for the Horse Show, or newspaper editors, or the King. In these bewilderments and shadowy opinions there was nothing to change our conviction (which is also that of the leading weekly paper of the Lord Lieutenant's own party) that so far from containing offences for any sincere and honest mind, Mr Shaw's play is a high and weighty argument upon the working of the Spirit of God in man's heart, or to show that it is not a befitting thing for us to set upon our stage the work of an Irishman, who is also the most famous of living dramatists, after that work had been silenced in London by what we believe an unjust decision.

The statement then went on to repeat the points made the previous day.

Shaw in Parknasilla, however, was indignant when he saw the papers of 21st August with the Abbey's first public statement in them. He wrote to Yeats on 22nd August, protesting [ALS: Berg NYPL]: 'The statement that you have bowdlerised the play practically confesses that it is not fit for representation. Also, the bowdlerised version is to me nothing but a message of despair and death'. He went on to demand the insertion of a new speech in lieu of the passage about the croup which had been cut from Blanco's part and enclosed the text of it in his letter. He then continued:

And make a further statement to the press that since the last statement Lady Gregory has written to me pointing out that a certain speech was open to misconstruction, and that I immediately rewrote it much more strongly and clearly; consequently the play will now be given exactly as written by the author without concessions of any kind to the attacks that have been made upon it, except that to oblige the Lord Lieutenant I have consented to withdraw the word 'immoral' as applied to the relations between a woman of bad character and her accomplices. In doing so I wish it to be stated that I still regard those relations as not only immoral but vicious; nevertheless, as the English Censorship apparently regards them as delightful and exemplary, and the Lord Lieutenant does not wish to be understood as contradicting the English Censorship, I am quite content to leave the relations to the unprompted judgment of the Irish people. Also, I have consented to withdraw the words 'Dearly beloved brethren', as the Castle fears that they may shock the nation. For the rest, I can assure the Lord Lieutenant that there is nothing in the other passages objected to by the English Censorship that might not have been written by the Catholic Archbishop of Dublin, and in point of consideration for the religious beliefs of the Irish people the play compares very favorably with the Coronation Oath.

This extract from Shaw's letter to Yeats was duly given to the press, and appeared in the *Evening Telegraph* of Monday, 23rd August, an issue which also contained an interview with the Lord Lieutenant in which he dismissed the letter as 'characteristic' and 'an excellent advertisement'. However, on 24th August the *Evening Telegraph* carried a note from the Chief Secretary's office saying that the previous day's interview with the Lord Lieutenant had been entirely unauthorised. The paper also contained a further statement from Lady Gregory clarifying exactly what alterations had been made and when, adding at the end that 'we have received a letter from Miss Horniman approving of our action'. *Blanco* continued to get wide and extensive coverage in all the papers, including a letter from Francis Sheehy-Skeffington, the well-known Dublin political figure, in the *Freeman's Journal* of 24th August, demanding the whole play and nothing but the play and condemning Yeats for having made any cuts at all.

LADY GREGORY TO SHAW
[ALS: HRC]

Nassau Hotel. Dublin
Tuesday [24th August 1909]

[Charlotte Shaw had arrived in Dublin with her sister, Mary Cholmondeley, having written on 21st August to reserve tickets for the first night and to announce that Shaw himself was definitely not going to come. The 'synopsis of the religious significance of the play' was in all probability the statement on 'The Religion of Blanco Posnet' written by Yeats and published in a special issue of *The Arrow*, the Abbey's house organ, on 25th August. In Shaw's letter to Yeats of 22nd August, he had warned that the actor playing Blanco must not 'funk' the new speech written for him. The 'express order from Marienbad' would have been from Edward VII, who was there from 10th August to 4th September. The performance of W.B. Yeats's and George Moore's *Diarmuid and Grania* by the English actor F.R. Benson and his company for the Irish Literary Theatre was in October 1901.]

Dear Mr Shaw

I send evening papers. The Herald poster has 'Mr Yeats accuses Castle of Sinister Designs!' It is such a pity you can't see it all. A press man asked for you yesterday at the Abbey and was told you are not in Dublin. He said 'We know he is, but Mr Yeats has him hid some place'.

You were quite right about that croup passage and we felt its omission weakened the play. Yet in itself the first impression it gave was of being sudden and not clearly explained. My son heard someone at a cricket match say yesterday 'The L. L. objects to "immoral"—perhaps "commercial" would be a better word'. 'Sinn Fein' and the Gaelic League are going to support us, against the censorship. The *Irish Times* Editor told me last night the danger would be either from Archbishop Walsh (who has a private telephone to the Freeman Office) or the Moderator of the [Presbyterian] General Assembly [John Courtenay Clarke], who I had never heard of before, but it seems is the head of Lord Aberdeen's church.

I have sent Lord Aberdeen privately 'not as part of the fight but under a flag of truce' a synopsis of the religious significance of the play, with which to meet the arguments of his Pope. Poor man, the same Editor told me he had banned our interview with him and 'if he wasn't the Viceroy I'd say he was in a funk!' We are still a little anxious lest it should be stopped tomorrow, but I think nothing but an express order from Marienbad could bring that about. No fear of the actors shirking [?] their words, they are in high spirits, but alas! Miss Allgood does look very virtuous for a fallen woman!

Mrs Shaw will give you fuller news, and I hope the reception may be so encouraging as to bring you up. We have had to substitute apple paring for shucking nuts. Nuts aren't ripe enough and we must consider the seasons. I remember Benson in 'Diarmuid and Grania' set his heart on shearing a sheep on the stage, but it came off in October, and the sheep hadn't grown their wool.

I like the play better and better. Of course you will have the jealousy against you of priest and preacher, who think the pulpit has a monopoly of sermons.

Yours affectionately
A. Gregory

Blanco Posnet was at last to be produced as scheduled on 25th August in a triple bill, preceded by Yeats's *Kathleen Ni Houlihan* and followed by Lady Gregory's *The Workhouse Ward*. The controversy over the play and the issue of censorship had drawn international attention to the production. There were special representatives at the opening from virtually all the principal English papers, including the *Daily Mail, Daily News, Daily Chronicle, Daily Telegraph, The Standard, Westminster Gazette, Evening News, Morning Leader, Manchester Guardian*, and *The Times* (which sent its reviewer A.B. Walkley). There were also reviewers from *The Spectator*, *The Athenaeum*, *The Stage*, the *Belfast Newsletter*, the *Gaelic American* (whose representative, only arriving on the day of the performance, was unable to get a ticket), the *Corriere della Sera*, Milan, and the *Frankfurter Zeitung*. James Joyce, who was in Dublin at the time, reviewed the play for the *Piccolo della Sera*, Trieste.

Inevitably present was Joseph Holloway, the architect commissioned to convert the Abbey theatre building in 1904, who, being an inveterate theatre-goer, voluminously recorded Irish theatre activities for nearly half a century in the manuscript journal he called *Impressions of a Dublin Playgoer*.

JOSEPH HOLLOWAY: *IMPRESSIONS OF A DUBLIN PLAYGOER*

[Holograph journal: NLI]

25th August 1909

Henderson told me to be down at 7 o'clock. Accordingly I went down at that hour and found but a faint stir about the place. Only a few of the company had arrived and a few stragglers peeped through the Vestibule doors. Soon life began to stir and the attendants, Henderson all business, and a few of the critics arrived ... A row of chairs was placed at the back of the pit (the heavy curtain being removed for the time being) for the accommodation of the critics. I was told off to capture half of the tickets at the stalls entrance as the audience passed in. I had a word with Miss Allgood and Miss [Maire] Walker [the Abbey actress] and others before the doors were opened—they had caught the excitement as well as everyone else and wondered what the night would bring forth. Crowds were assembling outside as it approached the time for opening and Henderson began to fear a rush would be made by people not having tickets to get into the theatre, but no such thing occurred though many sought admission in vain and lingered on all the night about the Vestibule in the hopes of getting in. ... The people came pouring in from the time the doors were opened. All artistic, literary and social Dublin passed in a rapid succession ... John

McCormack ... George Russell ('AE') ... William Orpen ... Sheehy Skeffington ... Mrs Shaw, W.B. Yeats, Lady Gregory, R. Gregory. Lords and ladies were present a galore, and many 'nice people with nasty ideas' had come on the off chance of hearing and seeing something strongly unpleasant. These were doomed to disappointment as Shaw's play proved a sort of sermon set in vivid melodramatic frame and all the audience at its conclusion wondered only why the censor vetoed it and put the bad name on it. ... Excitement was intense when the curtains were drawn aside, and the town hall in a Territory of the United States [of] America was disclosed to view. All held their breath and listened with all their ears — an event of a lifetime was taking place. The drama was followed with intense interest right up to the end and heartily applauded. The stirring events leading up to the conversion of Posnet were like a page torn out of Bret Harte and brought to life on the stage ... The acting of the Abbey company gave reality to the scene. The swaggering daredevilry of Fred [O']Donovan as Posnet was of vital value to the success of the piece; and Sara Allgood's Carmenesque 'study' of Feemy Evans, the loose woman who tries to get Posnet hanged was picturesque. ... Yeats came before the curtains at the end of Shaw's play on repeated calls for 'author' being demanded, and said Mr Shaw was not in the house but he was sure Mrs Shaw, who was, would convey the play's triumph to her husband.

LADY GREGORY AND W.B. YEATS TO SHAW

[Telegram: *Irish Independent* 26 August 1909]

[Dublin]
[25th August 1909]

GLORIOUS   RECEPTION   SPLENDID   VICTORY
WHERE IS THE CENSOR NOW

YEATS
GREGORY

LADY GREGORY TO SHAW
[ALS: HRC]

[Dublin]
Midnight! [25th-26th August 1909]

['The Lower Castle Yard' is a comic ballad from 1858–59, written by Dr Thomas Nedley, later Principal Medical Officer to the Dublin Metropolitan Police, commemorating a legal incident involving a printer of patriotic ballads, during the Lord Lieutenancy of the Earl of Eglinton (1858–59), appointed by Lord Derby, soon after replaced by the Earl of Carlisle (1859–64). The ballad was published in the *Irish Times*, 17th May 1915.]

Dear Mr Shaw

The shouts are still in our ears! Never was such a victory. From first line to last of the play sustained and intense attention, and applause—and much applause at the end! You *ought* to have been there and you must come before the week is over, and see what your countrymen think of you —and your countrywomen too.

The poor police, I pitied them. They were planted outside to carry us or rioters to gaol, and went home like fishermen with nets empty. Poor Aberdeen! I have been teaching our actresses tonight the old song of 'The Lower Castle Yard' the praise of the rebel poet 'his lays they banished Eglinton, and tore Lord Derby down; but far from town their grief to drown they took to drinking hard; while he had tea with old Carlisle in the Upper Castle Yard!' You will yet be teacher of your race.

Yours affectionately
A Gregory

Though the press was on the whole favourable towards the production, all the papers pointedly commented on the anticlimactic lack of any disturbance or anything in the play likely to have caused a disturbance. A long and respectful notice in the London *Times* gave the verdict that 'As a piece of dramatic art the play is not up to its author's highest level; as a study in

morality Mr Shaw's latest notion seems to us the most serious
and sound he has yet worked into drama' (26th August). The
novelist George Birmingham (the pseudonym of Canon J.O.
Hannay), who reviewed the play for the *Manchester Guardian*
(26th August 1909) wrote enthusiastically: 'The play is not a
blasphemy, and it is not indecent. It is a sermon on the working
of the spirit of God in the heart of a man'. There was some
cynicism about the publicity which had been created by the
controversy and some doubts expressed about the merit of the
play itself; more than one critic commented on Shaw's
indebtedness to Bret Harte, the American regional writer
('slices of Bret Harte served with G.B.S. sauce', Holloway
noted in his journal), but on the whole the production was
widely praised.

The Abbey directors did not fail to press home their advantage with an aggressive public statement on 26th August
[*Dublin Evening Mail*]: 'Now that the danger of interference is
over, we wish to protest against the grave anxiety and
annoyance we have been put to by the endeavour to force an
incompetent and irrelevant Censorship upon Ireland'. They
continued to make an issue of the need to keep theatrical
censorship out of Ireland, concluding: 'we are but little concerned with the question of the Censorship now being fought
out in London, but very much concerned in keeping the liberty
we possess'.

SHAW TO LADY GREGORY
[ALS: Berg, NYPL]

Parknasilla
27th August 1909

[This was Shaw's delayed statement intended for publication. Sir
Harry Poland was a noted criminal lawyer who, after his retirement in
1895, became a leading advocate of law reform. George Edwardes, a
theatrical manager, was best known as the managing director of the
Gaiety Theatre, the principal home in London of musical comedy and
other popular entertainments. Beerbohm Tree had been knighted in
the Birthday Honours list of 1909. *Press Cuttings* was by this time

passed by the censor with the names of the characters changed, hence the reference to the 'licensed' play offered to the Abbey in lieu of *Blanco Posnet*.]

Now that the production of Blanco Posnet has revealed the character of the play to the public, it may be as well to clear up some of the points raised by the action of the Castle in the matter.

By the Castle, I do not mean the Lord Lieutenant. He was in Scotland when the trouble began. Nor do I mean the higher officials and law advisers. I conclude that they also were either in Scotland, or preoccupied by the Horse Show, or taking their August holiday in some form. As a matter of fact the friction ceased when the Lord Lieutenant returned. But in the meantime the deputies left to attend to the business of the Castle found themselves confronted with a matter which required tactful handling and careful going. They did their best; but they broke down rather badly in point of law, in point of diplomatic etiquette, and in point of common knowledge.

First, they committed the indiscretion of practically conspiring with an English official who has no jurisdiction in Ireland in an attempt to intimidate an Irish theatre.

Second, they assumed that this official acts as the agent of the King, whereas, as Sir Harry Poland established in a recent public controversy on the subject, his powers are given him absolutely by Act of Parliament (1843). If the King were to write a play, this official could forbid its performance, and probably would if it were a serious play and were submitted without the author's name, or with mine.

Third, they assumed that the Lord Lieutenant is the servant of the King. He is nothing of the sort. He is the Viceroy: that is, he *is* the King in the absence of Edward VII. To suggest that he is bound to adopt the views of a St James's Palace official as to what is proper to be performed in an Irish theatre is as gross a solecism as it would be to inform the King that he must not visit Marienbad because some Castle official does not consider Austria a sufficiently Protestant country to be a fit residence for an English monarch.

Fourth, they referred to the Select Committee which is now investigating the Censorship in London, whilst neglecting to inform themselves of its purpose. The Committee was appointed because the operation of the Censorship had become so scandalous that the Government could not resist the demand for an inquiry. At its very first sitting it had to turn the public and press out of the room and close its doors to discuss the story of a play licensed by the official who banned Blanco Posnet; and after this experience it actually ruled out all particulars of licensed plays as unfit for public discussion. With the significant exception of Mr George Edwardes, no witness yet examined, even among those who have most strongly supported the censorship as an institution, has defended the way in which it is now exercised. The case which brought the whole matter to a head was the banning of this very play of mine, The Shewing-up of Blanco Posnet. All this is common knowledge. Yet the Castle, assuming that I, and not the Censorship, am the defendant in the trial now proceeding in London, treated me, until the Lord Lieutenant's return, as if I were a notorious convicted offender. This, I must say, is not like old times in Ireland. Had I been a Catholic, a Sinn Feiner, a Land Leaguer, a tenant farmer, a laborer, or anything that from the Castle point of view is congenitally wicked and coercible, I should have been prepared for it; but if the Protestant landed gentry, of which I claim to be a perfectly correct member, even to the final grace of absenteeism, is to be treated in this way by the Castle, then English rule must indeed be going to the dogs. Of my position as a representative of literature I am far too modest a man to speak; but it was the business of the Castle to know it and respect it; and the Castle did neither.

Fifth, they reported that my publishers had refused to supply a copy of the play for the use of the Lord Lieutenant, leaving it to be inferred that this was due to my instructions as a deliberate act of discourtesy. Now no doubt my publishers were unable to supply a copy, because, as it happened, the book was not published, and could not be published until the day of performance without forfeiting my American copyright, which is of considerable value. Private copies only were available; but if the holiday deputies of the Castle think that the Lord Lieutenant found the slightest difficulty in obtaining such copies, I can only pity their total failure to appreciate either his private influence or his public importance.

Sixth, they claimed that Sir Herbert Beerbohm Tree, who highly values his good understanding with the Dublin public, had condemned the play. What are the facts? Sir Herbert, being asked by the Select Committee whether he did not think my play would shock religious feeling, replied point blank, 'No: it would heighten religious feeling'. He announced the play for production at his theatre; the Censorship forced him to withdraw it; and the King instantly shewed his opinion of the Censorship by making Sir Herbert a knight. But it also happened that Sir Herbert, who is a wit, and knows the weight of the Censor's brain to half a scruple, said with a chuckle, when he came upon the phrase 'immoral relations' in the play, 'They wont pass that'. And they did not pass it. That the deputy officials should have overlooked Sir Herbert's serious testimony to the religious propriety of the play, and harped on his little jest at the Censor's expense as if it were at my expense, is a fresh proof of the danger of transacting important business at the Castle when all the responsible officials are away bathing.

On one point, however, the Castle followed the established Castle tradition. It interpreted the patent (erroneously) as limiting the theatre to Irish plays. Now the public is at last in possession of the fact that the real protagonist in my play, who does not appear in person on the stage at all, is God. In my youth the Castle view was that God is essentially Protestant and English; and as the Castle never changes its views, it is bound to regard the divine protagonist as anti-Irish and consequently outside the terms of the patent. Whether it will succeed in persuading the Lord Lieutenant to withdraw the patent on that ground will probably depend not only on His Excellency's theological views, but on his private opinion of the wisdom with which the Castle behaves in his absence. The theatre thought the risk worth taking; and I agreed with them. At all events Miss Horniman will have no difficulty in insuring the patent at an extremely reasonable rate.

In conclusion, may I say that from the moment when the Castle made its first blunder I never had any doubt of the result, and that I kept away from Dublin in order that our national theatre might have the entire credit of handling and producing a new play without assistance from the author or from any other person trained in the English theatres. Nobody who has not lived, as I have to live, in London, can possibly understand the impression the Irish players made there this year, or appreciate the artistic value of their performances, their spirit, and their methods. It has been suggested that I placed Blanco Posnet at their disposal only because it was, as an unlicensed play, the refuse of the English market. As a matter of fact there was no such Hobson's choice in the matter. I offered a licensed play as an alternative, and am all the more indebted to Lady Gregory and Mr Yeats for not choosing it. Besides, Ireland is really not so negligible from the commercial-theatrical point of view as some of our more despondent patriots seem to suppose. Of the fifteen countries outside Britain in which my plays are perform-ed, my own is by no means the least lucrative; and even if it were, I should not accept its money value as a measure of its importance.

G. Bernard Shaw

SHAW TO LADY GREGORY
[ALS: Berg, NYPL]

Southern Hotel. Parknasilla
29th August 1909

[Lady Gregory did not give Shaw's long letter of 27th August to the press, but published it in full in an appendix to *Our Irish Theatre* in 1913. Ben Iden Payne, Miss Horniman's manager at the Gaiety Theatre, Manchester, did apply for a licence for *Blanco Posnet* but was refused on the grounds that the play was still virtually identical with the version turned down earlier in the year. Shaw did not visit Coole until 1910.]

Dear Lady Gregory

I sent up to Charlotte a statement for your consideration which she had to bring back, as it did not reach her until you and Yeats had started for Galway, and she herself was getting into her cab.

Also, after I sent it, I saw your statement [of 26th August]. I suppose the business is now too stale to do anything more: still, if you think Dublin would still read about Blanco and the

Castle, the statement is at your disposal to publish where and how you please, or to pitch into the waste basket.

My chief reason for writing it is that I think we ought to divide the Castle, and make the officials thoroughly afraid of meddling again without instructions from the L. L. What I have tried to convey all through is that they made fools of themselves; that the subordinates acted ignorantly, insolently, improperly, and without authority; and that when the really important people came back the subordinates were thoroughly snubbed and the matter set right. This will save the face of the L. L., and establish the notion that he is on the side of the theatre in his capacity of cultured and liberal minded patron of the arts.

I am suggesting to Miss Horniman that she should apply for a licence for Blanco in Manchester.

You and W.B.Y. handled the campaign nobly. You have made the Abbey Theatre the real centre of capacity and character in the Irish movement: let Sinn Fein and the rest look to it.

It is raining cats and dogs. When we finish our stay here, I hope we shall be able to arrange our journey back so as to pass your way. Charlotte's sister Mrs Cholmondely has just joined us; and for the moment we want to wallow in the stationary delights of boating and bathing here. But it certainly doesnt look encouraging this morning.

Yours sincerely
G. Bernard Shaw

P.S. I have said that the Castle interpretation of the patent was erroneous on the strength of what Yeats said to Charlotte on the subject. If there is any doubt about it the parenthesis '(erroneously)' can be struck out without damage to the literary structure.

SHAW TO LADY GREGORY
[TLS: Burgunder, Cornell]

10 Adelphi Terrace. London
6th November 1909

[The Abbey was planning a performance of *Blanco Posnet* in London under the auspices of the Stage Society as part of a tour of England and

Ireland. Lady Gregory had evidently suggested a joint production of the Abbey company and the Stage Society, each performing at least one play, to which Shaw had replied by telegram on 5th November, urging her against the plan. Frederick Whelen, long-time Fabian associate of Shaw, secretary to Sir Herbert Tree and founder of the Stage Society, had sought Shaw's assistance in persuading Lady Gregory that a mixed programme was undesirable.

Lord Dunsany, the nephew of Sir Horace Plunkett, was an Irish playwright and man of letters who had reviewed the Dublin production of *Blanco Posnet* for the *Saturday Review*. William J. Henry Brayden was the editor of the *Freeman's Journal* 1892–1916. It is not quite clear how Brayden 'saved the situation' for the Abbey but, in view of the suggestion in Lady Gregory's letter to Shaw of 24th August that the *Freeman's Journal* had very close links with Archbishop Walsh, Brayden may have used his influence to stop Church intervention on the side of censorship in the *Blanco Posnet* controversy.]

Dear Lady Gregory

The Stage Society will take anything you can give it and be thankful. I do not think there is any serious risk of bad notices, because the bulk of the criticism will be so taken up with Blanco Posnet that the failure of an experimental work would mean, at worst, three lines at the end of the notice to say that such and such a play was also presented, but proved of no particular interest.

I am not, I confess, quite sure as to whether you should give us your best new work. In the ordinary theatrical routine, I should say without hesitation that the press notices to a performance to which the general public could not obtain admission would be a first rate advertisement; but as your audience is a small and select one and may overlap the membership of the Stage Society, I am not so sure about it in your case. Perhaps the best card to play would be Lord Dunsany, as he may be able to work you up a good house outside the Stage Society set.

Then there is the consideration of what plays will best fit in to the Blanco cast.

We must leave it altogether in your hands. Whelen telegraphed to me yesterday; and I replied to him mentioning that the S.S. ought to engage to cover the extra expenses involved by the additional plays. I need hardly say that we have great difficulty in making both ends meet at the Stage Society. When we have paid your expenses we shall have used up all that we can solvently allot to a single performance; and this is at the bottom of Whelen's anxiety to avoid a mixed program. However, I would not have considered this—even if it had involved our giving one performance less this season—if I had not believed that any confusion of the interest in your visit by the production of a new English or foreign play would have been even less desirable in your interests than in ours. The truth is, some of the critics would be only too glad of an excuse for saying as little as possible about Blanco Posnet and spreading themselves on any alternative offered them. Personally, I should like to see your three-act comedy [*The Image*]; but you must save that up for your own season.

I hope Yeats shewed a due sense of the service done us by Braydon in saving the situation. The more fathers the Abbey Theatre can adopt, the better, especially fathers in command of newspapers.

Yours sincerely
G. Bernard Shaw

[*Blanco Posnet* was duly produced, together with *Kathleen Ni Houlihan* and *The Workhouse Ward*, in two private Stage Society sponsored performances by the Abbey company at the Aldwych Theatre on 5th and 6th December 1909, both of which the Shaws attended. *Blanco* was on the whole well received. Yeats wrote to Lady Gregory, who could not come over to London, (postmarked 4th December 1909): 'I think we shall give a good performance. Shaw has rehearsed the company twice and improved them very much. He is an excellent teacher and I think he is pleased' (ALS/p: NLI). This would appear to be the only time Shaw actually worked with the Abbey actors.]

In the autumn of 1909 Miss Horniman made an offer to the Abbey directors to take over her leases of the theatre buildings, due to expire in 1910, for £1428, which was no more than she had paid originally. She promised to continue to pay the

Theatre subsidy until the end of 1910. Negotiations on this offer dragged on, as the directors did not feel they could close with it unless they could be sure of raising an endowment to keep the theatre running, and to pay the considerable costs of an application for a new Patent in 1910. By December 1909, Miss Horniman was insisting that the offer should be accepted before the end of the year, or it would be withdrawn and the theatre let to another tenant. She was particularly incensed by a public statement, made by the directors on the issue, which she felt misrepresented the position.

Shaw, who was on good terms with Miss Horniman, tried to mediate fairly between her and the directors, describing her offer to the Abbey as a generous one. However, a lower than expected valuation of the theatre premises gave the directors a new bargaining tool, and by January 1910 they were hoping to buy Miss Horniman out for no more than £1000. Lady Gregory at this stage was in London, staying with her friend Lady Layard, and a meeting between herself and Miss Horniman seems to have made the latter even more recalcitrant. Yeats, incensed by Miss Horniman's attitude, reacted angrily, in a letter to Lady Gregory from Dublin on 30th January, to what he considered to be Shaw's meddling [ALS/p: NLI]: 'If Shaw had ... not interfered I have no doubt that by this we should have got the theatre for a £1000 or close [to] it and this would have enabled us to get on without raising capital. ... Shaw's conduct is utterly inexcusable but there is no use saying that for we need his help clumsy as he has the reputation of being. We need his help because Miss Horniman is afraid of him'. The next day, 31st January, Miss Horniman wrote to Shaw outlining an elaborate proposal by which one or more hypothetical individuals 'of decent standing' should take over the leases of the theatre for a transitional period of three years, at a total cost of some £1200, after which it should be theirs outright. The point of this scheme was to avoid Yeats involving himself 'in a company with liabilities, got up among "Patriots"'[ALS: BL]. This letter Shaw passed on to Yeats and Lady Gregory.

The upshot of the bargaining was an agreement on 20th February 1910, by which the directors were to pay Miss Horniman £1000 for all her rights in the theatre, while she was to continue to pay the subsidy until the end of the year. This, however, was not the end of the story. When the Abbey, by mischance, remained open on the occasion of the death of King Edward VII in May 1910, a further dispute ensued, with Miss Horniman resolving to withdraw the remaining instalments of the subsidy and the directors retaliating by withholding the purchase payment. The dispute was finally resolved by arbitration in 1911, with the decision going in favour of the directors.

SHAW TO LADY GREGORY
[APCS: Berg, NYPL]

10 Adelphi Terrace. [London]
7th February 1910

[Mr Drucker, a London financial adviser who had been consulted on the transactions involving the takeover of the Abbey from Miss Horniman, was possibly a member of the stockbrokerage firm of Drucker & Morris.]

Unluckily I have an important committee at three tomorrow which will keep me busy all the afternoon. However, there's not really much for me to do on the accountant's report. I should shew it frankly to Mr Drucker, and ask him what he makes of it. Any figure named for endowment must be more or less a fancy figure, as you will go on with what you can get over and above the £1500 needed to buy out Miss H. or secure her for the three years. It would be absurd to ask for less than £5000 and extravagant to ask for more; so I should keep it at that, and take what Providence sends over and above the half of it.

G.B.S.

SHAW TO LADY GREGORY
[ACCS: Berg, NYPL]

10 Adelphi Terrace. [London]
9th March 1910

[Shaw's invitation was to *Misalliance*, which had opened at the Duke of York's Theatre on 23rd February 1910. Yeats attended, presumably with Lady Gregory.]

Dear Lady Gregory
Please come to my box tomorrow afternoon, with Yeats. I enclose the ticket. I will join you in the course of the performance—probably a little late.

Yours sincerely
G. Bernard Shaw

LADY GREGORY TO SHAW
[TLS: BL]

Coole Park. Gort
7th April [1910]

[Shaw had served on the Council and Committee of Management of the Society of Authors since early 1905. Harold V. Neilson was an actor-manager, best known in the English provinces. The 'Aerated Bread Shop young lady' is a reference to a passage in *John Bull's Other Island* where Larry Doyle comments on the charm of vocal novelty: 'When I first went to London I very nearly proposed to walk out with a waitress in an Aerated Bread shop because her Whitechapel accent was so distinguished, so quaintly touching, so pretty'. Curtis Brown did become Lady Gregory's literary agent. The 'chance' which Shaw had given the young and inexperienced Lennox Robinson was a nominal temporary secretaryship to Harley Granville Barker, which enabled him to attend rehearsals taken by Barker and Shaw, preparatory to assuming the managing directorship of the Abbey.]

Dear Mr Shaw
You have been so kind about my plays I wonder if I may ask you to advise me as to enclosed offer. I shall feel after June that my plays have done all they can do for our Theatre, and that I

may try to make something out of them with a quiet conscience. Please dont refer me to the Society of Authors, as you say is your principle; I do go to them about agreements and general business, but your plays having been given by Neilson, I think you would give the best advice. I have not yet taken an agent, and Curtis Brown is still hovering round me. I like him, but perhaps it is because he is so American, like your Aerated Bread shop young woman who is so fascinating to those to whom she is a new type. The Society of Authors say Curtis Brown is as good as anyone else, and if I let out any plays I should have some one I suppose to collect fees, but I dont know if I should let him deal with Neilson? or what I should ask?

Blanco is at Belfast this week, and did very well in Dublin in Easter week. I wish some friendly enthusiasts would arrange for some performances in London in June.

[Lennox] Robinson is getting on all right, he had a row or two with Miss Allgood, but writes from Belfast that she is an angel. We owe a great deal to you for the chance you gave him. Our Theatre fund advances slowly, we have been given or promised over £1800. In June we must make another effort, but meanwhile we shall be able to buy out Miss Horniman and get Patent, pay lawyers, decorate etc with our own £1700 and £300 from subscriptions, and that leaves us £1500 towards an endowment. And I have got together a financial committee, a temporary one, in Dublin to go into our affairs and make out a working scheme for the future, and this I hope will lead to a permanent finance committee and a business Director. Altogether, to quote your favourite Pilgrims Progress, I feel like Christian when the strings of his burden began to unloose.

With best regards to you both,

Yours truly
A. Gregory

Shaw and Charlotte, on an extended motoring tour of Ireland, paid their first visit to Coole from 15th August to 27th August 1910.

Yeats was a fellow guest at the time and it was here that Shaw came to appreciate Yeats's true qualities for the first time. Earlier, Shaw confessed in a letter to Stephen Gwynn on 28th August 1940, he had not taken Yeats quite seriously, regarding him as the incarnation of Gilbert and Sullivan's outrageous poet Bunthorne in *Patience*: 'Not until I spent some time in the house with him at Lady Gregory's ... did I learn what a penetrating critic and good talker he was; for he played none of his Bunthorne games, and saw no green elephants, at Coole' [TLS: Ellen Clarke Bertrand Library, Bucknell University].

SHAW TO LADY GREGORY
[APCS: Berg, NYPL]

[Central Hotel. Tralee]
27th August 1910

After an exciting road race, pursued by the execrations of the maddened peasantry, I drove the car into one end of Limerick Station exactly as the 1.28 train came in at the other. Mrs Chumley [Shaw's sister-in-law] was duly taken on board; and the drive to Tralee finished in torrents of rain that would have astonished Noah. The change from last night is very fearful; but the hotel is quite good; and we shall stay until Monday. Coole must seem very quiet now that I have stopped talking. Charlotte sends many messages; but I have left no room for them.

G.B.S.

SHAW ON LADY GREGORY
[Transliteration of shorthand draft: BL]

[Curtis Brown, Lady Gregory's literary agent, had urged her to obtain from Shaw for publicity purposes a written text of his eulogy of her work given in a speech on behalf of the Abbey delivered in London on 3rd February 1910. In Parknasilla, on 27 September 1910, Shaw drafted a statement which was intended to read like a verbatim transcript of the original remarks.]

Mr Bernard Shaw, speaking at a meeting in London in 1910, alluded to Lady Gregory's plays in the following terms:

'I know of no more conclusive refutation of the theory of irresistible vocation in fine art than the case of Lady Gregory. No dramatist, living or dead, has shewn the peculiar, specific gift of the born playwright—the gift of Molière, for instance— more unmistakeably than Lady Gregory. If ever there was a person doomed from the cradle to write for the stage, to break through every social obstacle to get to the stage, to refuse to do anything but write for the stage, nay, to invent and create a theatre if no theatre existed, that person is the author of Hyacinth Halvey, of The Workhouse Ward, and of The Rising of the Moon. There are authors who have achieved considerable reputation and success as writers for the theatre, who have not had a tenth of her natural faculty for the work. Yet it never, as far as I know, occurred to her spontaneously to write a play at all. She had, on occasion, turned her hand to writing, with invariably entertaining results; but it always was "on occasion": she does not seem to have volunteered anything. I see no reason to suppose that she would ever have written a line if nobody had asked her to. Her activities as the wife of an active member of the governing class were to all appearances quite enough for her.

'Fortunately for the world the public duty of nursing the Irish National Theatre thrust itself on her before it was too late. In those early days of the struggle of that institution for existence, everybody had to do what they could. I must not say that the actors had to shift the scenes, and the actresses to darn the wardrobe, the authors to write the playbills and paint the scenes, and the managers to sweep out the box office and so forth; but I feel quite sure that whenever anything was wanted, whether it was a scrubbing brush or an Irish play, Lady Gregory was appealed to as general housekeeper to supply it. The scrubbing brush she bought, and may even have wielded; but as the oilshops did not keep Irish plays, and Mr Yeats and the other great writers on the staff could not keep up with the demand, she had to produce them herself; and thus was discovered one of the most remarkable theatre talents of our time. There never was a clearer proof of the fact that it is not your hopelessly stage-struck, or book struck, or paint struck, or music struck monomaniac that makes our great artists, but rather the practical geniuses who will do anything in the air, and who respond to a public need and not to their individual ambition or vanity.

'Lady Gregory's success needs no confirmation from me. They never fail to do the one thing which we all demand from a play, which is, not as stupid people say, to amuse us—though Lady Gregory's plays are extremely amusing—but to take us out of ourselves and out of London and out of the stuffy theatre whilst we are listening to them. The early ones, from Spreading the News to The Workhouse Ward, have fun and bustle enough—what people call action—to make excellent Variety Theatre turns in the hands of capable Irish comedians. The later ones: The Image and the sequel to Hyacinth Halvey, are subtler and finer: they present to us a group of Irish people to whom absolutely nothing at all happens; and yet their imaginations work so furiously that at the fall of the curtain they have gone through a whole tragedy of what they would themselves call "heartscalding" experience. In this double command of the world of fancy, and the world of the vividest, funniest fact, Lady Gregory's genius strongly resembles that of Molière; and I am not surprised to learn that she has translated several of his plays for use by the Irish National Theatre'.

LADY GREGORY: *SEVENTY YEARS*

[June 1911]

[Lady Gregory was once again in London with the Abbey players, staying with her nephew Hugh Lane. *Fanny's First Play*, first performed at the Little Theatre on 19th April 1911, was to become Shaw's longest-running play to date. Shaw licensed *Blanco Posnet* to the Abbey for the American tour at a royalty of £5 a performance.]

Thursday night [2nd June] when I got to the theatre, I had a message that Bernard Shaw could see me if I came round to the Little Theatre. I had been deputed by the agents to find out how much he would demand for *Blanco*, which he is giving us leave to take to America, and they were afraid he would ask a prohibitive price. So I went there, and found *Fanny's First Play* going on, and went into his box, and between the Acts did my business, and he did not name a price but said I might set my mind at rest, that it would be all right. I lunched with him and Mrs Shaw yesterday. Delius the musician and his wife there. Music talked of. ... Delius attacked Strauss, said he was jerky and irresponsible and ought to stick to comic themes and pantomime tricks. Shaw defended him, and said at the end, 'I can't but feel that all you have said of him has been applied to G.B. Shaw!' which was just what I had been thinking. ...

After lunch he went through the proposed American agreement with me and said that if we had to pay any share of the royalties on *Blanco* he would give us back that share, very good of him.   .

The Abbey's first American tour began in Boston in September 1911; for the greatest part of the company's six-month visit, Lady Gregory accompanied them. In the Abbey's repertoire was *Blanco Posnet*, T.C. Murray's realistic play *Birthright*, which shocked Irish-Americans by its grim vision of Irish life, and the controversial *Playboy*. There was some hostility to the *Playboy* in Boston, attempts to have it banned in Providence and New Haven, and active Catholic church opposition in Washington. In the forefront of the campaign against the *Playboy* and the Abbey from the beginning were Irish-American organisations, including Clan na Gael and the New York-based *Gaelic American*, edited by John Devoy. And it was when the play appeared in New York, at the Maxine Elliott Theatre on 27th November 1911, that serious disturbances broke out, with eggs, vegetables and stink bombs thrown at the stage. 'New York's Protest Against a Vile Play' was the *Gaelic American*'s front-page headline [2nd December]:

Hostile Demonstration Unparalleled In The History Of The City Greets 'The Playboy'—Actors Hooted Off the Stage In First Act, The Police Reserves Called Out And More Than A Hundred Citizens Ejected—Supporters Were Largely English—Barefooted Women Act Like Prostitutes in Dublin Slums Capturing Drunken Soldiers And Sailors— Disgraceful and Disgusting Spectacle

The article was representative of Irish-American opposition to the play, attacking its obscenity and, above all, its lack of truth to Ireland and the Irish experience, even questioning, on the basis of their bare feet, whether the Abbey actresses were authentically Irish:

> No such feet ever came out of Ireland before. They were typically Anglo-Saxon feet—big, clumsy and flat ... Irish women have the daintiest feet in Europe, but there wasn't a foot or ankle in that crowd that would pass muster in Ireland.

Already in an Associated Press release from London on 25th November, Shaw had come to the defence of the beleaguered Abbey company, turning the tables on the Clan na Gael by attacking *their* Irishness:

> I warned Lady Gregory America was a dangerous country to take a real Irish company to, as there are not half a dozen real Irishmen in America outside of that company. You would suppose that all of these Murphys, Doolans, etc., that call themselves romantic names like Clan na Gael are Irishmen.
>
> As to Boston's Devoy, that is not an Irish name. I was brought up an Irish land agent and know more about Irish names than any one outside of a professor. [*Gaelic American*, 2nd December]

On 9th December, the New York *Evening Sun* published a long 'interview', entirely composed by Shaw, in which he further pursued the inauthentic Irishness of the Clan na Gael, defended the *Playboy* as representative of a new and healthily critical reaction within Ireland to the patriotic idealism of the past, and pointed out that Irish-American protesters against *Blanco Posnet* (which had also been a target for *Gaelic American* abuse) were aligning themselves with Dublin Castle:

> you will observe that the Clan na Gael instinctively takes the side of Dublin Castle; for without Dublin Castle there would be no Clan na Gael—nothing to blow up—no subscriptions. But Lady Gregory fought and routed Dublin Castle; and in America she will simply walk over the Clan na Gael unless it has the sense to understand that she is the greatest living Irishwoman, and that cultivated Americans will attach much more importance to anything she says or does than to splut-

terings of Bostonian sham Irish peasants who do not know the difference between Wycherley and Goldsmith and shriek in the same breath that Irishwomen are the purest in Christendom and that Lady Gregory is a disgrace to her sex.

In spite of the riots, in part because of them and the publicity they generated, the company did excellent business in New York and the tour was extended. But in Philadelphia, when the *Playboy* was produced at the Adelphi Theatre on 15th January 1912, they ran into further trouble. A meeting of the Irish American Club committee, chaired by Joseph McGarrity, a prominent member of Clan na Gael, on the day before the first performance, resolved that, as they had not succeeded in persuading the Mayor to prohibit the play, they should organise a protest demonstration to disrupt the performance [Hol. minutes: McGarrity papers, NLI]. Eighteen members of the Club volunteered to attend and protest. Many of the protesters, including McGarrity, were ejected from the theatre and arrested. After further disturbances at the second performance of the play, on Wednesday 17th January McGarrity brought an injunction against further performances, stating in a formal deposition that 'The Playboy ... is a gross misrepresentation of Irish Peasant Life. ... The thing is immoral and blasphemous almost from start to finish' [TMS deposition: McGarrity papers, NLI]. The result was the mass arrest of the cast.

Shaw, informed of the arrest, gave his reaction to the press in a statement widely publicised on both sides of the Atlantic:

> The occurrence is too ordinary to be worth any comment. All decent people are arrested in America. That is the reason I have refused all invitations to go there. Besides, who am I that I should question Philadelphia's right to make itself ridiculous?
>
> I warned the Irish Players that America, being governed by a mysterious race—probably one of the lost tribes of Israel—calling themselves American Gaels, is a dangerous country for genuine Irishmen and Irishwomen. The American Gaels are the real Playboys of the Western World; and they are naturally angry with Synge for showing them up, though really that does not excuse the Americans for allowing themselves to be made the cat's-paw of the Playboys.

We are none the less grateful on this side to Colonel [Theodore] Roosevelt [the former president, who had appeared in Lady Gregory's box at the second night of the *Playboy* in New York] for his public and no doubt representative expression of contempt for this blackguardly agitation against the art and literature which have made the names of Synge, Yeats and Lady Gregory famous, and have called the attention of Europe to the fact that Ireland is a nation with a specific and splendid national genius, and not merely a province of England [*Pall Mall Gazette*, 19th January].

LADY GREGORY TO SHAW
[ALS: BL]

Hotel Algonquin. New York
23rd January [1912]

Dear Mr Shaw

I feel you are the only one to deal with this censorship! I have written from day to day a letter, duplicate to Robert and Yeats, and I have asked John Quinn to have a copy made for you (I am just off to Pittsburgh and other towns on the way to Chicago). You may quote anything not marked, if you care to write about it. This is the 6th day since the arrest of the players—and they are still under bail and imputation, the judge not having given his decision. I am furious! Philadelphia is so pompous—and lets itself be governed by little political cliques of publicans and the like. Our whole tour has been very amusing and successful, and I like America very much indeed in spite of all—it is a great excitement seeing a new country at my time of life, and since Philadelphia I feel any romantic adventure possible!

Yours ever
A Gregory

LADY GREGORY: LETTER/JOURNAL
[TMS: BL]

Philadelphia
4.30 17th January [1912]

[This letter/journal, as Lady Gregory indicates in the previous letter, was sent in duplicate both to Robert Gregory, to whom it is addressed, and to Yeats. John Quinn posted Shaw's copy on 23rd January with a substantial covering letter [TLS: BL], explaining the context of the arrest in Philadelphia and reiterating Lady Gregory's restriction on using the marked passages (identified below by italic setting) in the journal. He added a further caution:

> Lady Gregory asked me to say to you that in her opinion it was of the utmost importance that no allusion whatever be made to the religious question or to the testimony of the priest; that that would be hurtful in Ireland. She suggested that in any statement you might make you keep off the religious question altogether. It would be a great mistake, in my judgement, to make any allusion to the religious question.

Shaw did not make any public use of the letter/journal material, possibly, as Yeats conjectured in a letter to Lady Gregory of 9th February 1912, because of his involvement in the renewed controversy over censorship: 'A great effort is being made to abolish the English censorship. Prosecution before the Courts will be the substitute. If Shaw were to use your letter he will have to go into a lot of explanation to show that the English Court would not be open to the same objections. Your letter on the face of it would give a popular argument on the other side' [TLS/p: NLI]. Her journal, discreetly edited, was to form the basis of Lady Gregory's account of the American tour in *Our Irish Theatre*.
   Mr and Mrs Henry La Barre Jayne were Lady Gregory's hosts, with whom she always stayed during her visits to Philadelphia. The Adelphi was one of the string of theatres, including the Maxine Elliott (where the *Playboy* had been performed in New York), owned by the Shuberts.]

Darling R.
   At 2 o'c. I was just finishing lunch alone ... when I was rung up by Mr [Walton] Bradford, our manager at the Adelphi, to say that he had warning from Lieblers [the theatrical agency handling the Abbey's American tour] that we might have to

change the bill tonight and take off Playboy. I said that could not be done, but he said that it might be necessary, there is some legal point and that we might all be arrested if we go on. I said I would rather be arrested than withdraw the play and could answer for the players feeling the same. He said there was also a danger Shubert to whom the Theatre belongs might close it. I said that would be bad but not so bad as withdrawing Playboy, for it would be Shubert's disgrace not ours, though that might not be much help in the public view. I was anxious, *for Shubert is a 'yellow cur' and apologized to the Irish at New York.* I told Bradford not to consent to anything without consulting me. Then I called up John Quinn at New York, got him at his office, and asked him to see the Lieblers, and said I need not tell him I would sooner go to my death than give in. He said he would do it at once, and will be here this evening, as he had intended. At 4 o'c. I heard again from Bradford. He said it had been decided to go on, and that a bail bond has been prepared, and asked if there was anyone to represent me in case of arrest. I said I would wait to consult Quinn. It is such a mercy he is coming. My only fear is lest they should get out an injunction to stop the matinée tomorrow, even that would be claimed as a victory. They had told me at the Theatre this morning there would probably be trouble tonight. The men arrested [for disturbing the performance the night before] were let out, had their money returned, and were escorted through the streets by an admiring crowd. *I don't wonder at Lynch law being adopted here, the police are so timid, afraid of 'civil actions' against them.* However they were warming up last night and will I hope be hot tonight. I should like to avoid arrest because of the publicity, one would feel like a suffragette.

Thursday 18th. When Quinn arrived we went straight to Theatre, 7.15, and found the whole cast had already been technically arrested! The tactics of the enemy had been to arrest them in the Theatre at 8.o'c. and so make a performance impossible. But the Theatre lawyer, [William H.] Redhefer, had managed to circumvent them, and the chief of Police, now our warm friend, had said he would not only refuse to let his men arrest them but he would have anyone arrested who came on the stage to do so. In the end the warrants of arrest were issued and the Manager of the Theatre signed bail bonds for the appearance of the company on Friday morning. *The laws are extraordinary here.* The warrants are founded on a bill passed last year in the municipality before S. Bernhardt, forbidding immoral or indecent plays. Our accuser is a publican, *and he got the warrants through* [James A.] *Carey, a corrupt magistrate entirely discredited amongst decent people, but who is to try our case!* I should have been completely bewildered by the whole thing, but Quinn seemed to unravel it. We had a consultation with Mr Redhefer and Mr Jayne's partners, Mr [Charles] Biddle and Mr [Howard H.] Yocum, whom he had sent to help me. The question seems to be whether it is best to have the hearing put off and brought before a judge, or whether to have it settled straight off tomorrow. The danger is our being let in for a trial after some weeks, bringing us back here, and having the Devoyites boasting that we were under bail. Quinn is this morning seeing all the lawyers here, and some decision as to our course will be come to. *The Manager* [Leonard A.] *Blumberg thinks more can be done through political influence and other influence than by law; for instance, our publican prosecutor is rather in dread of the Chief of Police lest his license should be stopped. He has not a good record.* The Commissioner of Public Safety [George D. Porter] attended the play last night, and said the attack on it must be a joke. I have been interrupted in this by the correspondent of the Telegraph coming to ask if it is true as stated by the Irish Societies that I am an envoy of the English Government. I referred him to Mr [James] Bryce [British Ambassador to the United States] who I suppose would be my paymaster.

Saturday 20th. I have been too anxious and hardworked to write since Thursday. That was the last performance (matinée) of Playboy, and there was an immense audience. I could not get a seat. Even the little boxes at the top—it is a very high theatre with eight boxes at each side—were all taken. I had made appointments with reporters and others, and had to get a high stool from the office put in the passage and sit there or at the back of stage. It was the record matinée of the Adelphi. There was tremendous enthusiasm and not a sign of any disturbance. Of course we had a good many police, to the great regret of the management who had to turn so much good money away. So that was quite a cheerful day. Someone in the audience was heard declaring that the players are not Irish, but all Jews. I had an anonymous letter from someone who accuses me of the usual crimes and winds up 'I have not seen the plays, but I have read all about them and you'! That is the way with most of the letter writers, I think.

Yesterday Friday morning we attended the Magistrate's Court at 9 o'c. We had to wait nearly an hour in a tiny stuffy room. When the trial began I was given a chair behind the Magistrate, but the others had either to sit at the back of the inner room where they could not see or hear, or stand, as they did, for over an hour. *The witnesses brought against us were the most villainous looking creatures.* I wanted to get a snapshotter but could not get through the crowd. Their faces would have been enough to exonerate us. The liquor-seller, our prosecutor, was the first witness; he had only stayed till Shawneen's 'coat of a Christian man' was left in Michael James' hands, he made a disturbance then and was turned out, but was able to find as much indecency even in that conversation as would *demoralise a monastery. His brother, a priest, had stayed all through and found we had committed every sin mentioned in the Act, (which had been made in preparation for the visit of Sara Bernhardt whose performance of La Samarataine was stopped here). Another priest swore that sentences were used in the play and that he has heard them, that are not either in book or play. Both priests made orations as if to their own congregations.* Several witnesses were examined or asked to speak, giving all the same story 'or if it were not the same story anyway it was no less than the first story'. Our actors were furious. [J.M.] Kerrigan says it was all he could do to keep from breaking out and risking all when the priest was attacking his ('Shawn Keogh's') character and intentions. At last all got tired, the counsel for the prosecution, Mr [William A.] Gray, demanded that the actors should be 'held for court', but Quinn knowing what would happen had arranged for this, and our lawyers (who had been quite useless in cross-examination) sued out writ of habeas corpus (I hope this is the right expression) and had arranged with Judge [William Wilkins] Carr to try the case in the afternoon. Mr Gray tried then to have it tried at once, said he had to leave town in the afternoon, but in the end the Judge said he could not have us before three o'clock. This gave time to telephone to J. Quinn who had thought it was not to be till next morning, and was attending cases of his own in New York, but answered he would come if he possibly could, and then there was a message that he had missed the train by one minute, but had caught another, ten minutes later. At three o'clock we went to the court, a large one this time, and the Judge had a nice face. He had been to my lecture here the first time I came *and is a friend of the Jaynes.* He didn't know anything of the play, and had to be told the whole story as it went on, just like old Wall [the magistrate who tried the *Playboy* rioters] in Dublin at our first riot, so before the case was over audience and officials were in a broad grin. Mr McGarrity the liquor dealer got a different hearing this time, was asked some pertinent questions instead of being simply encouraged, as by Magistrate Carey ('a bad name' say the players), but you will see that in the papers. The dramatic event was the arrival of Quinn *while a priest* [Father P.J. McGarrity, brother of the publican] *was being examined. We had got leave from the Judge for him to cross-examine, and the priest had to confess that the people of Ireland do use the name of God at other times than in blessing or thanking those who have been kind to them, (and in gratitude or prayer), as he had at first asserted upon oath. Also when he based his attack on indecency on the 'poacher's love' spoken of by Christie he was made to admit that a few sentences earlier marriage had been spoken of 'in a fortnight's time when the banns will be called'. Whether this made it more or less moral he was not asked to say. He called the play libidinous.* The players beamed and the audience enjoyed themselves, and then when the Director of Public Safety was called and said he and his wife had enjoyed the play very much and seen nothing to shock anybody, the enemy had received as Quinn said 'a body blow'. He made a very fine speech then, there is just a little bit of it in the North American, but Mr Gray made objections to its being reported, but anyhow it turned the table completely on the enemy. It was a little disappointment that the Judge did not give his verdict there and then, that we might have cabled home. There is no doubt what it must be, but we are still awaiting it. ... A lot of people have been expressing sympathy. A young man from the University who had been bringing a body guard for me on the riot nights has just been to say good bye and says the students are going to hold an indignation meeting. The Drama League, 600 strong, has so far done or said nothing, though it is supposed to have sent out a bulletin endorsing the favourable opinion of Boston on our plays a week after we came, not having had time to form an opinion of its own. ... I think the very name League leads to impotency. Can you imagine their allowing such a thing to happen here as the arrest of a company of artists engaged in producing masterpieces, and at such hands! The Administration has been reformed of late and is certainly on the mend, *but there is a lot of corruption about still, although* the city has an innocent look as if it had gone astray in the fields, and its streets are all named after trees. The company are in a state of fury. *It will be very embarrassing if I have to bring home a company of Protestants!* But they adore John Quinn, and his name will pass into folklore like those stories of O'Connell suddenly appearing at trials. He spoke splendidly with fire and full knowledge. You will see what he said about the witnesses in the North American, and even [Lennox] Robinson says he 'came like an angel'.

Sunday 21. Yesterday a little depressing for the Judge has not yet given out his decision, so we are still under bail and the imputations of indecency etc. The Philadelphians say it is because the Act is such a new one it requires a great deal of consideration. A reporter came yesterday to ask if I considered Playboy immoral. I said my taking it about was enough answer, but that if he wished to give interesting news he would go to the 26 witnesses produced against us, and try to get at their opinions and on what they were founded. He answered that he had already been to ten of them that morning, that they all answered in the same words, not two words of difference—that their opinion was founded on the boy and girl being left alone in the house for the night. *They can hardly have heard Quinn making the priest withdraw his statement that immorality was implied by their being left together.* I advised him also to look at the signed articles on the Play in so many English and American magazines, and to remember that even here the plays have been taught at the dramatic classes in the University of Pennsylvania, and Miss [Martha Carey] Thomas [the President] of Bryn Mawr had me to lecture, and Yeats before that, and had invited the Players to the College for the day, and sent a large party of students to the last matinée of Playboy, leave being asked to introduce them to me. He might print all this opposite the witnesses' opinions and it would be amusing. Yesterday's matinée—Rising of the Moon, Well of the Saints and Workhouse Ward—was again so crowded that I could not get a place, and went and sat in the sidewings, where a Cinematograph man came to ask if I would allow Playboy to be made a moving picture of, as it would be 'such a good advertisement for us'! Last night also very good audience. We took just one dollar short of eight thousand dollars in the week. Such a pity the dollars were returned to the disturbers or we should have been over it. ...

I was to have started with the Company this morning for another six towns, on the road to Chicago, but the delay in the Judge's decision keeps me here till tomorrow partly to be able to cable and partly another point. Quinn advised that as soon as we get the decision we ought to take an action in the name of the Players against McGarrity for malicious arrest. It would be a splendid dramatic coup. *He said that we need not go on with it longer than we liked; it could be easily dropped after a while.* Mr Jayne was well enough to see me yesterday, he is a very good lawyer and gives very clear advice, and he said he thought it an excellent idea, and that we should sue for 50,000 dollars, the cost of starting proceedings would be very little, and we could not be forced to continue them. I have just been called up by J.Q. from New York, and he has given some further advice about it. Of course if the Judge's decision is not clearly for us we can't do it. I am more anxious about this cable than anything, for I think our situation in Ireland is made much more difficult by this business here. *It is the first time they have had two priests on oath proclaiming the play blasphemous, immoral and indecent.* It is quite likely that it has already been cabled, and that we may be denounced even now, from the altars of this morning, and that the Abbey may be cleared of Catholics for a while. It may be the fight has come and that we must face it. But if we can show that the charge is brought by publicans *and sinners of a low type*, judgment will at all events be suspended for a little while and the truth become known. I would not send any cable up to this, because we have no victory to announce. ...

Monday 11 o'c. Still waiting for the Judge's verdict. I forget what I have written, but I don't know if I have explained that we were allowed no witnesses either at Magistrate's or Judge's

Court, and with our hastily instructed lawyers we should not have been able to make even any defense through them but for the miraculous appearance of John Quinn. And this is the fifth day we have been under bail on charge of indecency, and its like.

N.Y. Had to come here with no decision: off to Pittsburg tomorrow.

With love
M.

[On 23rd January Judge Carr at last gave judgment, discharging the company, though without making further comment. The tour continued through several other cities to Chicago: Lady Gregory received death threats, but there was no further major trouble for the players. They returned to Ireland at the beginning of March.]

SHAW TO LADY GREGORY
[ALS: Berg, NYPL]

10 Adelphi Terrace. [London]
18th June 1912

[Lady Gregory was once again in London with the Abbey players, staying with Hugh Lane. Shaw was here honouring his undertaking made the previous year to return to the Abbey any royalties they had to pay for performances of *Blanco* in America. Two performances of the still censored *Mrs Warren's Profession* were given in a private theatre club production on 16th and 18th June.]

Dear Lady Gregory

My secretary hands me a memorandum of five payments made me for 23 performances of Blanco Posnet in America, amounting to £105–17–10. I enclose a cheque for that sum. Is it correct as far as the number of performances is concerned? If so, it is probably all right as to the money, as this was checked as the returns came in.

I enclose also the two seats for Mrs Warren this afternoon. The performance begins at 2. I shall perhaps see you there.

Yours sincerely
G. Bernard Shaw

LADY GREGORY TO SHAW
[ALS: BL]

Lindsey House. 100 Cheyne Walk. Chelsea
18th June [1912]

[Nugent Monck, an Irish actor who had trained in England with
William Poel and the Elizabethan Stage Society, had taken charge of
the Abbey School of Acting and produced a number of plays with the
School at the Abbey during the absence of the main company on their
American tour of 1911–12. He continued to be associated with
Lennox Robinson in the management of the Abbey for the next year
and was the manager of the company on their second tour of America
in 1913.]

Dear Mr Shaw

Very many thanks from us all, theatre and company, for your
cheque. [J.A.] O'Rourke expressed the feeling of the rest by
saying 'He is entirely too good a man'. It was a kindly and
generous act, and I am grateful.

Thank you also very much for the tickets, I could not get
there after all, and Yeats and [Fred] O'Donovan used them.

Our new manager question has been settled for the present
by Yeats casually remembering he had engaged Nugent Monck
for a year!

Yours always sincerely
Augusta Gregory

SHAW TO LADY GREGORY
[APCS: Berg, NYPL]

Ayot St Lawrence. Welwyn
14th September 1912

[The attack of asthma and bronchitis from which Charlotte Shaw was
now suffering was nearly fatal; she had to remain in bed for a month.]

Charlotte is a wreck: asthma at its worst, bronchitis, bed,
cylinders of oxygen, and all the horrors. She will recover
presently; but she will not be able to travel until she has

recuperated a little. I scrawl this in wild haste, within a minute of post hour.

G.B.S.

LADY GREGORY TO SHAW
[TLS: BL]

Coole Park. Gort
5th October [1912]

[The book that Lady Gregory was writing was published as *Our Irish Theatre* by Putnam in New York in 1913. Douglas Hyde had contributed to the early theatre movement some short plays in Irish, including *Casadh-an-tSugain* (The Twisting of the Rope) and *The Poorhouse*, a collaboration with Lady Gregory which she subsequently re-wrote as *The Workhouse Ward*. *Selected Passages from the Works of Bernard Shaw*, edited by Charlotte, had been published on 23rd September: Lady Gregory had been sent a copy. *The Playboy* was produced at the Abbey in Horse Show week; a new version of Yeats's *The Countess Cathleen*, first performed on 14th December 1911, had become part of the theatre's repertoire, with the title role played first by Maire O'Neill and subsequently by her sister Sara Allgood. Wilfrid Scawen Blunt, who was a close friend and had had a brief affair with Lady Gregory in 1882–83, agitated for Irish as well as Arab political causes, hence his connection with Charles Stewart Parnell. The correspondence between the actor, producer and actor-manager, John Martin-Harvey and Lady Gregory over his possible production of the *Playboy* does not seem to have survived, although there is an undated typescript text of the play in the National Library of Ireland that evidently was prepared as the prompt-book for a touring production by Martin-Harvey, apparently in 1907.]

Dear Mr Shaw

I have at last got to work on what I had meant to be one or two magazine articles, but I think will be a little book, on the Abbey Theatre, arranged something like this in chapters: 1. Making the Theatre. 2. The fight over the Playboy. 3. The fight with the Castle (or the Censor, but I think the Blanco fight with the Castle balances our fight with Nationalists better). 4. Helpers and friends, (Synge, Douglas Hyde, etc etc). 5. The visit to America. Last winter I determined not to go to America again without some such statement, I was so worried to death by being asked 'Please tell me the exact reasons for the objections to the Playboy' or to Blanco; or as one lady expressed it '*Lady Gregory's* play, the *Cowboy* of the Western World!' It will be a comfort not only being able to refer them to my little book, but to think I shall get a few cents on each sale.

I have had copies of the Blanco correspondence made, and I am enclosing those made of your letters; will you please look at them and say if you have any objection to my using those parts I have marked? Alas, I cannot publish the Lord Lieutenant's with his delicate flattery of my plays. 'Another which I thought very effective was one the title of which curiously I forget, but you would doubtless recognize it if I quote one or two phrases such as "Do you like Michael?", and "Woman of the House" and again (a pathetic touch) "Probably by some labouring man's ticket"'. I hope if anyone should ever think worth doing for me what Mrs Shaw has been so brilliantly doing for you, these passages of wit and wisdom will not be put in the front rank!

I am sorry to trouble you even so far now you are so full of work.

We go to America in December. I don't think we shall have Playboy rows this time, but country feeling here is still being stirred up by emigrants coming back on visits from America and reporting the attacks upon us there. However in Horse Show week there was just a little organised hissing on the first night, and none at all afterwards. And we have been playing Countess Cathleen in complete peace, and without the police protection necessary when we first produced it in Dublin.

Martin Harvey! He begged for the play for English provincial cities—was frightened by I believe some one on the Freeman's Journal—and wrote to announce his withdrawal, to the Irish papers only—'What a good boy am I'. He wrote to me less ambiguously than to the papers, saying he didn't want to offend his Dublin audience. 'You understand don't you?' Parnell said to Wilfred Blunt, 'an Irishman may betray us but an Englishman always does so', and it is what we have found.

Yours sincerely
Augusta Gregory

We are putting on Blanco Oct 21

SHAW TO LADY GREGORY
[ALS: Burgunder, Cornell]

Ayot St Lawrence. Welwyn
18th November 1912

[Shaw's mother had suffered a series of three strokes, which led to her death in February 1913. The three plays that Shaw had been rehearsing were *Overruled*, *Captain Brassbound's Conversion*, and *Caesar and Cleopatra* (the production in the provinces). Mrs Patrick Campbell, injured in a taxi-cab accident, had been confined to bed.]

My dear Lady Gregory

Three times at least I have begun letters to you; and I cant remember finishing or sending them off. Charlotte's been seriously ill; my mother is dying, they say, but *wont* die — makes nothing of strokes—throws them off as other women throw off sneezing fits; and since the middle of September I have rehearsed and produced three plays, one of them in the provinces. Also Ive been violently in love with Mrs Patrick Campbell because you told me I ought to. I *did*; and such reams of outrageous love letters as I have poured into her sick bed when I ought to have been attending to my wrecked business and hopeless arrears of correspondence have never before been penned. I scorned the danger; thought I was more dangerous than she; and went in head over ears before I had been thirty seconds in her presence. And this at fifty-six, and worn out at that by overwork. Is there no age limit?

By all means make any use you please of my letters. But I still think your pugnacity undervalues the importance of making it clear that Lord A. was treated with the most distinguished consideration all through, and that the thing began in his absence with officious blundering on the part of the Castle bottle washers. The grand manner becomes us in Ireland: we are the only people in these islands who can still do it. Let the opposition to Abbey Street appear as the work of vulgar persons and toadies of the English Lord Chamberlain as far as possible; and leave to be imagined a higher plane on which Lady G. and Lord A. have fought a duel in which Lord A. has been vanquished, but not without gallantry and saving of honor. When you cannot exterminate your foe, build a bridge of silver

for him: it makes his flight more probable in a second battle—
and we may not be at the end yet.

In haste to catch the village post.

Yours sincerely
G. Bernard Shaw

———————————

The next public issue in Ireland for which Shaw's help was
enlisted was the cause of the Dublin Municipal Gallery of
Modern Art. The Gallery had been established in January 1908
by Hugh Lane, who had been the moving force behind it, and
was initially housed in Harcourt Street, where Shaw visited it in
September 1908. Lane had made available on loan, and offered
to give to the city, a very important personal collection of
modern French paintings, including some fine Impressionist
works, on condition that the Corporation would undertake to
build an appropriate gallery to house the collection. After years
of delay, he had warned the city authorities in November 1912
that he would take the collection away from the Gallery unless
the new building was decided upon by January 1913. The Lord
Mayor, Lorcan G. Sherlock, called a public meeting at his
official residence, the Mansion House, for 29th November to
enlist support for the cause. Lady Gregory evidently wrote to
Shaw asking for a letter to the Lord Mayor.

———————————

SHAW TO LADY GREGORY
[APCS: Burgunder, Cornell]

Ayot St Lawrence. Welwyn
19th November 1912

[Sir Thomas Devereux Pile, Lord Mayor of Dublin in 1900, had not
in fact been a member of the Dublin Corporation since 1904. He was
Shaw's classmate at the Wesleyan Connexional School in 1867.]

Our letters crossed.

I'll write to the Lord Mayor. Who is he, by the way? He might be an old schoolfellow, like Tommy Pile.

G.B.S.

SHAW TO LORCAN G. SHERLOCK

[London]

[Having wired Lady Gregory 'Is the Lord Mayor Right Hon., or what?' (quoted by Lady Gregory in *Hugh Lane's Life and Achievement*), Shaw composed this letter on 25th November and hastily struck it off in galley proof. It was duly read out at the Mansion House meeting.]

My dear Lord Mayor

I understand that you have convened a meeting to consider the question of providing a suitable gallery for the collection of works of art brought together by Sir Hugh Lane and now stored in a very handsome dwelling house in Harcourt Street. ...

When I was a boy in Dublin I did not know that our Dublin National Gallery was, for its size, one of the very best in Europe: that is, in the world. I found that out when I had travelled and seen other collections. We owe that eminence practically to the genius of one man, [Henry] Doyle [Director of the National Gallery 1869–92]. ...

Dublin has had the extraordinary good fortune to have had not only a collector of genius in the person of Doyle for its national gallery of old masters, but later on an equally gifted collector of modern pictures. ... Sir Hugh Lane, in making a great collection of the modern French school... and of the works of those painters, especially Irish painters, who assimilated its technical discoveries and responded to that French audacity of spirit which is so congenial to our own national temperament, has placed in the hands of the Corporation of Dublin an instrument of culture the value of which is far beyond anything that can be expressed in figures by the City Accountant.

I speak on this point with strong personal feeling. The taste and knowledge of fine art which I acquired as a boy in the National Gallery of Dublin not only made it possible for me to live by my pen without discrediting my country, but are built into the fabric of the best work I have been able to do since. I was sometimes the only person in that gallery, except the attendants. If a member of the Corporation with a turn for false economy had looked in on these occasions he might have asked whether it was not monstrous that all the cost of maintaining such a building should be incurred for the entertainment of a single idle boy. But I hope I was not so bad a bargain after all. A few of us must spend our boyhood in this way if Irishmen are to keep and extend their share in forming the mind of the world: a share which we may with just pride claim to be large out of all proportion to our numbers and our opportunities. ...

I have nothing more to say except to beg you to allow the importance of the subject to excuse the length of this communication. And as your Committee may be curious to know whether I am sufficiently in earnest to back my opinion, I shall be glad, if contributions are invited from private sources to assist the Corporation in providing a suitable gallery, to put down my own name for one hundred guineas.

> I am, my dear Lord Mayor,
> yours faithfully
> G. Bernard Shaw

LADY GREGORY TO SHAW
[ALS: BL]

> Coole Park. Gort
> 30th November [1912]

[*Bombastes Furioso*, a burlesque tragic opera in one act, by William Barnes Rhodes, was first performed at the Theatre Royal, Haymarket, in August 1810, and enjoyed enormous popularity throughout the nineteenth century. Lady Gregory was due to leave on the Abbey's second American tour at the end of December 1912, during which funds were raised by the company for the Municipal Gallery. The Home Rule meeting took place in the Memorial Hall, London, on 6th December 1912; Shaw's speech at it was published in a pamphlet, *What Irish Protestants Think: Speeches on Home Rule* (London 1912).

The Cuchulain quotation is from Lady Gregory's own *Cuchulain of Muirthemne* (London 1902). It is not clear what the 'headless portraits' were that Lady Gregory was returning, possibly badly judged photographs by Shaw in which the heads were out of frame and the subjects therefore unrecognisable.]

Dear Mr Shaw

That letter is splendid, it ought to do a great deal. And then that final and inspiriting sentence! Is it not in Bombastes Furioso (it ought to be in Arms and the Man) the army is tipped—

'So give five shillings to these loyal men'—

Captain (aside) 'They haven't seen as much, the Lord knows when!'

You have put the case so clearly and convincingly no one can pretend to ignore it. I should like to take some copies to America. If you have any more to spare you might let me have them, if not I will get them reprinted. In the Philadelphia row we were told 'there is no one Americans *feel* but Bernard Shaw'.

Yeats has just been dictating a letter about that Home Rule meeting at which he had promised to speak, but has been turned off by the circular.

One is not afraid of R.C. intolerance, for as I quote from Cuchulain 'Good as the attack is the defence will be as good', but one might as well say there will be no whisky.

I return the headless portraits which are still a mystery. I should have preferred the head, if given my choice. My love to Mrs Shaw. I do hope all is quite right again.

Yours always truly
A Gregory

SHAW TO LADY GREGORY
[APCS/p: Colin Smythe]

10 Adelphi Terrace. London
18th December 1912

[Shaw's two-sentence letter appeared in the *Irish Worker* on 30th November 1912. An unidentified Canadian friend of Hugh Lane had promised £2500 towards the building of a Municipal Gallery to house

the Lane collection provided the remainder of the necessary funds
were subscribed by January 1913, a promise which was announced at
the same Mansion House meeting of 29th November at which Shaw's
letter offering one hundred guineas had been read out.]

Who is the treasurer of the Hugh Lane Gallery Fund? I have
just recollected that I have not yet made my bluff good; and I
have heard nothing from the Lord Mayor or anyone else.
   Who is the wretched Canadian who played me off the stage?
And I thought I was going to cut a most munificent figure!
   Did you see the Irish Worker, which got out on that very day
my denunciation of Dublin as 'a city of derision and invincible
ignorance'?

G.B.S.

SHAW TO LADY GREGORY

[TLS: Berg, NYPL]

10 Adelphi Terrace. London
24th June 1913

[Liebler, the theatrical producers who had again been responsible for
the Abbey's second American tour, went into bankruptcy in 1914.]

My dear Lady Gregory
   I have just squeezed Lieblers successfully for fees that were in
arrear for an American tour; but I do know that they are in
shallow water at present. As far as I am concerned, I do not need
the money on the nail; and therefore it would be mere spite on
my part to refuse to accommodate them by accepting the notes.
And if your enterprise is in the same happy circumstances, then,
as you probably do not make more interest on your capital at the
theatre than the notes will bear, I do not see why you should
force the situation. Notes are really a better security than a
theatrical contract, as it is a very serious commercial misdemea-
nour not to meet a bill when the bank presents it, whereas
nobody attaches the smallest importance to a theatre contract.

Yours sincerely
G. Bernard Shaw

SHAW TO MRS ROBERT GREGORY
[APCS: Sotheby, 24.7.79]

Folkestone, en voyage
6th September 1913

[Margaret Gregory had written from Coole asking Shaw if he would be godfather to her daughter Catherine.]

Never. I am continually defending children against these outrages. How do you know that she will not abhor my opinions, or that I may not be hanged yet?

You really must not tattoo an infant with a political and religious trademark. Choose some nonentity whose name will never be connected with anything.

Besides, if I undertook at the font to see to her religious education, I should do it; and then where would she be?

G.B.S.

SHAW TO LADY GREGORY
[TLS: Berg, NYPL]

10 Adelphi Terrace. London
29th November 1913

[The proposed scheme for a gallery to house the Lane Collection had collapsed in September 1913, partly because of Lane's insistence on the adoption of the plan for a bridge-gallery spanning the Liffey, designed by the English architect Sir Edwin Lutyens. That portion of the money raised for the Gallery by the Abbey performances in America was finally returned to the actors, after a dispute with the directors in which both they and the actors resorted to taking counsel's opinion.]

My dear Lady Gregory

I am afraid that the question of the disposal of the funds raised by the Abbey Theatre for the Picture Gallery is not so simple as you think. It seems reasonable, now that the project has fallen through, that the funds raised by the Abbey Theatre be returned to the Abbey Theatre exactly as the sum which I personally subscribed will be returned to me; and your impulse to hand it back to the company as a welcome windfall is a very natural one.

Unfortunately, this money was not contributed by your people at the Abbey directly out of their private incomes: it was collected from the public by means of performances at which the tickets were sold at enhanced prices avowedly for the benefit of the Picture Gallery. This complicates the transaction very considerably. You cannot find out all the people who attended the performances, and give them back their admission money, because you cannot identify them; and even if you could there would arise the insoluble question as to the proportion in which they were influenced in parting from their money by the attraction of the performance and by their interest in the Picture Gallery. The only point that is quite clear is that one must not collect money for a public purpose and then put it in one's own pocket.

What then is the position at present of all that part of the Gallery fund which cannot be returned to the subscribers. Frankly, I dont know: it is a question for a lawyer. There are plenty of precedents to guide the lawyer in giving you his opinion. For example, it was once a well-known practice for people to leave money in their wills for the relief of Christian prisoners in the hands of the Turks. When the Christians got the upper hand of the Turks all this money was in the position of the Gallery fund: that is, it could neither be returned to the donors nor applied to the purposes for which they had bequeathed it. It used to go into Chancery until 1853, when the Charitable Trusts Act provided a body called the Charity Commission, which is now the proper body to deal with such matters. I believe you are legally entitled to demand their 'opinion, advice and direction' as to the disposal of your fund; and if you do so without misrepresenting your case, and follow their directions, you are completely discharged from all further responsibility as to your disposal of the money. This, I suppose, is what a lawyer would advise as the strictly proper and legal course, though, I repeat, mine is only a layman's guess at the law on the subject; and you should confirm it by resorting to that friendly legal advice which is no doubt always at the disposal of the Abbey Theatre. It is of course possible that the costs of applying to the Charity Commissioners and of obtaining from them a scheme for the disposal of the money might end in there being very little money left to dispose of. What's more, the commissioners might hand the money to some ordinary charity having no relation whatever to the fine arts, the net effect being simply to relieve the rates without relieving a single extra human being. Therefore, if the thing can be done without exposing the Abbey Theatre to a prosecution for misappropriation of money collected for public purposes, it might be as well to put the money in trust and simply sit on it until the time comes when it can be given as an act of public munificence on the part of the Theatre to some future project of the same character as the one which the Corporation has just let slip through its silly fingers.

That is all I can say on the matter. As far as you are personally concerned, the moral is that you must not, except under legal advice, make yourself a party to any private or commercial appropriation of what is virtually a trust fund.

Yours sincerely
G. Bernard Shaw

SHAW TO EDWARD McNULTY
[TL/d: BL]

Ayot St Lawrence. Welwyn
9th June 1914

[Matthew Edward McNulty, Shaw's closest boyhood friend, who had written four novels and several plays, had had a play, *The Lord Mayor,* accepted for production by the Abbey and had written to Shaw for advice on stage technique. The play had been already produced (on 13th March 1914) before Shaw got round to replying. His long letter to McNulty included a section on directorial methods subsequently published (revised) as *The Art of Rehearsal* (1928).]

...The success of the Abbey Street Theatre was due to the fact that when it began, none of the company were worth twopence a week for ordinary fashionable purposes, though some of them can now hold a London audience in the hollow of their hands. They were held down by Yeats and Lady Gregory ruthlessly to my formula of making the audience believe that real things were happening to real people. They were taught no tricks, because Yeats and Lady Gregory didnt want any, didnt know any, having found out experimentally only what two people of high intelligence and fine taste could find out by sticking to the point of getting a good representation. ...

I should think you would find Lady Gregory very useful in your production. In Blanco Posnet she spotted a sentence in the wrong place which made all the difference; and I rearranged half a page accordingly. Also, being a lady who knows the great world, she can correct social solecisms and rub out little vulgarities: things that are sure to crop up because everybody has weaknesses of that kind of which he is not conscious. After a time they all get pointed out; but a critic is useful at first.

In the spring of 1915 the Shaws paid what was to be their longest visit to Coole, from 13th April to 10th May. They had been staying with Horace Plunkett in Dublin from 1st to 12th April and had gone to a production of Lady Gregory's three-act play *Shanwalla* at the Abbey, which Shaw very much admired. Lady Gregory was able to quote Shaw's favourable opinion in a letter to Arthur Sinclair, who played the leading role and who was reluctant to have it included in the repertoire for the company's imminent London season because of its poor critical reception in Dublin: 'Like all fine actors Sinclair is a fool. What is it to him if the play is liked or not while he plays the part so finely as he does. He will be a success in London in it anyhow' (quoted in Joseph Holloway, *Impressions of a Dublin Playgoer*, 6th May 1915). Among those whom Shaw met at Horace Plunkett's home, and who was to be a fellow guest at Coole, was the Rt Hon W.F. Bailey, one of the Estates Commissioners and an active supporter and adviser of the Abbey Theatre, who took a series of photographs of Shaw during the visit.

The stay at Coole was prolonged partly in order to make it possible for Augustus John, who was a friend of Robert Gregory, to paint Shaw's portrait. The suggestion for the portrait had been Lady Gregory's:

Mrs Shaw was lamenting about not having him painted by a good artist and I suggested having John over, and she jumped at it, and Robert is to bring him over on Monday ...

Augustus John wired from Dublin yesterday that he would come on today. G.B.S. had his hair cut in Galway yesterday as a preliminary, but too much was taken off (*Seventy Years*, April 1915)

The results of the sittings Shaw described in a letter of 15th May 1915 to Mrs Patrick Campbell [TLS: State University of New York at Buffalo]:

Augustus John painted six magnificent portraits of me in eight days. Unfortunately, as he kept painting them on top of one another until our protests became overwhelming, only three portraits have survived: and one of these got turned into a subject picture entitled Shaw Listening to Somebody Else Talking, because I went to sleep while I was sitting, and John, fascinated by the network of wrinkles made by my shut eyes, painted them before I woke, and turned a most heroic portrait into a very splendidly painted sarcasm.

Details of Shaw's adventure in the Coole woods, mentioned in Lady Gregory's *Seventy Years* account of the visit quoted below, can be found in a letter of Lennox Robinson to him of 4th May 1943 [Shaw's holograph comments on Robinson's letter are set here in bracketed italics]:

I have been down at Gort lately and there is a story there that either you or Willie wandered into the woods one night after dinner, lost yourself and turned up in the little town at 11 o'c [*correct*], others say 4 o'c [*No*] in the morning, and knocked up Mr Lally, of Lally's Hotel, [*I called at the hotel and got a car to Coole*] who was very indignant at the disturbance and said 'Looking for the bloody Fairies'. [*He did not say this to me. He treated me with every civility.*] Men were out looking through Coole woods with a lantern and a pony and a bell, and what I want to verify is: whether it was you or W.B. who got lost. [*It was I. I have a very defective sense of direction, and thought I was making for Coole all the time until I found myself in Gort. I have no recollection of their having sent out a searching party.*] [TLS/p with hol. additions in Shaw's hand: Southern Illinois University Library]

Towards the end of Shaw's visit, on 8th May, came the tragic news of the sinking of the *Lusitania* in which Hugh Lane had been sailing from New York. Shaw asked Lady Gregory what he could do to help her in her distress: 'I said I longed to be alone, to cry, to mourn, to scream if I wished. I wanted to be out of hearing and sight' [Lady Gregory: *Memoirs*, manuscript, 7th (for 8th) May: Berg, NYPL]. Lady Gregory had in fact to leave for London on 9th May without knowing whether Lane was alive or dead, the confirmation of his drowning only coming some days later. The Shaws crossed back to England on 11th May on the ferry bringing home many of the survivors of the *Lusitania*.

LADY GREGORY: *SEVENTY YEARS*

16th April 1915

[To W.B.Yeats] The Shaws are here. They are very easy to entertain, he is so extraordinarily light in hand, a sort of kindly joyousness about him, and they have their motor so are independent. He says *Shanwalla* is the best ghost play he ever saw, and thinks Sinclair *very* fine in it ...

Wednesday 21st. A wire has come saying we must decide at once about taking the plays to London, followed by a letter to-day. I read it to G.B.S. He said decidedly we ought to go, and if we must die, die gloriously, and I was glad to have his definite opinion, for of course I realise the risk. ...

Thursday 29th. G.B.S. came in to photograph me ten minutes ago at my writing table, and I said it was one of life's ironies that I who had done so much literary work should be photographed writing, as I was, to engage a kitchen maid! Just after I had begun this letter he took another and said we must offer a prize to whoever could guess by the expression whether I was writing to the kitchen-maid or to you! ... Did I tell you of his being lost last Saturday in the woods, of which he declares there are seventy-seven. He didn't get home till 11.00 o'clock at night, having walked for five hours, when he got to Gort through Inchy, and took a car. The people all say already he was led 'astray'.

SHAW TO LADY GREGORY
[ALS: Berg, NYPL]

10 Adelphi Terrace. [London]
11th June 1915

[Lady Gregory, in London for the Abbey season, staying with her
friends Frederick and Clara Jackson at 64 Rutland Gate, had spent the
previous weekend with the Shaws at Ayot St Lawrence.]

Dear Lady Gregory
Are you engaged for lunch today? If not, will you lunch with
us at 1.30? Charlotte is in bed being massaged; and the operation crowds up her morning so much that she will not have
time for a walk to Rutland Gate. Besides, the notion of
Charlotte walking anywhere shews how little you know her
even yet. She never walks a yard when there is a vehicle—even a
wheelbarrow—to be had for love or money.
    Please give the boy an answer—yes or no scrawled on the card
will suffice. I enclose the writing materials.

Yours sincerely
G.B.S.

SHAW TO LADY GREGORY
[ACCS: Berg, NYPL]

10 Adelphi Terrace. [London]
11th June 1915

[H.W. Massingham, formerly editor of the *Daily Chronicle*, was a
long-time associate of Shaw.]

Dear Lady Gregory
We have put off lunch until two, because Massingham is
coming; and it is his printing day (he is editor of The Nation)
which makes it impossible for him to come at 1.30.
    But of course you will be welcome at any hour, if 2 is an
inconvenient fit-in. You can always settle down with the books
and papers here unmolested if you are at a loose end.

Yours sincerely
G. Bernard Shaw

SHAW TO LADY GREGORY
[Telegram: Berg, NYPL]

The Hydro. Torquay
2nd September 1915

LADY GREGORY COOLE PARK GORT
NOT A WORD WRITTEN YET WILL BEGIN IT
TOMORROW

SHAW

The subject for *O'Flaherty V.C.* had been suggested by the award of the Victoria Cross for conspicuous bravery to Lance-Corporal Michael O'Leary, 1st Battalion, Irish Guards, on 1st February 1915 (reported in *The Times* on 19th February). The idea for the play had germinated in Shaw's mind by April when he was at Coole (which was to provide its setting) and he promised it to Lady Gregory for the Abbey, waiving royalties for performance in Ireland. In spite of his 2nd September telegram, Shaw had in fact attempted a few lines of dialogue for *O'Flaherty V.C.* on 23rd July. A brief shorthand passage, subsequently crossed out, is to be found in the middle of the manuscript draft of the preface to *Androcles and the Lion* [Rutgers University]:

O'Flaherty V.C.

23/7/15

Cant you explain to her what the war is about?

Arra, and how the divil do I know what the war is about?

You shouldnt have enlisted if your conscience didnt tell [you] it was a righteous war[.]

I wouldnt have done it if I had been sober. What with the drink, and the offer of money, and me not being afraid of anything but my mother[,] I was overpersuaded.

But you know that the Germans are in the wrong, dont you?

Of course I do; and theyre trying to shoot me and gas me and kill and destroy me from morning till night.

SHAW TO LADY GREGORY

[ALS: Burgunder, Cornell]

The Hydro. Torquay
14th September 1915

[Richard, Anne and Catherine were Lady Gregory's grandchildren, who had been at Coole during the Shaws' visit there in the spring.]

My dear Lady Gregory

O'Flaherty V.C. may now, I think, be regarded as a certainty. I have finished the shorthand draft (most of which has been already transcribed); and even if I perish tonight, you could easily polish and finish it for the stage. I hope to be able to send it to the printer before the end of this week. The setting-up of the type and the revision of proofs will take some time; but everything should be complete well before the end of the month.

Played straight through without interruptions, applause, or riot, it ought to take from forty minutes to forty-five to get through—longer than The Workhouse Ward, but on that scale generally. It requires four performers: Sinclair, for whom the title part is written, and for whom no substitute is possible except possibly [J.M.] Kerrigan at a pinch; [Sydney J.] Morgan, as General Sir Pearce Madigan (God help him!); an old woman (Flaherty's mother) to whom Sara Allgood might, with an effort, condescend; and a young one, parlormaid (save the mark!) to Sir Pearce, and designated by Providence and Mrs O'Flaherty, though not, in the upshot, by the hero himself, as O'Flaherty's bride.

The scene is quite simply before the porch of your house, supposed for the moment to be the countryseat of Morgan. Small but important parts are played by a thrush and a jay. Properties: a garden seat and an iron chair (as at Coole), also a gold chain, looted by O'Flaherty for presentation to the parlormaid. O'Flaherty and the general are in khaki; and the two women are in correct local color. A band capable of playing a few bars of God Save the King and a little more of Tipperary has to be heard 'off'; and patriotic cheers will also be required, though the cheerers, like the band, will be invisible.

I think that gives you everything you will need. It is all quite cheap and simple, and can be done anywhere and anyhow.

Unfortunately I cannot be so reassuring about the play itself. When it came to business, I had to give up all the farcical equivoque I described to you, and go ahead quite straightforwardly without any ingenuities or misunderstandings. The picture of the Irish character will make the Playboy seem a patriotic rhapsody by comparison. The ending is cynical to the last possible degree. The idea is that O'Flaherty's experience in the trenches has induced in him a terrible realism and an unbearable candor. He sees Ireland as it is, his mother as she is, his sweetheart as she is; and he goes back to the dreaded trenches joyfully for the sake of peace and quietness. Sinclair must be prepared for brickbats.

I am sorry: *c'était plus fort que moi*. At worst, it will be a barricade for the theatre to die gloriously on.

Convey to Richard the assurance of my distinguished consideration. I kiss the hands of the blue eyed Annakin. Tiny Catherine I will talk to when she grows up. I shall be still on the right side of eighty.

It is really not so bad to be old after all, is it?

I am divided between my reluctance to put you to the trouble of writing a letter and my desire to have another glimpse of Coole.

Yours affectionately (really)
G. Bernard Shaw

PS We shall be here until the end of the month. Charlotte likes the place, and will hang on as long as she can.
PPS Did I ever tell you that Dr Jonathan E.A.G. Becker, M.B. (of Edinburgh) 24 Gordon Square, London W.C. (close to the Gwalior) can cure rheumatism in an amazing manner by injections of hyperchlorite of soda?

LADY GREGORY TO SHAW
[TLS: HRC]

Coole Park. Gort
19th September 1915

[Lady Gregory was going to America on a three-month lecture tour; she did not sail until 15th October. *Duty* was a one-act comedy by

Seumas O'Brien, which had been first produced at the Abbey on 16th December 1913, and played by members of the Abbey company in a tour of music-halls in Great Britain through the summer of 1915. Fred J. Harris was the Abbey Theatre's accountant; the theatre had been in financial difficulties earlier in the year. A. Patrick Wilson (known as Andrew P. Wilson in the Scottish theatre), whom Lady Gregory describes as the 'Scotch Rogue', was the actor, playwright and producer who had been manager of the Abbey since September 1913, but who had resigned in May 1915 after a quarrel with the directors. He had since been in dispute with them over theatrical contracts.

Robert Gregory had joined the 4th Connaught Rangers; he would transfer to the Royal Flying Corps in 1916, winning the Legion of Honor and the Military Cross in 1917. The bulk of the land on the Coole estate, some 3500 acres, had been sold to the Congested Districts Board, the state authority which had the responsibility on the western seaboard of Ireland for purchasing estates from landlords for re-distribution to tenant farmers. *The Golden Apple*, dedicated to Shaw, was published by John Murray (London, 1916). Maunsel, the Dublin publishing company run by George Roberts, had published most of Lady Gregory's work up to 1910; having fallen out with Maunsel, she was at this point in dispute with the company over sales of her books in the American market, which were infringing the rights of her authorised publisher Putnam.

Lady Gregory's optimism as to an early and happy outcome of the question of Hugh Lane's collection of French paintings was misplaced. Named as trustee in his will, she was to fight unsuccessfully for the rest of her life to have the claim of the London National Gallery, to which Lane had bequeathed the pictures in 1913, overturned in favour of the Dublin Municipal Gallery, which had been the beneficiary in a later unwitnessed codicil. In the event, Lane's fine personal collection of pictures from his London home, Lindsey House, was not all sold for the benefit of the National Gallery of Ireland, which was his residuary legatee, but a selection of it was transferred to the Gallery. Robert Ross, the art dealer and connoisseur, had been the close friend of Oscar Wilde. John Pentland Mahaffy, Provost of Trinity College Dublin, was Chairman of the Board of Governors of the National Gallery. Thomas Bodkin, a friend and associate of Lane, who had been specifically requested in Lane's will to assist in the matter of the Municipal Gallery, was passed over in favour of Walter Strickland as Lane's successor in the directorship of the National Gallery. He eventually became its director in 1927, publishing *Hugh Lane and his Pictures* (Dublin 1932), at the request of the Irish government, as a statement of Ireland's case for the return of the pictures from England.

Lady Gregory's plans for handing over the Abbey to the state were based on the assumption that the bill giving Home Rule to Ireland, which had been passed in 1914 but suspended for the duration of the war, would come into force, as intended, as soon as the war was over. The Abbey players frequently performed some of their repertory of one-act plays during the summer as music-hall 'turns'. *Handy Andy* (1842), written by Samuel Lover, was to provide one of the types of the comic Irishman; Mickey Free is the faithful servant of the eponymous hero of Charles Lever's *Charles O'Malley* (1841). Mr Dooley was an American comic fictional character, the pseudonym of Finley Peter Dunne, who had been a friend and supporter of Lady Gregory in America.

Lady Gregory commonly read aloud to Yeats plays that had been submitted to the Abbey for consideration; it was presumably the impression of some thirty to forty of these that *O'Flaherty* was needed to efface.]

Oh my dear G.B.S. your letter was a great cheer up, though such is my confidence in you that from the moment you had first spoken of O'Flaherty I had never a moment's doubt as to his coming punctually into being.

I long to see him, and do please send any sort of rough copy before I go. I leave this Oct 1. and sail from Liverpool on the St Louis, American Liner, Oct 2. Of course what I hope is that O'Flaherty will get us an American engagement. We have had quite enough of Great Britain and *Duty*, and the actors are growing demoralised, and unmanageable so that I have at last got the financial side into the hands of our Auditor Mr Harris, who had been always reproaching us for giving them such high salaries, and now has to deal with them face to face and try to cut them down. Wilson, that 'Scotch Rogue', cabled to America and got the English Vaudeville rights of *Duty* from the author, and threatened us with an injunction if we went on playing it, but we have taken no notice, our contract seeming all right. But we want to get rid of it anyhow. It does not even do very well in some places. From what you say, O'Flaherty may do for Royal and Command performances!

I am not very light-hearted, for Robert is carrying out his desire of this time last year, and is going to the war. He couldn't go then because there was no one to look after the sale and transfer of the estate, but now that is done, and the desire comes uppermost again, and he is in London and wires that he will be home tomorrow, that all is settled, he has ten days leave. He has got a commission, but I don't know whether he is going in for the Artillery or for Flying, he wanted one or the other. Whether he is right to go I don't know. I daresay I should go if I were in his place, but I feel just now and since the Lusitania I should like to kill Germans, and I don't think he is so ferocious. The only thing I [am] sure of is that he ought to make up his own mind about it, and so I would say nothing. But when I look at Margaret and the little things and think in what an unsettled state Ireland still is, my heart breaks.

Before this was settled I had written to try and defer my American trip, but it was not possible, too many engagements had been made. It is just as well perhaps. I shall only be four months away, and better able 'to buy a little rabbit skin, to wrap my baby buntings in'. I have just been seeing a mason about mending the demesne wall. But not expecting to go so soon, I have a great mass of work on hand. I have been arranging my big book of folk-lore, *Visions and Beliefs* [not published until 1920], which has been too long on [my] hands, delayed by some notes Yeats was doing for it. And I am correcting proofs of *The Golden Apple*. And I am trying to get myself out of the hands of Maunsel and Co; and [G. Herbert] Thring [secretary of the Society of Authors] and all his merry men have not been able to prevent him from selling 3000 copies in sheets of the Seven Short Plays to a fellow rogue [John W. Luce] in Boston, which will probably lose my American copyright, and spike Putnams' guns. Then the matter of Hugh's pictures gives me a good deal of work, but so far as the Corporation providing a building I am full of hope; the want of money is the drawback, the Government won't allow them to borrow at high interest, but it has just been discovered that the Carnegie Trustees have lately been empowered to assist in other things besides libraries, [like] Church Organs and Public baths, and none of these being in great request in Ireland they might help the Gallery. Horace Plunkett is one of the Trustees and says it is quite within their scope. It will then rest with the Trustees of the N.G. London, to resign their claim which is not a very clear one, and if a Bill is necessary, [Augustine] Birrell [Chief Secretary for Ireland] will run it through Parliament. I am hoping also that the best pictures from Lindsey House will be brought over to our N.G. and not sold for its benefit. Dublin should be a great Art Centre then. I am very anxious still about a successor to Hugh at the National Gallery. Two very good, first rate men are ready to come: Robert Ross who Mahaffy and others object to on moral grounds, and another even better expert. But young Bodkin meanwhile is using every means with the trustees to get their promise on various grounds unconnected with art, of which he knows little or nothing. If he should be appointed, he would remain there till the age limit removes him in forty years. And the poor gallery would be given up to teaparties meanwhile.

As to the Abbey, I don't think we should have had patience to go on as we are now, but that, partly from my talk with you, my mind cleared itself; and I felt that if we can keep it alive till the end of the war and the beginning of Home Rule, we can give it over to the nation, buildings, company and stock in trade. We should give it into the hands of trustees, more or less Nationalist, anyhow those who are anxious to help the new government on, and let them do their best with it. Yeats approves of this idea and so does Bailey, and that makes us very anxious to keep or get it solvent, and not let the Company scatter.

My summer work has included the writing of a little play, one act, *Hanrahan's Oath*, I think it would amuse you. Hanrahan, under the impression he has sent a friend who killed a gauger to transportation through too much talk, makes a vow of dumbness for a year and a day and the scene is conveniently laid in a wild and rocky place where is the bed of a saint. There he is beset by some who believe him to be a new saint, and by his young woman who thinks he is funning her, and by his landlady who has stolen his boots and he is not able to reprove, and can only make faces at. Finally the friend who was not transported, and had but inflicted a slight injury on the gauger, turns up, and when Hanrahan is at last able to talk, it is like the bursting of Niagara from captivity. No chance of acting it now, with the Company at the [music-]halls, but I feel glad to have done even a scrap of creative work, and feel my mind hasn't quite gone.

Also I have two lectures to write and compose, that also

hurriedly. One I have roughly finished. It was demanded by
Pond [the American lecture bureau that booked the speaking
tour], 'laughter (or humour) in Ireland'. I begin by conclusively
proving there is none; there is certainly none and never was
among the Gaelic speakers and writers—they had no audience
for it. Then I say, with the Union came an English and English
speaking audience and Handy Andy and Micky Free began,
and set the pace to all the facetious and artificial humour made
ever since for the English market. I liken the two schools to Don
Quixote and Sancho Panza, one retiring brokenhearted from
the Ducal Court, the other seeing his profit and saying 'very
well let them come and play bo-peep, let them spite and
backbite me, but he that comes to shear may go away shorn'.
Well, (here I quote from my Mss.) 'the jocose, the facetious
school had come in with the Union, the school of the satirists
came in eighty years later at the time of the Union of Hearts.
The satire of the old bards was still in the blood, the satire that
used to raise blisters on the face of the person satirized. I take
Mr Bernard Shaw as the chief figure of that reaction. Mr Yeats
says of him that he has done more than any living man to shatter
the complacency, to shake the nerves of the English. He says
like Sancho, "All right, let them play Bo-Peep, I am ready". He
turned the tables and the English gasped. They never thought
we would turn on our paymasters. And the worst of it was they
couldn't close their ears. They had got the habit of listening and
couldn't leave off'. Haffigan and Broadbent come in very nicely
on this, and then Mr Dooley. I have Mr Dooley on the Hague
Conference and the Olympian games, and he speaks of England
with the detachment, the freedom from illusions of a wife who
has obtained her divorce and is able to discuss with her present
husband the weak points and the clumsiness of her first. If I can
remember to give all this extemporaneously, it will go well I
think. To keep up the harshness and gloom I am keeping the
detachable jokes I give to those uttered by judges, lawyers, and
prisoners in the dock.

Oh if you were coming to America, and Charlotte, what a
different prospect it would be! What shall I say to them is your
present opinion on the war? That is the first thing they will ask.
The only thing that rewarded me for my study of Lever was the
duel between Harry Lorrequer and Beamish [in the novel *Harry*

Lorrequer], in which the combatants hoped the executors would be able to tell the cause of the quarrel.

Richard and Anne were very much pleased by your messages, Richard I think a little jealous at hearing Anne's hands were to be kissed. He still keeps asking when you are coming back. Tiny Catherine is as Nurse says 'quite a fruitarian' and devours everything before her, from unripe apples to yew berries, without the slightest ill effect. Poor darlings, I don't know how I shall leave them. I hope Margaret may go over for a while if Robert is training in England, and they will go to my sister. Thank you for the Doctor's address. I may try him some time. I am much better though and can walk as well as anybody, except that there is a tender spot developing on the back of my right hand, just where enthusiastic Americans stick their thumb to show appreciation after a lecture. Yeats will be in London early in October, he is still here and will report all late news to you about state of theatre etc. O'Flaherty will take away the flavour of between thirty and forty bad plays I have read aloud. I wrote you a card yesterday, but there is reason to believe the Kiltartan letter box was not cleared last night. It was once left unopened for a fortnight so I think I had better keep this for Gort tomorrow.

Love to Charlotte, and to you.

Yours indeed, affectionately
A Gregory

SHAW TO LADY GREGORY
[ALS: Berg, NYPL]

The Hydro. Torquay
23rd September 1915

[Shaw by this time made a consistent practice of using unpublished proofs of his plays as rehearsal copies, a practice begun with *Blanco Posnet*. Lady Gregory must have sent to Shaw the wording of her dedication to him of *The Golden Apple*, possibly by the card from the Kiltartan post-box referred to in the previous letter. The final dedication, from which the reference to Shaw's influence on her grandchildren was removed, ran: 'To George Bernard Shaw the gentlest of my friends'.]

My dear Lady Gregory

If my printer [R. & R. Clark, Edinburgh] plays up promptly
I shall be able to send you half a dozen copies of the play —
enough to rehearse with—before you start. If he runs it very
close I shall send them to Liverpool.

Do you know that a play can be copyrighted for performing
purposes in America without being printed there? As plays are
very seldom printed, the Copyright Acts had to except 'dramatic compositions' from the printing clauses. If you send a
copy of a play, whether typewritten or printed in Ireland does
not matter, to the Librarian of Congress in Washington, with a
dollar for registration fee, it will be registered and your performing rights saved.

Thring ought to threaten your publisher with an action for
damages if he goes beyond his agreement to your damage. He
certainly ought to give you time to register.

Naturally I like the dedication: but you must leave the infants
out. Your works will live as long as they will; and in the
meantime I may be hanged, or Richard may be defeated at an
election at a critical moment of his career by placards quoting
your testimony to my early and infamous influence on him. I
often have to stop people from christening their children
George Bernard: there is a passage in Getting Married about the
unfortunate high Churchman whose Nonconformist parents
improvidently christened him Oliver Cromwell. A child, and
even a grandchild, has a sacred right not to be tattooed. Imagine
an archbishop called Tom Paine Gregory!

Your news about Robert does not make me feel any the more
amiable about the war. They will have to capitulate all round
when they are nine tenths ruined.

Are you taking the company out with you, or do you lecture
and make arrangements for them? If the latter, what do they do
meanwhile?

I must stop, as I have one of my headaches and the pen is
screwing my eyes out. I will write again when O'Flaherty
arrives.

Ever
G. Bernard Shaw

SHAW TO LADY GREGORY
[ALS: Berg, NYPL]

The Hydro. Torquay
26th September 1915

My dear Lady Gregory
This is the first proof [of *O'Flaherty V.C.*], all in the rough. I have scribbled in all the corrections that are not merely technical. Those on pages 21–22, which seem superfluous, are necessary for the timing of the speeches, as I found when I came to count the words.

I hope to have corrected copies in time to catch you before you sail; but if this proves impossible, you will at least know what you have to deal with.

When do you leave Coole? Do you go straight thence to Liverpool?

If any of the locutions are wrong, please let me know at the earliest possible moment; so that I may put them right. Anything very bad would justify the extravagance of a wire.

Ever
G. Bernard Shaw

SHAW TO YEATS
[ALS: HRC]

The Hydro Hotel. Torquay
12th October 1915

[With Lady Gregory off to America, Yeats took over the arrangements for the production of *O'Flaherty V.C.* W. Angus McLeod was one of the two directors of the London-based theatrical agency Daniel Mayer & Co, with whom the Abbey had dealt in arranging the music-hall tour. There seems, at this stage, to have been a plan to have *O'Flaherty V.C.* produced at the London Coliseum.]

My dear Yeats
Lady Gregory's speeded-up departure made it impossible for me to send her the final copies of O'Flaherty to take with her. They are passed for press; and I have instructed the printer to send you half a dozen for use at rehearsal, or to send out to her.

allowances, ever since the war began, bad luck to them that made it.

TERESA [*coming from the porch between the General and Mrs O'Flaherty*] Hannah sent me out for to tell you, sir, that the tea will be black and the cake not fit to eat with the cold if yous all dont come at wanst.

MRS O'FLAHERTY. Oh, Tessie darlint, what have you been saying to Denny at all at all? Oh, oh—

SIR PEARCE [*out of patience*] You cant discuss that here. We shall have Tessie beginning now.

O'FLAHERTY. Thats right, sir : drive them in.

TERESA. I havnt said a word to him. He—

SIR PEARCE. Hold your tongue ; and go in and attend to your business at the tea table.

TERESA. But amment I telling your honor that I never said a word to him ? He gave me a beautiful gold chain. Here it is to shew your honor thats it's no lie I'm telling you.

SIR PEARCE. Whats this O'Flaherty? Youve been looting some unfortunate officer.

O'FLAHERTY. No, sir : I stole it from him of his own accord.

MRS O'FLAHERTY. Wouldnt your honor tell him that his mother has the first call on it ? What would a slip of a girl like that be doing with a gold chain round her neck ?

TERESA. Anyhow, I have a neck to put it round and not a hank of wrinkles.

At this unfortunate remark, Mrs O'Flaherty bounds from her seat ; and an appalling tempest of wordy wrath breaks out. The remonstrances and commands of the General, and the protests and menaces of O'Flaherty only increase the hubbub. They are soon all speaking at once at the top of their voices.

MRS O'FLAHERTY [*solo*] You impudent young heifer, how dar you say such a thing to me? [*Teresa retorts furiously ; the men interfere ; and the solo becomes a quartet, fortissimo.*] Ive a good mind to clout your ears for you to teach you manners. Let me not see you casting sheep's eyes at my son

Be ashamed of yourself, do ; and learn to know who youre speaking to. That I mightnt sin, but I dont know what the good God was thinking about when he made the like of you.

again. There never was an O'Flaherty would demean himself by keeping company with a dirty Driscoll; and if I see
you next or nigh my house I'll put you in the ditch with a
flea in your ear: mind that now.

TERESA. Is it me you offer such a name to, you foul-
mouthed, dirty minded, lying, sloothering old sow, you? I
wouldnt soil my tongue by calling you in your right name
and telling Sir Pearce whats the common talk of the town
about you. You and your O'Flahertys, setting yourself up
against the Driscolls that would never lower themselves to
be seen in conversation with you at the fair. So the back
of my hand to you, Mrs O'Flaherty; and that the cat may
tear your ugly old face!

SIR PEARCE. Silence. Tessie: did you here me ordering
you to go into the house? Mrs O'Flaherty! [*Louder*] Mrs
O'Flaherty!! Will you just listen to me one moment?
Please. [*Furiously*] Do you hear me speaking to you, woman?
Are you human beings or are you wild beasts? Stop that
noise immediately, do you hear? [*Yelling*] Are you going
to do what I order you, or are you not? Scandalous, disgraceful! This comes of being too familiar with you. O'Flaherty:
shove them into the house. Out with the whole damned
pack of you.

O'FLAHERTY. Here now: none of that, none of that. Go
easy, I tell you. Hold your whisht, mother, will you, or
youll be sorry for it after. [*To Teresa*] Is that the way for
a decent young girl to speak? [*Despairingly*] Oh, for the
Lord's sake, shut up, will yous? Have you no respect for
yourselves or your betters? [*Peremptorily*] Let me have no
more of it, I tell you. Och, the divil's in the whole crew
of you. In with you into the house this very minute and
tear one another's eyes out in the kitchen if you like. In
with you.

*The two men seize the two women, and push them, still violently
abusing one another, into the house. Sir Pearce slams the door
upon them savagely; and immediately a heavenly silence falls on
the summer afternoon. For a long time nothing is said. Sir Pearce*

But you had better keep the six for the theatre and let me know Lady G's address in America. I can then send her a couple to tempt managers with.

I find that I may have to come up to London for one night on Friday this week; and before Friday next week I must be up for good. I can't recall who McLeod is; but I am quite willing to read the play to him; and if the Abbey St company is now in London and you could arrange for Sinclair and Sidney Morgan to be present, all the better. It is important that Sinclair should get the hang of it from me.

It is by no means sure that it will be licensed in England; and a few preliminary trials in Dublin might do no harm. I agree that it is much safer for Ireland and America than for England.

Yours ever
G. Bernard Shaw

SHAW TO LADY GREGORY
[ALS: Burgunder, Cornell]

The Hydro Hotel. Torquay
19th October 1915

My dear Lady Gregory
On the point of returning to London I receive a letter from Yeats with your American address.

Packing prevents expatiation.

Did you say you'd send me Hanrahan? If so, you didnt.

I enclose a couple of O'Flahertys. Yeats has a further supply for rehearsal. Do not let them get into hands you cannot trust, as publication of them, or any part of them, would be ruinous to my publishing contracts.

Yours ever
G. Bernard Shaw

On 21st October, the *Manchester Guardian*, reporting the appointment of St John Ervine as the new manager of the

Abbey, announced that he would 'produce, among other plays, a new piece in one act by Mr Bernard Shaw, entitled "Michael O'Flaherty VC"'. There was, however, a problem with the casting, as Arthur Sinclair, for whom Shaw had written the part of O'Flaherty, had just left the company in a dispute over a contract agreement, and the part was to be given instead to J.M. Kerrigan. Shaw was not happy with this decision.

SHAW TO YEATS
[ACCS: NLI]

Ayot St Lawrence. Welwyn
8th November 1915

My dear Yeats

I wrote to Ervine on Sunday, explaining why I committed myself to Sinclair subject to his rejoining the company. Kerrigan is really the only male member of the company who has charm; and if 'O'F' were a romance of illusion, instead of a comedy of disillusion, and ended with the hero's union to a colleen bawn, he would be perfect in it; for he has not only charm but youth. I think his Fenian in [Lady Gregory's] The Rising of The Moon one of the best things in the repertory. But he lacks variety, and is not a real comedian. People want a happy ending for him; but for Sinclair, who *is* a comedian, they want confusion, disillusion and bathos. It is Kerrigan's tragedy that there is so little romance in the repertory: he is always character-acting, which is a mechanical business; and Sinclair gets all the fat. Writing for Kerrigan, I should have done quite another sort of part. ...

I come up to town tomorrow (Tuesday) until the end of the week; but this, of course, requires no answer.

G.B.S.

The result of Shaw's intervention was that Sinclair was re-hired by the Abbey, initially just to play the part of O'Flaherty rather than as a regular member of the company. The opening of the play was set for 23rd November.

Then on Friday, 12th November, there came the first news of trouble with the authorities over *O'Flaherty V.C.*, as Yeats, who was in London at the time, reported subsequently in a letter to Lady Gregory [TLS: Berg, NYPL]:

> I had a wire from [W.F.] Bailey saying that the Bill for November 23rd will have to be changed. That Bill was Shaw's play. I went off to Shaw and found him in the middle of lunch. I pointed out that the telegrams must mean that the authorities objected to his play. He wired to Bailey who replied that it was the military. Shaw then wrote a detailed letter to [Sir Matthew] Nathan [Under Secretary at Dublin Castle] putting the case before him. I should say that my very first sentence had been that it was out of the question our fighting the issue. Shaw, I thought, was disappointed. He said, if Lady Gregory was in London, she would fight it, but added afterwards, that he didn't really want us to but thought you would do it out of love of mischief. I told him that was a misunderstanding of your character.

Later that day Shaw wrote to Yeats.

SHAW TO YEATS
[ALS: NLI]

10 Adelphi Terrace. [London]
12th November 1915

My dear Yeats

I got overwhelmed by a mass of business after you left; and the end of it was that I could not write to Bailey nor copy my letter to Nathan, which got posted at Euston at the very last moment.

Plunkett wired that Sir M. is at the Under Secretary's Lodge all right. Bailey wired later that the difficulty is not with the Castle, but with the military authorities. On the whole, I had rather deal with them than with the Castle. Nathan is a colonel, and will perhaps be as useful on the military as on the civil side.

The line I took was that the suppression of the play will make a most mischievous scandal, because it will be at once assumed that the play is anti-English; that this will be exploited by the Germans and go round the globe; that there will be no performances to refute it; and that a lot of people who regard me as infallible will be prevented from recruiting, shaken in their patriotism etc etc. I enclosed a copy of the play in my letter, and explained that I had not presented it for licence here because the Lord Chamberlain would not pass the description of the queen, though she herself would like it, and that his refusal would start the same mischief of false reports of my pro-Germanism. I dwelt on the hardship to the starving theatre, and altogether made a strong and quite genuine case for letting the performances proceed.

Ever
G.B.S.

YEATS TO SHAW
[ALS: BL]

[10 Adelphi Terrace. London]
[c. 13th November 1915]

[This note, written on 10 Adelphi Terrace stationery, Yeats appears to have left for Shaw while the latter was at Ayot for the weekend.]

My dear Shaw

I have just seen our agents. The Coliseum see no difficulty about 'O'Flaherty'. They suggest a few slight cuts and apart from that say the play is too long—should play 30 minutes. I leave you the marked copy (which agents want back as it is their only copy). It may be useful to you with Nathan or the like; I have written to Bailey to say that we should, if military do not give way, give a private performance inviting all Dublin notables and taking up a collection. I may have to go to Dublin tonight.

Yours ever
W.B. Yeats

McLeod says no theatre here would object to the play.

W.F. BAILEY TO YEATS
[ALS: BL]

3 Earlsfort Terrace. Dublin
Sunday [14th November 1915]

My dear Yeats
    As regards the play: I have read it over again carefully—I had
only time to glance at it when I wrote you on Friday. It seems to
me on a careful reading better than I first thought and with
some alterations it might be made all right. I sent it to the
military authorities and they are reading it. I think the view is
that with an 'educated' audience it would be all right but the
danger is that it may be misinterpreted and the house be made
an audience of warring factions which of course would be bad
for the theatre. I am arguing in its favour—subject to certain
alterations—not many—and I think they are quite reasonable
so far: but it has to be read by the higher command yet. I shall
know what he thinks tomorrow, and if necessary I shall go to see
the censor tomorrow. Nathan asks me to go and talk it over with
him tonight.
    The danger is that people will consider it rather an insult to
'*Lieutenant* Michael O'Leary V.C.' and if he sees it I'd imagine
that he would be very angry and take very strong steps indeed.
On careful reading it seems to me a better play than I thought at
first but it would not do to risk losing our stalls audience and I
know that some of the Dublin papers on both sides of politics
would combine to hound us down if they come to the conclusion that it is intended to depreciate and degrade Michael
O'Leary. Already many inquiries are being made as to this
point. The title of the play raises suspicion in a city which is
placarded with pictures etc of 'O'Leary V.C.'
    I shall know tomorrow what the military authorities decide
and if they think it should not be done we should 'postpone' the
production and see what our future policy should be. It will be
easy to give a satisfactory reason. I would not be surprised
however from my talks with them that they may pass it with
'some emendations'. They think it is rather on the border line at
present. There is no use in threatening them—they are not in
the mood for that and when I wired you on Friday they spoke of
closing the theatre if the play proved objectionable. That of

course would be ruin to us and as things are going very promisingly now under St J. E.'s management it would be a great pity.

There would not be much harm in withdrawing the Bill for 23rd as I suggested and putting it on after with the approval of the military people.

I believe the actors themselves are very doubtful as to its reception as it is now.

Shaw says that it could be made a good recruiting play I hear. Well that may be but it is hardly one at present. Having regard to the manner in which it impartially hits all sides I would not be afraid of it but for the feeling that it may be regarded as an insult to O'Leary—'the Irish Hero'. Such a play would be all right at any time but the present when the whole question of recruiting is in a very critical stage.

Very sincerely yours
W.F. Bailey

YEATS TO SHAW
[ALS: BL]

18 Woburn Buildings. [London]
Monday [15th November 1915]

My dear Shaw

I enclose Bailey's last letter. I see that the military authorities do take action or rather threaten action so that our first impression was right. I cannot go to Dublin. I have spent the day in bed with asthmatic attack and bad cold but hope to be able to go out tomorrow. However, Bailey will manage all right and better than I could in my new mood.

Yours
W.B. Yeats

SHAW TO YEATS
[TLS: Sotheby catalogue, 8th July 1969]

Ayot St Lawrence. Welwyn
15th November 1915

[Shaw's proposal here was for a special performance of *O'Flaherty* for the military staff.]

... There should be tea for them [*i.e.*, the military staff]; and extraordinary care should be taken to have the theatre as warm as possible. And there must be no middle class persons about under any pretext whatever. They must see nobody but the people they see every day; and the more of *them* there are the better, short of overcrowding the generals ...

If the play makes them laugh, they will pass it cheerfully without the smallest regard to its meaning or tendency. If not, they will stop it, and would even if it were crammed with loyal sentiment and contained a dozen Remember Belgiums on every page. In which they will be perfectly right ...

It is written so as to appeal very strongly to that love of adventure and desire to see the wider world and escape from the cramping parochialism of Irish life which is more helpful to recruiting than all the silly placards about Belgium and the like, which are the laughing stock of Sinn Fein ...

G. Bernard Shaw

SIR HORACE PLUNKETT TO SHAW
[TLS: BL]

[Dublin]
15th November 1915

[In his diary for this date, Plunkett noted that he had written 'begging Bernard Shaw to postpone the production of his play O'Flaherty V.C. which would provoke riots in Dublin just now'(Plunkett Diaries [microfilm]: NLI).]

My dear Shaw

I hear you are in direct communication with Sir Matthew Nathan, so I have little to say about 'O'Flaherty', but I will give you my opinion for what it is worth.

I should think it improbable that the military authorities, who would alone be concerned with the stoppage of a play open to no possible objection except on the ground that it might be prejudicial to recruiting, will take action. But I chanced to hear that Mr Commissioner Bailey, a most sensitive barometer in these matters, is greatly alarmed at the possible injury your desire to help the Abbey Theatre (of which he is one of the Maecaenasses—the spelling is awkward) may do and that some other people, friendly both to you and the theatre, feel likewise. I had a quiet read over the play and I am afraid that in the present state of feeling in Dublin its presentation might be made the occasion for a riot in the theatre. The trouble would begin by demonstrations from one side or the other and these would provoke counter demonstrations. On the first night there would certainly be a considerable number present who were on the look out for such an opportunity of making fools of themselves and trouble for others.

There are some passages in the play which would hurt people just now who were not ordinarily oversensitive. If the play were postponed awhile it seems to me that, with very small amendments, it might be safely produced and what to me is its moral is so good that it would be a pity that it should be lost in minor issues. The change wrought in O'Flaherty by his outlook to the world beyond his parish is to my mind a valuable contribution to Irish progress. It seems rather a pity to teach the lesson when the attention of the important pupils is elsewhere. When this conscription question ceases to trouble all could laugh and learn. ...

Yours ever sincerely
Horace Plunkett

[In London eight days later, Plunkett recorded in his diary:
'Lunch with G. Bernard Shaw who was in a delightful (and chastened) mood. He has offended people about the war—quite unintentionally for he is strongly pro-Ally—and wants to get back his influence' (Plunkett Diaries [microfilm]: NLI).]

SIR MATTHEW NATHAN TO SHAW
[ALS: BL]

Dublin Castle
16th November [1915]

[Since his acknowledgement of Shaw's letter a day earlier and indication that he had read the play 'with excitement and interest', Nathan had consulted with Bailey, Plunkett and the Lord Lieutenant, Lord Wimbourne (to whom he sent a copy of the play).]

Dear Mr Bernard Shaw

I have now had an opportunity of consulting confidentially on the subject of 'O'Flaherty V.C.' several persons in whose judgment I have confidence and I find they are definitely of opinion that the representation of this play at the present moment would result in demonstrations which could do no good either to the Abbey Theatre, or to the cause that at any rate a large section of Irishmen have made their own. By such demonstrations the fine lesson of the play would be smothered while individual passages would be given a prominence you did not intend for them, with the result that they would wound susceptibilities naturally more tender at this time than at others and be quoted apart from their context to aid propaganda which many of us believe are inflicting injury on Ireland as well as on my country. In these circumstances, I think, and so does [Major] General [L.B.] Friend [Officer Commanding the Troops in Ireland] that the production of the play should be postponed till a time when it will be recording some of the humour and pathos of a past rather than of a present national crisis. I am in a way sorry to have to suggest this as, though it may be presumptuous on my part to say so, I feel strongly that the main idea as you quote it in your letter to me is entirely right, that this war does give to the most thinking of all peasantries the chance of contact with the wider world which will enable them to rise above the hopelessness derived from their old recollections and surroundings.

Yours sincerely
Matthew Nathan

On 16th November the papers carried the announcement that the production of *O'Flaherty V.C.* had been postponed, though rumours were flying in Dublin that it had been suppressed by the military authorities under the Defence of the Realm Act, or that it had been so heavily cut by the British Censor that the attempted Dublin production was an effort to evade the Censor, as with *Blanco Posnet*. Such rumours Shaw and St John Ervine tried to squash in the press, as can be seen in the article published in the *Manchester Guardian* on 17th November:

Mr Bernard Shaw in an interview with a London representative of the *Manchester Guardian* to-night [16th] on the report that his new play *O'Flaherty V.C.* has been suppressed said:

'The report is extremely inconsiderate because, thanks to the folly of the London press, the claims which the Germans have been intelligent enough to make that I am what is called a pro-German has been very widely circulated on the Continent, in America, and even in Morocco. This is not my fault. I can state an unanswerable case against the Germans, but I cannot make the English intelligent enough to see that it is a better case than the kinematograph heroics with which they hope to impress Europe as well as amuse themselves.

'Now, this silly report will probably be picked up by the Germans and circulated abroad in the form of a statement that I have written a play which the English Government is suppressing because the poet Shaw has again raised the cry of "Deutschland über Alles". I therefore appeal to the press, if they must circulate an unfounded report, at all events to make it clear that the author has no more desire to discourage recruiting in Ireland than the military authorities themselves.

'The report, moreover, is absurd, because there is no censorship in Ireland. There are two authorities—the Castle authorities and the military authorities. The Castle authorities have not intervened, and neither I nor the Abbey Street Theatre would think for a moment of producing a play if the military authorities felt that it could do the slightest harm to recruiting or to anything else. As a matter of fact the play, which appeals strongly to the Irishman's spirit of freedom and love of adventure, would, in my opinion, help recruiting rather than otherwise.

'But the military authorities will be the judges of this, and there will be no attempt to disregard their wishes should they for any reason prefer that the Abbey Street Theatre should adhere to its original intention to produce the play in America'.

A Dublin correspondent, telegraphing late last night, says: 'Mr Shaw's play has not been suppressed. Its production is merely postponed'.

Mr St John Ervine, the manager of the Abbey Theatre when questioned about the production of the play, said that it had not been either suppressed or withdrawn, but had been merely postponed for the present owing to difficulties in connection with the rehearsals. 'The play will be produced' he said, 'as it was written by Mr Bernard Shaw, and no passages have been deleted either by the Censor in England or at the request of the military authorities in Dublin'. The latter had not approached the management of the theatre in any way in reference to the production.

As to when the play will be produced in the Abbey Theatre Mr Ervine was unable to fix a definite date.

In an interview with the *Irish Independent*, published on 18th November, Shaw was at pains to dissociate the play from the real Michael O'Leary V.C., which had been heightened by the mistaken titles *Michael O'Flaherty V.C.* and *O'Leary V.C.* that had appeared in the press:

It happens that the hero of my play is an almost entirely ignorant Irish peasant lad who has been greatly startled and disillusioned by the spectacle of the great world which has been opened up to him by his travels and his warfare. It must be quite clear from the rapid promotion of Lieut. O'Leary to his present rank—a promotion which would be impossible in the case of a man, however brave, of the O'Flaherty type— that the gratuitous identification of O'Flaherty with O'Leary is extremely annoying to me, and may possibly be offensive to Lieut. O'Leary. I can only take this opportunity of offering him my apologies, protesting that I am entirely innocent in the matter.

Shaw went on to parry the question of just when or where the postponed production would take place:

The play was written for production in America, and possibly in Australia, during the forthcoming tour of the Irish Players, and it is not yet settled whether it will be performed in Dublin before or after that tour. Naturally the American managers would prefer to have the first bite.

Although he here put up a cover of semi-truths—Lady Gregory had wanted the play for an American tour; an Abbey tour of Australia had been mooted—Shaw still had hopes that *O'Flaherty V.C.* might be produced in Dublin with whatever cuts were necessary.

SHAW TO YEATS
[AccS: NLI]

10 Adelphi Terrace. London
17th November 1915

I have received a quite friendly letter from Nathan. I have written to Bailey about the private performance, telling him to say that I can easily cut or modify any lines that may jar on the military staff. Probably the result will be some cuts and a safe performance. ...

G.B.S.

SHAW TO W.F. BAILEY
[TL (signed for Shaw by his secretary Ann Elder): NLI]

10 Adelphi Terrace. London
17th November 1915

My dear Bailey
I enclose a copy of a letter I have just received [from Nathan]. I feel that we should not hesitate for a moment about withdrawing if they demand it; but I still think, now that the play has been announced, that less mischief might be done by the performance of a carefully cut version than by what would

appear to the public as a suppression, in spite of all possible disclaimers. I have written to Sir Matthew in this sense. What do you think, yourself?

Yours ever
G. Bernard Shaw

SIR MATTHEW NATHAN TO SHAW
[ALS: BL]

Dublin Castle
23rd November 1915

Dear Mr Bernard Shaw

I have been delayed by much work of a rather troublesome nature in replying to your letter of the 17th . . . and now Bailey, with whom I thought myself justified in talking it over, has told me that he will be seeing you tomorrow or the next day when he will give you the views we hold in common in the matter. Possibly, even more than he does, I should like to see the play produced here with certain elisions to avoid hurting excited susceptibilities. For it would I feel sure be valuable in stimulating those real motives from which you say men enlist, especially if at the time it is put on the recently inaugurated recruiting campaign, now meeting with a certain measure of success, shall then have spent its novel force.

Possibly when I myself am in London in a week or two's time you would allow me to go and see you not only with regard to this play but also about the big subject of this country where much is dark to me that you could I believe illumine.

Yours sincerely
Matthew Nathan

In spite of the hopes still held out in this letter of Nathan, the postponement of *O'Flaherty V.C.* was to be an indefinite one; the play did not receive its first production until 17th February

1917, when it was performed by Officers of the 40th Squadron, R.F.C., on the Western Front, with Robert Loraine creating the part of O'Flaherty. It appears never to have been performed by the Abbey, though there was a production of the play at the Abbey Theatre by a visiting company in 1927.

Nathan did, in fact, call on Shaw when in London on 2nd December and 'told him something of the state of affairs with the Sinn Feiners in Ireland', as he recorded in a memorandum of the interview [Hol: Nathan, Bodleian]:

> I suggested the possibility of some counteracting literature to the stuff they circulate and the necessity for it to be on rather a high plain. He asked me to send him copies of leaflets issued by the Sinn Feiners and also by the Recruiting Department and he would see what he could do.

Sir Matthew duly sent Shaw specimens of anti-recruiting and recruiting literature on 11th December. Shaw's response was a draft poster dispatched from Ayot on 29th December 1915, which Nathan, replying on 3rd January 1916, thought 'splendid'. However, he confessed, he 'funk[ed] a little exhibiting it' and he preferred 'a distribution in leaflet form through the post on the lines of the similar distribution of some of the Sinn Fein literature' [ALS: BL]. It is not clear whether the leaflet was eventually distributed in Ireland, but Shaw continued to support recruiting in Ireland, eventually in 1918 contributing the pamphlet *War Issues for Irishmen*, which was rendered obsolete by the Armistice.

LADY GREGORY TO SHAW
[TLS: BL]

Coole Park. Gort
12th August 1916

[St John Ervine was discharged from his managership of the Abbey on 16th July 1916. Although for much of the winter 1915–16 his management was financially successful, he had quarrelled with the company and as a result many of the actors had left and formed their own touring company, the Irish Players, under the leadership of Arthur

Sinclair. Sir Horace Plunkett had suffered very badly from X-ray burn in the summer of 1916 as a result of incompetent treatment by a Harley Street dermatologist. Carleen Shedden was a member of the second Abbey company in 1914 while the first was on tour in America, and had played in revivals of Lady Gregory's *Mirandolina*, adapted from Goldoni's *Locandiera*, and *Kincora*. Robert Gregory was to become good friends with Robert Loraine, the actor who was all but a surrogate son to the Shaws and Gregory's commanding officer in the Royal Flying Corps. Burren is a little village on the south coast of Galway Bay, not very far from Coole; Robert and Margaret Gregory's house there, Mount Vernon, given them by Lady Gregory as a wedding present, was used as a summer home by the whole family.

Shaw had worked hard to try to save Roger Casement, who, convicted of treason for his part in the Easter 1916 Rising, was executed on 3rd August. Eoin [John] MacNeill, the Celtic scholar, had been the commander of the Irish Volunteers. He had not approved of the Rising but, when arrested and tried, accepted responsibility with the other leaders. Sentenced to life imprisonment in Dartmoor, he was released under a general amnesty in 1917.]

Dear G.B.S.

I set out the day before yesterday from Burren to Dublin, and having been on the road nine hours arrived there just as Theatres were opening. I went up to see how we were to begin rebuilding, Ervine having scattered our Company and spent our money. We are free of him now, and have taken on J. Augustus Keogh as Manager; he has been in various companies as stage manager or actor and seems competent; and anyhow there was no one else to be had. He is putting on this week as his own speculation (we are not paying him yet) Widowers' Houses. I thought the performance very good and very well produced. The leading lady was hopeless (Miss [Elizabeth] Young an amateur with every bad stage trick) but the men very good. [O']Donovan and Kerrigan had come in from the [Irish] Film Co they had joined, and did well, there was a young clerk, Earl Gray (just another!) very promising, and Keogh was excellent as Lickcheese. There was a good audience and it went extremely well, every point taken up, and great applause on the slum question. So a brilliant thought struck me, to turn in

Napoleon's way a defeat to a victory; and our peasant plays
being for the moment knocked on the head, to do an autumn
season of G.B.S.—our Irish Shakespeare—I hope for an annual
festival of him! If we could put on your plays through say six
weeks of September and October, we could at the same time
begin classes and rehearsals of peasant work, and be ready to
put it on about end of October. I would like to put on John Bull,
(written for us and never acted by us); Devil's Disciple, which
should appeal to the romantic side of our audience; Doctor's
Dilemma, not my favourite but which I am inclined to think
acts best of all—and anyhow a hit at doctors has been appreciated since Molière's time, and poor Horace Plunkett having
been experimented on so lately would give it topical interest.
And I should like much to put on Androcles, if we could borrow
the lion—it is so delightful, and religious discussion should be
popular here. As to a leading lady, I tried Miss [Maire] O'Neill
but she says she would rather wait and do some of her old parts
later. So I want to get Carleen Sheddon, have you ever seen her?
She is partly Spanish though not Irish; speaks beautifully; we
had her for voice production classes and want her again. She did
Goldoni's Locandiera (Kiltartan translation) extremely well for
us, and Gormleith from my Kincora, and I think you would be
pleased with her. Of course I don't know what you, the victim,
will think of all this, but I don't think you would be displeased
with the shows. Keogh will write to you, this is just to prepare
your mind. I have just arrived from Dublin and in an hour or
two go back to Burren, to the children. I think Margaret will
soon be back with them now, for Robert was to go to the front
probably this week. I should find a letter at Burren to tell me if
he has gone. He likes Loraine, to whom I gather you had
written; many thanks.

We are still hoping to see you before the daylight saving is
over.

I couldn't feel much enthusiasm for Casement, but I wish
something could be done for John McNeill, a scholar to the
backbone and most generous in his help to learners. There are
such masses of MSS to be translated, while he is making sacks
in gaol. He is our business because of what he has done for the
intellectual life of Ireland.

My love to Charlotte—and you—and I hope to see you both
soon.

Ever yours
A Gregory

J. Augustus Keogh was an enthusiast for Shaw's plays; during
the 1916–17 season he was to direct six of them at the Abbey:
John Bull's Other Island (25th September 1916); *Widowers'
Houses* (9th October 1916); *Arms and the Man* (16th October
1916); *Man and Superman* (26th February 1917); *The Inca of
Perusalem* (12th March 1917); *The Doctor's Dilemma* (26th
March 1917). In most of these the leading roles were taken by
Maire O'Neill and Fred O'Donovan. The Abbey did eventually
produce *Androcles and the Lion* (4th November 1919), and *The
Devil's Disciple* (10th February 1920).
    The pressure for Shaw productions at the Abbey came from
Keogh rather than the directors. When Lady Gregory lunched
with the Shaws on 12th November 1916, she recorded in her
journal: 'Shaw had had letters from Keogh begging him to press
for his plays to be put on but had answered "Lady Gregory has
me on a string and I can't do anything without her leave" '.

SHAW TO LADY GREGORY
[TLS: Burgunder, Cornell]

10 Adelphi Terrace. London
22nd August 1916

[Robert Loraine had named Shaw as his next-of-kin to notify in the
event of his death. Isabelle M. Pagan, theosophist and astrologer, was
the adapter of several Ibsen works, whose *Fantasy of Peer Gynt done
into English Verse*, published in 1909, had subsequently been given
two private performances. No version by her of *The Master Builder*

was published or licensed for production. J. Augustus Keogh's own company produced *Candida* at the Abbey Theatre, for the week of 21st August, with Maire O'Neill in the title role. Shaw had not only protested vigorously against the shooting of the main leaders of the Easter Rising in May 1916, but had sought to achieve a reprieve for Casement: hence his bitterness against the 'present Terrorist Government'. Francis Sheehy Skeffington, whom Shaw had publicly supported the previous year when he was imprisoned for pacifist anti-recruiting activity, had been arrested while attempting to stop looting during the Rising and had been summarily executed at the command of a deranged British army officer. Although *John Bull's Other Island* had not been produced at the Abbey, it had been performed in Dublin by a number of other companies, the earliest occasion being in November 1907 at the Royal Theatre.]

My dear Lady Gregory

I have at last heard from Robert Loraine—a letter enclosing his Military Cross and a few other personal belongings for safe custody, the first view of which made Charlotte exclaim tragically 'He's dead'. The letter was written on the day of his departure for the front; and he mentions in the course of it that he has been looking after your Robert, whom he declares a man of merit, personally and professionally.

Charlotte is at Parknasilla with her sister Mrs Cholmondeley; but unless you happen to be in Dublin when she is returning in the middle of September I am afraid she will not have the pleasure of seeing you, as she has economically taken a return ticket direct from Euston, and therefore cannot without extravagance swerve from her journey in your direction. She has had a brilliant idea concerning the Abbey Theatre, which is, that you should break new ground by playing Ibsen. I think this is an inspiration. Ibsen has always paid on the Abbey Street scale, though never on the London West End scale. The plays are very cheap to stage: all domestic interiors of the sort you are accustomed to, except Peer Gynt, which your people could do to perfection as far as the acting is concerned; and though it seems impossible from the scenic point of view, I believe you could suggest the atmosphere as successfully as in Riders From the Sea or The Image.

However, for the moment it is a question of the domestic interior plays. Charlotte sends you the enclosed new translation of The Master Builder, made by Miss Pagan, a very remarkable and very nice Scottish lady who performed Peer Gynt in Edinburgh. You ought to invite her to Coole merely to see how you would get on with her. I think you would. I think she is old enough to be your grandmother, but so pretty that she would certainly become Richard's first love. Anyhow you ought to know her.

By the way, I am not quite sure about the copyright of her translation. I am writing to ask whether she has taken any steps to legalize it. But Archer's translation is available as an alternative.

Now as to my plays. I have given Keogh leave to try Candida with Miss O'Neill, though it is obviously less suited to his resources than Widowers' Houses. If it fails, it will teach him his limits: if not, so much the better. The Devil's Disciple is a sleeping dog that must be let lie: I think its effect just now, though exciting, would be purely mischievous. Besides, it is expensive and troublesome, involving five scenes, two of which have to be changed with an instantaneousness impossible on the Abbey stage, with crowds, real soldiers, and a military band. The military authorities would not give you the last two requisites. The Doctor's Dilemma is, I think, quite beyond your resources: it requires *polished* acting by a cast of cockney stars.

John Bull's Other Island is of course available; but I am afraid it is rather hackneyed in Dublin by this time. Arms and the Man, tried after great misgivings the other day in Birmingham, went very well indeed with soldier audiences and provoked not the slightest disapproval. You Never Can Tell always goes with a decent cast; but it is also somewhat polished and artificial.

On the whole, if Widowers' Houses and Candida have any success, I should stick to their period, and boldly try Ibsen: I believe he might give the theatre a new lease of life. And it would be a labor of piety too: he is the greatest of educators; and Ireland needs him badly.

I refuse flatly to put foot in Ireland without a safe conduct from the present Terrorist Government. If I do not fear the fate of Skeffington, at least I can pretend to. Tomorrow I start for Glastonbury in Somerset, where I shall be (Crown Hotel) until

Saturday next. Thence I go to Sedburgh, Yorkshire (White Hart Hotel) until the 9th September. After that, God knows where if not back home.

No: I have never seen Carleen. The name does not suggest Spain.

Casement's cousin, Gertrude Bannister, has been dismissed from the school in which she taught for seventeen years because she visited him in prison. Such is the union of hearts!

Ever
G. Bernard Shaw

PS As I cannot, in the hurry of packing, say all that about Ibsen over again to Keogh, may I leave him in your hands? By the way, Keogh is not paying my fees and has sent me only three returns. I have therefore had to tell him that unless he cashes up this week I shall stop his performances.

SHAW TO LADY GREGORY
[ALS: Burgunder, Cornell]

The White Hart. Sedbergh
3rd September 1916

[In responding to Shaw's suggestion of producing Ibsen at the Abbey, in a letter which is unfortunately not extant, Lady Gregory must have made allusion to the debates early on in the theatre movement between George Moore and Edward Martyn, who strongly advocated Ibsen and used him as a model for their own dramatic work, and Yeats, Synge and Lady Gregory herself, who were opposed to Ibsen's realism and his middle-class settings. Ibsen had been a major influence on Lennox Robinson, and in recent years the Abbey had increasingly produced realist plays by Robinson, T.C. Murray, and St John Ervine, among others, a necessity that both Yeats and Lady Gregory were inclined to regret. Lady Gregory had translated three of Molière's plays into Kiltartan dialect and all of them had been produced at the Abbey: *The Doctor in Spite of Himself* (1906), *The Rogueries of Scapin* (1908) and *The Miser* (1909). She eventually wrote a version of *The Would-be Gentleman*, first performed at the Abbey in 1926. Yeats had a long-standing interest in Sophocles' *Oedipus* and the Abbey produced his translations of both *Oedipus the King* (1926) and *Oedipus at Colonus* (1927).

Shaw had written a long Preface to *Three Plays by Brieux*, one of
them translated by Charlotte Shaw (1910). Max Reinhardt's spectacu-
lar production of Karl G. Vollmöller's *The Miracle* was first performed
in London in the cavernous Olympia, converted for the occasion into
a baroque cathedral, with the audience becoming the congregation.]

My dear Lady Gregory
    I dont at all agree about Ibsen; and I implore you to struggle
with your Irish propensity to throw back to the past and to
classical models. I am with Synge in thinking that the Irish
should do their own Ibsenizing; and in fact all your successes
have been nothing else than that as far as they have been
concerned with the works of young Irishmen. But the present
crisis has been produced by the drying-up for the moment of
that source; and you are going to tide over the famine (mixed
metaphor, *that*) by giving Dublin a turn of foreign work,
including mine, of one sort or another.
    Now Molière can do nothing for Dublin but encourage it in
that derision which is its curse and its sin. And Sophocles is a
deliberate and shameless exploiter of cruel superstition and
prejudice, the curse and sin of the whole Irish nation, especially
in that abominable play which leads up to nothing but a man
tearing his eyes out because he discovers that his wife is also his
mother: a really filthy insult to the human heart. For Euripides
there is something to be said: he was no cynical trader in the
vices of public opinion. If you must have antiquity, play
Euripides.
    But Ibsen is a great modern poet and teacher whom the Irish
especially need, and whom they have a right to know as a part of
their culture. He is the only real successor to Swift; and he is
centuries ahead of Swift in his diagnosis of the odiousness of our
society and his discovery of the cause in the idolatry of ideals.
His Norwegian interiors are equally true as West Kensington
interiors and Rathmines interiors. To have Ibsen under your
hand and deliberately go back to Molière and Socrates [for
Sophocles] is a crime against civilization. If Ibsen has set
[Lennox] Robinson and Co imitating him, all the more reason
to give the original.
    There is Brieux, too; but the new departure, if you make it,
should be consecrated by the depth and power and glamor of

Ibsen's poetry. The north of Ireland should hear Brand, and the south Peer Gynt. And Merrion Square and Rathmines and Kingstown need A Doll's House and The Wild Duck to save their souls. Dreamers all round the coast need The Lady from The Sea; and Hedda Gabler needs shewing-up everywhere as much as Blanco Posnet.

As to Androcles, how on earth could Keogh get it on to the Abbey Street stage? There is hardly room for the lion: one spring would carry him half way to the G.P.O. Where are you to put those towering stairways, surmounted by the emperor's box? How are they to revolve and shew the arena side of the Coliseum? Where are you to put those groups of Christian martyrs on the one side, and of gladiators (mostly all-but-naked) on the other, and leave a big floor between for the action of the piece? You might as well propose Reinhardt's Miracle.

I cannot decipher the end of the sentence beginning 'Poor Edward Martyn, who has a real gift for ideas, has'—? It looks like 'crushingly broken his wings'.—Here I am interrupted and must abruptly stop without adding anything nice—

G.B.S.

SHAW TO LADY GREGORY
[APCS: Burgunder, Cornell]

White Hart Hotel. Sedbergh
3rd September 1916

[The Abbey company did not revisit America until 1931. O'Flaherty VC was not actually performed there until 1920, when it was given its first professional production anywhere by the Deborah Bierne Irish Players in New York.]

What are the prospects of the Abbey Players ever revisiting America? When I say 'ever', I mean two years or thereabouts. The reason I ask is that I am being heavily pressed to let O'Flaherty loose there; and as by next January my direct war taxation will have amounted to considerably over £10,000, the policy of holding up plays for vague or remote contingencies is financially impossible. O'F. is a war play, and may be valueless twelve months hence. Is there any reasonable reason for not letting it go?

This is only a postscript to a letter in reply to yours which will reach you via Parknasilla, as I had better secure my domestic comfort by convincing Charlotte that I have defended her Ibsen suggestion.

G.B.S.

SHAW TO LADY GREGORY
[APCS: Berg, NYPL]

10 Adelphi Terrace [London]
13th October 1916

[The accident-prone Charlotte had apparently got caught up in a dog-fight and had been knocked down by one of the combatants. The evening meeting was of the Fabian Society, with Harry Johnston, friend of Shaw and author of the sequel novel *Mrs Warren's Daughter*, as speaker. The lunch was with Charles Charrington, whose actress wife Janet Achurch had died on 11th September.]

Charlotte has fallen down and damaged her knee. She is at Ayot; and though she can now get about on crutches, I have to be at hand to put on a sort of putty poultice every day twice. I have dashed up to town for a moment, having to attend a meeting this evening. But I must go back early tomorrow afternoon; and I have to lunch a man whose wife has just died and who has to talk to me very privately about her. I may be able to make a rush to Cheyne Walk in the forenoon if you are not going out, and if the morning's mail does not crush me with a heavy block of immediate business. If you are going out perhaps you will be so good as to ring me up (331 Gerrard) and warn me not to attempt the journey. And I shall know by ten o'clock whether I can get away. Forgive me for making myself scarce in this fashion; but I am really rather fussed by the shortness of the time I can spend in town.

G.B.S.

LADY GREGORY: *JOURNALS*

Ayot St Lawrence
19th [November 1916]

[Lady Gregory was in London throughout November staying with
her niece, Ruth Shine, and lobbying for the return of the Lane
collection to Ireland. She had seen Shaw several times and was
spending the weekend with him at Ayot. Shaw's short story, 'The
Emperor and the Little Girl', written for the Vestiaire Marie-José, a
Belgian war charity for children, was first published in the *New York
Tribune Magazine* on 22nd October 1916; he collected it in *Short
Stories, Scraps and Shavings* (1932). Composition on what was to be
Heartbreak House had been started on 4th March 1916.]

... I lunched with the Shaws at 10 Adelphi Terrace. Mr and Mrs
Parry there, she was Miss Gertrude Bannister who had been
turned out of a school for being Casement's cousin but this had
led to her marriage so it was all for the best. There was some talk
at lunch about spiritualism. G.B.S. said his mother had been
very much given to table-turning and that the spirit used to
come who gave his name as Matthew Haffigan, a name he has
used later in *John Bull*, and who was a most awful liar. They
tried to verify some of his statements and they were always
false. His mother, however, went on quite happily. G.B.S.
himself became an adept at cheating at séances and gave no
belief to anything in them. He says his mother's real love was
for gardens, that he used to say that if he were run over by a dray
she would say 'Oh poor fellow' but if a beautiful rose had been
crushed she would go out of her mind with grief.

We came on here in snow but the house is warm and bright
with fires in every room and pots of chrysanthemums. ...

Last night G.B.S. read me a story he had written. He had
been asked for one for a Gift Book to be sold for the Belgian
Children's Milk Fund and had refused, saying the Society of
Authors objected to these Gift Books. But the lady [Carmen
Goldsmid, who was Mrs L. Haden Guest] came again to say she
had got leave from the Society of Authors to print it, if she gave
them a percentage. He was quite taken aback and said he hadn't
promised it, but in the end sat down and wrote it straight off.
Then the lady brought it back in a few days to say she wouldn't

put it in the Gift Book but Mrs Whitelaw Reid had offered £400 for it to put in the *New York Tribune*. So the Belgian children will get plenty of milk for that.

He read it and it is beautiful and touching, about a child and the Kaiser. He said that his idea was to show that the Kaiser is not quite a demon. ... He read also the first act of a play, very amusing, 'The House [Studio] in the Clouds' (afterwards *Heartbreak House!*) but says he doesn't know how to finish it, it is so wild, he thought bringing my 'fresh mind' to bear on it might be a help.

He had been to Birmingham to see a new little play of his own [*The Inca of Perusalem*], and has seen [John] Masefield's *Chimney sweepers of '98* not good; but at the end when someone says 'At the next Rising I shall be too old' or some such words, he found his eyes full of tears.

SHAW TO LADY GREGORY
[TLS: Burgunder, Cornell]

10 Adelphi Terrace. [London]
22nd January 1917

[The 'Russian lady' was Vera Donnet, whose ballet *La Pomme d'Or*, performed under the auspices of the Stage Society in London in February 1917, brought to public attention Marie Rambert, later founder of the Ballet Rambert. Yeats's 'broadside' in *The Observer* (21st January 1917) was his most recent contribution to the campaign for the return of the Lane pictures. D.S. MacColl, Keeper of the Tate and, at this time, of the Wallace Collection, had been invited by Lady Gregory to write a life of Hugh Lane. However, he incurred her enmity by writing repeatedly against the Dublin claim to the Lane collection, at one point quoting from unpublished letters of Lane to Lady Gregory to enforce his argument (*The Observer*, 14th January 1917); in the circumstances he felt obliged to give up his commitment to the biography. In spite of Shaw's attempts to mollify Lady Gregory, she still regarded MacColl as 'the principal spokesman of our opponents' as late as 1926. Jeanne E. Vandervelde was the wife of the Belgian Minister of State, Emile Vandervelde, operating from London 1914–18. The rough sketch in plaster for Rodin's Balzac (depicted in a bulkily draped dressing gown) had so angered the conservative Society of Men of Letters in 1898 that it withdrew its commission for the work. Shaw was to visit the Western Front from 28th January to 5th February; while there he dined with Robert Gregory and Robert Loraine.]

My dear Lady Gregory

I have talked to the Stage Society people about The Golden Apple; and they are greatly concerned to hear that their attitude towards you, as conveyed at two removes through their present provisional secretary [Alice Fredman] and our friend Thring, has lost something of its Bayard-like bloom. They beg me to assure you of their most distinguished consideration (they are quite sincere about it), and to say that they will make the strongest representations to the Russian lady as to the extreme inconvenience, and (unless she unluckily knows better) the illegality of using your title, and will call her ballet Pomme d'Or at their performance.

I hope this will dispose of the matter; but the difficulty is that there is no copyright in such a title as The Golden Apple, which, since the days of the gardens of the Hesperides, has been used again and again. Androcles and The Lion is in the same category; and one author protested vehemently that it was 'his title'. I appeased him by pointing out that my play would probably revive his, which had been dead for a long time. I told the S.S. to explain to the Russian Lady that if her ballet had the same title as your play she would not be able to check American piracies by watching the reports in The Dramatic Mirror, and that she would find managers refusing to book dates on the ground that 'We have had that before'.

I have just been reading Yeats's final broadside in The Observer. You have certainly had a tremendous press: your campaign has been like the Hundred Days campaign of Napoleon; but it will end the same way, I am afraid. I thought you were going to win when the National Gallery Bill was at stake; but when that evaporated I concluded that we were lost; and I hold that opinion still. Just suppose the boot had been on the other foot: that Hugh had made a valid will leaving the pictures to Dublin, and that the unwitnessed one left them to London. We should not have let them go. Then why should we try to persuade ourselves that the English will let them go? I shouldnt in their place. The best thing that can happen is the adoption of MacColl's suggestion that the pictures should circulate. If that were applied to the entire national collections, it would be a great advance on the present plan of chaining all the masterpieces to a post hundreds of miles from everywhere except itself.

There is nothing more to be done on our side now. The press has been worked to exhaustion: no editor would let me start it all over again. Do not quarrel with MacColl: he is still the best man to write the life; and though you are indignant with him for using those letters he has a very strong case for the use he made of them. By the way, dont quarrel with me, either, for saying these things: I have considered it very carefully and with all my bias on your side; but when a bequest of great value was staked by us on the state of mind of the testator, I do not see how you could possibly have refused MacColl leave to publish the letter if he had asked you for it. That he was canny enough to mak siccer [play safe] by doing it without asking, gives you an opening for a gentle reproach to him for not asking; but his reply is pat: 'As I had quite made up my mind on public grounds to publish the letter leave or no leave, I thought it was honester not to pay you an idle compliment and risk putting myself in a false position if you had refused'.

I saw Yeats yesterday at Madame Vandervelde's. He still hopes, though, like me, he would like a catastrophe to rub into the Corporation for their emulation of the French municipality which turned down Rodin's Balzac. I am not so sanguine: I know too well that the innate British admiration for chivalry and self sacrifice is—except when practised by others—subject to the wholesome condition that it shall not involve any substantial loss and thereby discredit itself by making it impossible to recall its exercise with pleasure.

Robert was of course inevitably an officer from the first. Men accustomed to that position and able to assume it with any grace are so scarce that they will presently make him a field marshal.

Ever
G.B.S.

SHAW TO LADY GREGORY
[TLS: Berg, NYPL]

10 Adelphi Terrace. London
28th April 1917

[Keogh, who was shortly to be replaced as manager of the Abbey by
Fred O'Donovan, had continued to mount productions of his own
even while at the Abbey. One of the sources of dissatisfaction with his
Abbey managership had been the relatively poor returns of the Shaw
plays he insisted on producing.]

My dear Lady Gregory
    I am rather bothered about the extreme enterprisingness of
the energetic Keogh. He is launching out on his own account,
and of course wants to have the run of my plays. He wanted You
Never Can Tell for the Gaiety in Dublin; and I replied, in
effect, that my Dublin custom would only support one shop.
He also wanted to get Pygmalion, whereupon I retreated
behind Mrs Patrick Campbell. He now says that he is going to
start in Cork. This is all right: I am quite prepared to let him do
in Cork what he has done in Dublin but he adds 'of course I will
tour all the larger towns in Ireland as well'. This raises a
difficulty. It is not reasonable to confine him to Cork, which
could hardly support a repertory theatre singlehanded. I should
have to allow him a circuit. The question is, will the Abbey
Street Players undertake anything in the same line. If so, there
ought to be an understanding as to the circuits. For the present
I can tell Keogh that I will licence him for Cork only, leaving
other places to be dealt with as they come up; but the question
of Belfast will come up very soon.
    I foresee a rather awkward situation. Keogh's trump card,
which he has already thrown down boldly, is that when he
leaves the Abbey Theatre there will be no more of my plays
there as they do not 'meet with the approval of Mr Yeats for
production at the Abbey'. I understand exactly what this
means; so you need not soothe my unwounded feelings, as I
take it that you and I and Yeats are very much of the same
opinion in the matter. But if we act on that opinion, and find
such action successful: that is, if it should prove possible to
keep the Abbey going by fresh native work and by what I call
the quartier Latin cum Bedford Park cum Gaelic League

School (to distinguish them from the Irish school, which so far buzzes apart as a bee from your own bonnet), then it will inevitably happen that Keogh, if he can keep going, will be exploiting my plays vigorously all over Ireland, and asking me whether I seriously mean to impoverish myself and break his back by keeping them out of Dublin for the sake of a rival theatre which never performs them at all, and never did except as a stopgap in a desperate emergency. Under these circumstances I should have to hold a pistol to the head of the Abbey Theatre by saying that it must either give me a minimum number of performances every year or else see my plays go to Keogh.

Even if Keogh breaks down another Keogh may turn up and reproduce the situation. It is not in the least pressing as yet, and may never become so; but I want the Abbey Theatre to foresee its possibility, especially as we may all be dead when it matures, and my executors will have to take a purely commercial view of the matter.

The immediate object of this letter is to induce you to gossip to me a little about Keogh.

Ever

G. Bernard Shaw

SHAW TO LADY GREGORY
[TLS: Burgunder, Cornell]

10 Adelphi Terrace. London

4th May 1917

[In a letter to the *Boston Evening Transcript* published on 28th June 1917 Shaw explained publicly his reasons for withholding *The Devil's Disciple* during the war. J.A. Keogh did produce *You Never Can Tell* with his own company in Dublin at the Gaiety Theatre during the week beginning 18th June, followed by *Candida* and *How He Lied to Her Husband* the next week. C. Haviland-Burke had acted in three of Shaw's plays during Keogh's season as Abbey manager but there is no record of his having produced any Shaw with his own company, which performed in the Queen's and the Tivoli Theatres in the summer of 1917. Shaw's three 'articles on the Front' had appeared in the *Daily Chronicle* on 5th-8th March, under the title 'Joy-Riding at the Front'.]

My dear Lady Gregory

I have practically pledged myself not to allow The Devil's Disciple to be played during the war. There has been a considerable clamor for it in America; and I believe it has been actually played in Germany. The demand for it is partly a direct pro-German demand, and partly a commercial demand aiming at the exploitation of pro-Germanism. As to Androcles, how is it possible to do Androcles on your little stage? Even if the stage were large enough, how much do you think the cast and the costumes would come to? In London, where it unfortunately drew only £800 a week, the season was only rescued from bankruptcy by the hasty substitution, just before the shutters went up, of The Doctor's Dilemma.

To Keogh's demand for You Never Can Tell has now been added one from Haviland-Burke. Now You Never Can Tell is a champion money maker if only it is well cast and played. What I really want to get at is whether there is sufficient chance of your doing these comparatively unpoetic plays of mine at the Abbey to justify me in making a corner in them for you in Dublin.

I am rather alarmed at your making [O']Donovan your producer. It is likely to have two results: one being to ruin him as an actor and to spoil the performances, and the other to make him the absolute master of the Theatre; for when, with the reputation he has acquired as an actor, he has qualified himself completely as a manager and producer as well, he will be in a position to take the whole thing out of your hands the moment he feels solid ground under his feet commercially. This may be a quite desirable solution when you and Yeats get tired of the drudgery of running a theatre; but it will turn the Abbey into some thing very like what the old Lyceum here was under Irving's management: that is, it will have no opportunity of growth in it.

My articles on the Front were shocking: it was a most demoralizing experience. I send you a set of the papers containing them. The first article has a good many blunders and misprints, as it was printed not from my corrected proof, but from a resetting in smaller type which occurred at the last moment.

Charlotte is much bent on going to Ireland this summer. I expect to have to stay here during August, for Fabian [Summer

School] purposes; but there's nothing to prevent me from joining Charlotte in Ireland (if she goes) for September. However, nothing is settled as yet. The war is still very disturbing in spite of the extent to which we have settled down to it.

Ever
G.B.S.

SHAW TO LADY GREGORY
[APCS: Burgunder, Cornell]

10 Adelphi Terrace. [London]
[26th July 1917]

[Robert Loraine and Robert Gregory visited the Shaws at Ayot on 21st July. Shaw had lobbied unsuccessfully to be appointed to the Irish Convention, an assembly of political and non-political figures representing a range of opinion, convened by the British government to discuss a possible Irish constitutional settlement, which met from July 1917 to April 1918. He had to be content with offering detailed advice privately to Sir Horace Plunkett, the Convention's chairman.]

He literally *was* hovering over our chimney pots with Loraine; but our lawn is too tiny and beset with trees for a descent; so they came down two fields off, to the unspeakable admiration of the whole village, the population of which multiplied tenfold in as many minutes. They dined with us and flew off before a huge and ecstatic audience at 9 o'clock. The day will be remembered for ever in Ayot St Lawrence. Robert looked excessively well.

I have seen Charlotte off at Euston. She will stay in Dublin at the Shelburne until Saturday, when she goes on to join her sister at Parknasilla. I did my best to get nominated to the Convention, but in vain; so I shall now stay here for the Fabian Summer School until the middle of August or thereabouts, when I shall go to Parknasilla if nothing intervenes.

G.B.S.

SHAW TO LADY GREGORY
[ALS: Burgunder, Cornell]

Ayot St Lawrence. Welwyn
27th November 1917

[The 'proof' enclosed was of *How to Settle the Irish Question*, a series of articles published in the *Daily Express* on 27th-29th November. Shaw had been in Parknasilla from 11th September to 12th October, and with Sir Horace Plunkett from 13th to 23rd October. It was on 23rd October that he had lunch at the RIC depot. Albert J. Kilsby was Shaw's chauffeur.]

My dear Lady Gregory

It *was* rather a pity that we missed Coole; but it was well into September before I could get across to Ireland; and I had to make time at the end for a week with Sir Horace Plunkett. I enclose a proof of the result. Keep it duly dark for me until it is published. You will see that I have at least been able to drive a wedge into the wooden solidarity of Ulster, and to give the real answer to Casement's scheme for an Irish independence made in Germany.

I found Ireland in a condition of insufferable self-conceit, and quite enjoyed lunching at the R.I.C. depot in Phoenix Park with [Brigadier-]General [Sir Joseph Aloysius] Byrne [Inspector General of the Royal Irish Constabulary] and the chief of the metropolitan police [Lt-Col. Walter Edgeworth-Johnstone], though I rather horrified them by my program of machine guns and Mills bombs.

The theatre was out of action during my Dublin visit.

Ervine is in the trenches. I heard from him the other day.

This remote village is now an armed camp bristling with guns and blazing with searchlights. Kilsby has just bade me a long farewell. Having evaded the recruiting officers successfully for three years, at the cost of an operation, he is now past military age, and has gone off to Woolwich to make aeroplane engines.

Yesterday I read O'Flaherty VC to 250 soldiers [at Stuarts Hospital, Blackmore End]. They gave me three cheers, and laughed a good deal; but the best bits were when they sat very tight and said nothing.

Ever
G.B.S.

PS I have just learnt that the publication of the articles has begun today.

SHAW TO LADY GREGORY
[APCS: Burgunder, Cornell]

Ayot St Lawrence. Welwyn
3rd December 1917

[Although Shaw declined Lady Gregory's invitation to lecture on this occasion, he did speak in Dublin the following year. He evidently sent her a copy of *How to Settle the Irish Question* in its pamphlet form, for it was in her collection in 1929, with the pages still uncut, as Shaw wryly remarked when signing it then (*Journals*, 11th January 1930).]

The articles are being republished as a sixpenny pamphlet, and will be out in a few days.

As to the lecture, NO. The very words nation, nationality, our country, patriotism, fill me with loathing. Why do you want to stimulate a self-consciousness which is already morbidly excessive in our wretched island, and is deluging Europe with blood? If we could only forget for a moment that we are Irish, and become really Catholic Europeans, there would be some hope for us. Since my recent visit I feel like putting up a statue to Cromwell.

G.B.S.

Robert Gregory was killed on 23rd January 1918. His plane was, in fact, shot down in error by an Italian pilot as he returned from a flight over enemy lines in Northern Italy, a detail that Lady Gregory was spared. His death was to provide the subject for a series of poems by Yeats, including the great elegy 'In Memory of Major Robert Gregory' and 'An Irish Airman Foresees His Death'.

For Shaw, Robert Gregory's death came as only the last of a whole series of deaths of the sons of close friends and colleagues, including those of William Archer, Carlos Blacker, and Mrs Patrick Campbell. In striking contrast to the tone of his letter of condolence to Lady Gregory is that to Mrs Patrick Campbell of 7th January 1918: 'It is no use: I cant be sympathetic: these things simply make me furious. I want to swear. I *do* swear. Killed just because people are blasted fools'. The original of his letter to Lady Gregory is not extant; what is given below is an extract that she transcribed in a letter to John Quinn.

LADY GREGORY: *SEVENTY YEARS*

[Coole Park. Gort]
[29th January 1918]

When I came home from Dublin ... I went to the wood where I was planting. I was vexed because in my absence timber had been given away, and there were men cutting the young ash that had come into sight with the cutting of the spruce and that with the blue hills showing through them I had thought Robert would enjoy seeing on his next leave. I had been planting broom and flowering trees also, and they would have pleased him. Next morning I determined to spend the whole day at the wood. I had a sandwich put up and the donkey carriage made ready, and went to the drawing-room to write some necessary letter. I was at my writing table when I heard Marian [McGuinness, the children's nurse] come in, very slowly. I looked up and saw she was crying. She had a telegram in her hand. ...

SHAW TO LADY GREGORY

[Extracted from TLS of Lady Gregory to J. Quinn: Berg, NYPL]

[10 Adelphi Terrace. London]
5th February 1918

I have just met [Henry] Tonks at the Burlington Fine Arts Club; he told me the news. These things made me rage and swear once; now I have come to taking them quietly. When I met Robert at the flying station on the west front, in abominably cold weather, with a frostbite on his face hardly healed, he told me that the six months he had been there had been the happiest of his life. An amazing thing to say considering his exceptionally fortunate and happy circumstances at home, but he evidently meant it. To a man with his power of standing up to danger—which must mean enjoying it—war must have intensified his life as nothing else could; he got a grip of it that he could not through art or love. I suppose that is what makes the soldier.

Only the other day Mrs Patrick Campbell's son, after years of service with the trench mortars (horribly dangerous), got promoted to the staff and was immediately killed in his dugout by the last shell from a German battery ceasing fire. Like Robert he was a very goodlooking man of a refined type, who left the Navy because they are all drunken Philistines there and took to art. Like Robert he never seemed able to find any full expression of himself in art or society. Like Robert he seemed to find himself in doing dangerous things. His mother thinks he got all the life he wanted out of the war and nothing else could have given it to him.

LADY GREGORY TO SHAW
[ALS: BL]

Coole
Friday 8th February [1918]

Dear G.B.S.

I was hoping for a letter from you. I knew it would be helpful. Just that—danger and authority and the sense of power to do more than he had ever done—intensified his life—were the high light in the picture.

Just this day a week ago I was here, at my writing table—about to go out for a whole day's planting in the woods—when the telegram came—my one thought was 'how shall I tell Margaret'. She was in Galway with the children. I had to go by train—the saddest task of my life—but of course when she saw me she knew, and I was free to cry.

I have been more serene since we have had letters—he was I think happy to the very last—for they were coming back from patrol over the enemy's lines and they say he fainted in the air and never recovered consciousness. Here, it has taken away the horror. I am glad to know the last thing he looked at was the Italian sky and not bursting shells or the faces of enemies. And all the people here thank God that he was laid to rest in the holy ground of Padua. Margaret is broken hearted—they were wrapped up in each other. We are here and the children with my sister in Galway. Poor little Richard does not know yet what his loss is. I had been so happy about his school days, thinking Robert would understand so well, and look after him there, as women cannot do.

The machinery of my life does not change much. I was planting last week for Robert—this week for Richard, but my heart is very sore for my fair haired child who to me never seemed greatly changed, gentle and affectionate as at the first. But I have missed already these two or three years his right judgment and clear thinking and intellectual grip. I am maimed without him.

My love to Charlotte and to you.

A Gregory

The Shaws, after their holiday in Parknasilla in September 1918, visited Coole again from 3rd to 11th October, their third and, as it was to turn out, their last visit, before going on to spend two weeks in Dublin. The British Government had failed to implement the recommendations of the Irish Convention that there should be a single Irish national parliament and had tried to introduce the profoundly unpopular measure of extending military conscription to Ireland. With the increasing strength of the Sinn Féin party in the south of Ireland demanding complete separation from England, and the Unionists of Ulster, led by Sir Edward Carson, ever insistent that they would not accept any Home Rule measure that united them with the nationalists, a partition of the country looked likely.

Lady Gregory was still very actively involved in the Lane pictures controversy, in which Sir Edward Carson had promised support for the introduction of a Bill in the House of Commons to have the collection restored to Ireland. In October 1918 she was much alarmed by a proposal from the Dublin Lane Picture Committee to have the dispute with the National

Gallery submitted to arbitration, as she felt that, if the arbitration went against them, there would be no possibility of
pursuing the claim further. Shaw, in Dublin at the time, went
to a meeting of the committee with Lady Gregory; she was
extremely grateful for his help in persuading the committee to
change its mind about asking for arbitration. After the meeting,
as she recorded in her *Journals*, she commented: "'When you're
in doubt lead trumps say cardplayers, and when I'm in doubt I
lead G.B.S.'', and he laughed and said ... "She always tells me
what to do, and I just do as I'm told"'.

SHAW TO LADY GREGORY
[TLS: Burgunder, Cornell]

10 Adelphi Terrace. [London]
14th November 1918

[Lady Gregory apparently suggested that Shaw join a deputation, led
by the Lord Mayor of Dublin, to both David Lloyd George, the Prime
Minister, and H.H. Asquith, his former colleague and now Leader of
the Opposition, to seek support in the Lane pictures controversy.]

My dear Lady Gregory
    I think you may regard the arbitration business [concerning
the Lane collection] as now finally shelved. I doubt if anything
can be done in the enormous excitement of the present
moment; but as Lloyd George has confirmed his surrender to
Carson [in agreeing to the principle of Irish partition], perhaps
Carson will join in pressing him to make some demonstration of
friendliness to Nationalist Ireland.
    Knowing how frightfully obstinate you are in your opinions
(usually, I admit, with good reason) I despair of convincing you
that I am the very worst person you could possibly send on the
deputation to the Prime Minister; but I certainly wont go and
play the poor Lord Mayor off the stage, and set Mrs Asquith
telling her husband that the deputation is a *deputation pour rire*
because I am on it, and that he must on no account make
himself ridiculous by helping it. It is quite useless trying to play

me off among these people as a trump card; I have the whole English press against me whenever I move; and the politicians will not do anything for anyone who has not a press backing. Plunkett's failure to get me nominated to the Irish Convention shews how sure they are that I am safely negligible, but dangerous if they gave me any chance.

Before I left Dublin I looked through the Municipal Art Gallery. Let me whisper to you that the collection seemed to me better balanced than it used to be. This does not reconcile me to the loss of the pictures, because I should like to see the balancing done at the National Gallery, and some specializing at the other. Still, the collection is not in the least disabled by the withdrawal of the bequest: it is still a very worthy monument to its founder.

We had a stormy voyage through the torpedoes: there was a Westerly gale; and the ship kept standing on its head all the way. But we got a cabin and were not sick.

We were not in London for the [Armistice] rejoicings [on 11th November]. The dozen unfortunates in khaki whose contribution to the great victory has been a year of idleness and boredom in this village assembled when the news came and cheered as if they had been over the top daily for four years; but that was all.

Give the infants the compliments of the Dhee Bee Ettha [the Gregory granddaughters' attempted pronunciation of 'G.B.S.']. I found Dublin loquacious as ever, but damnably dull after Coole, as there was nobody nearly as good company as you.

Ever
G.B.S.

LADY GREGORY: *JOURNALS*

Saturday [1st March 1919]

[Lady Gregory was in London from the middle of February 1919, continuing to pursue the issue of the Lane collection. Apsley Cherry-Garrard, a friend of the Shaws, who had been on the second Antarctic expedition (1910–13) led by Captain Robert Scott, now lived on his country estate, Lamer Park, within a mile of Shaw's Corner at Ayot. Kathleen Lady Scott, Captain Scott's widow, was a sculptor, to whom Shaw had sat the previous year. Fridtjof Nansen was the Norwegian Arctic explorer. John Henry Foley, the Irish sculptor, created the statues of Burke and Goldsmith erected at the entrance to Trinity College Dublin, and of O'Connell in Sackville (now O'Connell) Street. Shaw had started writing *Back to Methuselah* on 19th March 1918.]

... To Ayot St Lawrence. The Shaws in the train but didn't see me, I being third and they first-class. G.B.S. first attacked me about public schools ... and denounced Harrow and wondered we could send Richard there, they learn nothing but to hate Classics and all knowledge, and their mind closes up. I said that had not been the case with two Harrovians, my husband and Robert, which left him rather weakened. Then he told me he had dropped into the National Gallery the other day and seen the Lane pictures surrounded with a crowd with catalogues, much interested in them, and had felt convinced it was the right place for them whereas the Dublin National Gallery is a silent desert.

3 March. We lunched yesterday at Lamer with Mr Cherry Garrard, Lady Scott and Nansen, and dined there also.

To continue about the pictures, G.B.S. was really very good, for Mr Garrard asked me if we were going to get them, and I said I hoped so and I told him that G.B.S. said they were appreciated by more people in London. 'But', I said, 'George IV when very tipsy and entertaining a deputation from Cork, had news that the Italian Government was sending him some casts of statues, and in his good humour, made a present of them to the City of Cork. Probably very few people visited them there, but one poor boy did and was influenced by them, and so became our great sculptor, Foley; and so it might be if we had the pictures in Dublin, even if many visitors do not visit the Gallery'. 'But, I', said G.B.S., 'I am one whose whole life was influenced by the Dublin National Gallery for I spent many days of my boyhood wandering through it and so learned to care for Art'. We have been talking of it this morning and he is sympathetic. I said to him: 'I am more appreciated in London than in Dublin, but I spend more time in Dublin because I think I am more useful there'.

Last night at Lamer, he gave an account of a wonderful and
fantastic play he is writing beginning in the Garden of Eden,
before Adam and Eve, with Lilith who finds a lonely immorta-
lity impossible to face and so gives herself up to be divided into
Man and Woman. He had read me a scene in it (on the pier at
Burren) about a thousand years in the future with the Irish
coming back to kiss the earth of Ireland and not liking it when
they see it. ...

G.B.S. read me his play beginning in the Garden of Eden.
The first Act a fine thing, 'a Resurrection play' I called it. The
second, 200 years later, an argument between Cain, Adam and
Eve, the soldier against the man of peace. I told him I thought it
rather monotonous, an Ossianic dialogue, and he said he
thought of introducing Cain's wife 'the Modern Woman', or
perhaps only speaking of her in the argument. I said even that
would be an improvement, as Cain is unnecessarily disagreeable and one could forgive if he is put, by aspersions on his wife,
in a passion, for one can forgive where there is passion. It is like
drunkenness—'Ah, you can't blame him, he was drunk'—
when a man has cut your head open. He laughed and agreed, or
seemed to.

SHAW TO LADY GREGORY
[TLS: unlocated; p: Colin Smythe]

                                          Ayot St Lawrence. Welwyn
                                                    28th April 1919

[*The Dragon*, one of Lady Gregory's 'wonder plays', had been produced at the Abbey on 21st April to more favourable reviews than any
of her plays had received for some years. She had evidently written to
Shaw asking advice on where it might be produced in England. Nigel
Playfair abetted by Arnold Bennett had gone into management at the
Lyric Theatre, Hammersmith, in 1918, establishing a popular and
inspiring artistic centre. Oundle school, whose origins are rooted as
far back as the fifteenth century, stressed modernised education, with
a bent towards engineering, under its headmaster of the time, Frederick W. Sanderson. Despite Shaw's arguments, Richard Gregory was
sent to Harrow.]

My dear Lady Gregory

I rejoice in the success of The Dragon. Make the Birmingham Repertory Theatre do it. Then go for the Lyric, Hammersmith (Arnold Bennett and Nigel Playfair). There will soon be others.

I have found a proper school for Richard, and personally inspected it and talked to the headmaster. I found it out through H.G. Wells, whose boys are there, and who took me down [on 1st April] to see a school performance of Arms and The Man, the fusillades in which, performed by the entire School Rifle Corps behind the scenes, surpassed anything I have ever heard either at a professional performance or at the front.

I really cannot have Richard sent to that obsolete and thrice accursed boy farm which is an evil tradition in the family. Richard has a right to choose his fate. Shew him the picture postcards of the workshops, and tell him that the boys repair all the cars in the countryside, and test the farm seeds, and pick up Latin and Greek for fun in their spare time with such success that they beat all the other public schools at examinations, Eton and Harrow being nowhere, and Rugby, which has been modernized, the only feared competitor. Or, if you like, dont mention the Latin and Greek and mention only the workshops. You *may* mention, though, that there are no punishments, and that Sanderson, the headmaster, is rather like Granny in respect of calmly doing everything he wants to do, however subversive of established institutions, by simply walking in his heavy amiable way through every prejudice. It would be a crime to deliver Richard over to some imbecile don when men like that are about. Intellect is respected and athletics tolerated with due kindness, but no more.

You see, it was all very well to send Robert to Harrow: where else was there to send him? Besides, he was able to regain contact with the modern world through literature and art. But everybody has not the faculty for that; and it is not the best way anyhow. Now there is an alternative in Oundle, and the schools that are being headmastered by the men who have been trained at Oundle. Richard has a turn, not for Latin verse and football, but for mechanics. Richard's mother has not the Harrovian psychology; and Richard has a touch of his mother which you must not try to correct or Gregorize. By the time Richard is twenty Harrow will be unthinkable except for absolutely idiotic country gentlemen. If Richard is sent there he will spit in my face, and ask me why, after all my talk about education, I let his mother, or his grandmother, ruin him by sending him to such a place.

Think over it; and do not be indignant with me for interfering. Tradition is all very well if it is kept whole. But Robert broke the tradition when he married Margaret and became a painter. You cannot patch it up again; and Harrow at its most harrowing cannot make another Sir William out of the son of a Welshwoman. You must develop the new tradition, which is a healthy one; for Robert was just on the verge of being overbred: one more generation as fine drawn as that would have produced something that might have been pretty and would certainly have been effete. The Welsh sand came just in time to make good brick of the clay. Now Harrow is in the old tradition: Oundle is in the new. I say again, think over it.

I meant this letter to be all about the Dragon; but, after all, the dragon can take care of itself, and Richard can't.

I suppose there is nothing fresh yet about the pictures.

Ever
G. Bernard Shaw

SHAW TO LADY GREGORY
[APCS: Berg, NYPL]

Ayot St Lawrence. Welwyn
7th May 1919

[Eleanor Elder, sister of Ann Elder, Shaw's secretary, was manager of the just-formed Arts League of Service Travelling Theatre, whose first programme was a triple bill, directed by W.G. Fay, consisting of *The Workhouse Ward*, Gertrude Jennings's *The Rest Cure* and Harold Brighouse's *The Price of Coal*. It toured the provinces for a fortnight from 26th May. The new book by William Ralph Inge, Dean of St Paul's, was his volume *Outspoken Essays*, which Shaw was to review enthusiastically later in the year.]

As Eleanor Elder has none of your scruples about consulting me, I had already written to Thring on the subject when your letter arrived.

My solution is that Eleanor's League should pay the Authors' Society 5% on her takings every week, and say what plays she has performed. The Society then, in the case of the specimen program given, credits Lady Gregory with one third of the performance, Harold Brighouse with the same, and Gertrude Jennings with the same. If The Image is given, Lady G. is credited with three thirds. If Blanco Posnet and the Workhouse Ward are given, then Shaw is credited with two thirds and Lady G. with one third. Two plays of equal length would count as three sixths each. At the end of the quarter or half year or tour, the Society takes the total sum sent by the Eleanor League and divides it among the authors in proportion to the totals of the performances credited to them. They are spared the indignity of touching their hats (and sending receipts) for half crowns. They get one substantial remittance; and the Society's bookkeeping is very simple.

I must read Inge's book. Charlotte has it.

I hope Margaret wont be infuriated by my Welsh references if you send her on that letter.

G.B.S.

SHAW TO LADY GREGORY
[ALS: Burgunder, Cornell]

Penlee. Near Dartmouth. Devon
4th September 1919

['Mr Seaghan' was Seaghan Barlow, the theatre carpenter who created the scenery for *Androcles*, first produced at the Abbey on 4th November 1919. Shaw had been in Parknasilla from 5th July to 26th August. Though Shaw's suggestion in this letter was obviously intended to be ironic, *Cæsar and Cleopatra* did receive a production at the Abbey in 1927.]

My dear Lady Gregory

I wash my hands of Androcles. Let Mr Seaghan do his worst, since you are resolved to murder my poor play. The apron is

easy; but how are you going to manage the revolving scene? If
you make an interval before and after the arena business the
movement of the play will be destroyed. However, there is no
use talking to you: you are simply the most obstinate and
unscrupulous devil on earth; and I well know the vanity of
remonstrance.

I believe the American lion was sold years ago. You will
probably have to fall back on a real one from the Zoo.

I left Ireland on the 26th August, and came hither via
Glastonbury (musical festival—three days), Bray (the
Berkshire Bray—a week end with Madame Vandervelde and
Sir Edward Elgar), and so hither, where I am starring at the
Fabian Summer School.

Charlotte, who is going up to Dublin from Parknasilla to stay
with Horace Plunkett, wants to drag me back across the
channel to take her home (poor lamb!); but Androcles frightens
me off. It would drive me out of my senses; and we should
quarrel violently and end with Seaghan in Glasnevin [cemetery]
and myself in Mountjoy [prison].

Why did I not go to Coole, and nip this nefarious conspiracy
in the bud?

But—I repeat—it wouldnt have been any use. I now await
your production of Caesar and Cleopatra.

Ever
G.B.S.

LADY GREGORY: *JOURNALS*
9th November [1919]

[Shaw's review of G.K. Chesterton's *Irish Impressions* appeared in the
Irish Statesman on 22nd November 1919. Lady Gregory was working
on her memoir of Hugh Lane; it had originally been promised to
Grant Richards but she was considering a transfer to John Murray,
who eventually published the book in 1921. The *Daily News* had
invited well-known public men and women to contribute 'thoughts'
for the two-minute silent tribute requested by the King on the first
anniversary of Armistice Day; Shaw's reply was not among those
published.]

Fog in London yesterday. I came to Ayot St Lawrence; G.B.S. met me at the station and motored me home, the light flashing on the narrow lane and the hedges, still brown and yellow and bronze. The house full of comfort and fires. He had just been writing a review of Chesterton's book on Ireland, read aloud a good deal of the book in the evening—the review will be better. Talking of the Dublin statues he says he had, when a child, a dream one night that he went out and went through the garden and at the end of it opened a gate and saw the sky all filled with wonderful light, and in the centre was God. And He was in the form of the statue of William III in College Green.

I have been consulting him about my book and Grant Richards trying to get it. He strongly advises Murray and tells me to go to Murray at once. It was he, he says, who helped Grant Richards ... to start in business. At that time it was almost impossible to publish plays and when G.R. set up and came to ask him for something, he gave him his plays *Pleasant and Unpleasant* and they were a great success. But then G.R. went bankrupt and he took a great deal of trouble trying to get this through, and says he would have got through but that the binders who had part of his stock and to whom he owed money, sold it off to pay themselves.

But Charlotte says 'G.B.S. is like that, he never will speak ill of anyone. But Grant Richards treated him very badly, owed him hundreds which he couldn't pay and because he had spent the money on his wife's extravagances—paying thousands for a pearl necklace for her. And G.B.S. was poor then, and though I had money he wanted some of his own. ...' He is very indignant at the King's proclamation ('a lying proclamation too, because we are still at war') ordering all work to cease for two minutes on Armistice Day. He asked what I thought and I said I thought it dreadful, I felt it an impertinence. We who love our dead will think of them—as ever—and those whose work is hindered and have none to care for will think impatiently. But I am sorry he sent his message to the *Daily News* calling it 'tomfoolery', it will be misunderstood. He meant the 'tomfoolery' of the King stopping factories and upsetting business by his royal word. He says he was in such a rage about it when the *Daily News* request came that he wrote it hastily.

SHAW TO LADY GREGORY
[APC (in Ann Elder's hand) S: Berg, NYPL]

10 Adelphi Terrace. [London]
11th December 1919

[Grant Richards had written to Lady Gregory on 9th December threatening to consult his solicitor over her decision to take the memoir of Hugh Lane away from him.]

I should leave Grant to get what comfort he can out of his solicitor. There is much to be said for writing the book first and consulting the authorities afterwards. The book not only has a chance of being written, but of being a work of art instead of a collection of memoranda.

G. Bernard Shaw

SHAW TO LADY GREGORY
[ALS: Burgunder, Cornell]

Lucan House. Lucan
12th April 1920

[Shaw was in Dublin from 5th April to 16th April, staying first with Sir Horace Plunkett at his house, Kilteragh, in Foxrock, and then with Charlotte's niece Cecily and her husband Capt. Richard St John Colthurst at Lucan. The references to Edgar of Ravenswood and Manfred are presumably to Verdi's opera and Tchaikovsky's symphony as much as to Scott's novel and Byron's poem. Lennox Robinson, reappointed manager of the Abbey in March 1919, following the departure of Fred O'Donovan, had had a busy season through 1919–20, hence his lack of time to write his own plays.]

Dear Lady Gregory
    We were unlucky today in not being able to catch you on your return (as I surmise) through Dublin. We changed from Foxrock to Lucan; and it so happened that Sir Horace's car was in demand to such an extent that we could not without inconvenience to him stop it even for half an hour in passing through Dublin: the non-stop run to Lucan just fitted in. As it was, a job I had to do for him kept us rather late in starting; and altogether

a visit to the Gresham [where Lady Gregory was staying] was impossible.

I saw the Devil's Disciple on Saturday afternoon [10th April]: an execrable performance, not improved by the hideous nervousness my presence set up. I can imagine that in the evening, with a less depressing audience and in finer weather, it goes better; but they are not up to my stage tricks anyhow, poor lambs! Essie [Sheila O'Grady] was a helpless oaf, too young and unused to the stage for her job. Dick [Arthur Shields] tried to be smart all through, and had no suspicion that the part should be played like Edgar of Ravenswood plus Manfred, and is full of sombre music. He was horribly discordant. Anderson [Peter Nolan] was sincere and promising; but he could not touch the explosion at the end of the second act, and left the audience jeering at him for having run away.

Burgoyne [F.J. McCormick] was too nervous to make his key words audible, and so dropped most of his points; but I can understand his scoring on ordinary occasions. But he has no idea of how to make that interrupted exit with 'By the way, bring Mrs Anderson too'.

Christy [Philip Guiry] was absolutely perfect: the best on record. Judith [May Craig] was not bad in the second act; but the third beat her: she couldnt cry and couldnt go Fantee at Burgoyne. Mrs Dudgeon [Christine Hayden] had the general hang of her part, but took her husband's death as became a lady who knew all about it beforehand.

The gallows scene was of course frankly impossible on that tiny stage without a crowd, an army, and a street. And the omission of a great deal of my stage business (as I produce it) made a difference; but nobody can do all that but myself.

Lennox says he has no time to write. I think that's a pity.

On Friday we cross back to Holyhead and proceed by road homeward, arriving at Ayot on Monday evening.

The weather has been vile ever since we arrived on Easter Monday.

My sister [Lucinda Frances Shaw] died on the 27th March; and I am now the last of the family. I shall complete the cinder path at Golder's Green in due time.

Ever
G.B.S.

SHAW TO LADY GREGORY
[ALS: Burgunder, Cornell]

Lucan House. Lucan
16th April 1920

[In 1915 most of the outlying land on the Coole estate had been sold
to the Congested Districts Board for division among small tenant
farmers. It was now planned to offer the remaining grazing land
within the demesne for sale to the tenants. However, a group of the
tenants had formed themselves into a 'committee' to try to negotiate
an exclusive purchase of the land and, having made an offer which
was too low to be acceptable, were pressing to be accepted as grazing
tenants. The situation was a very difficult one, with the local Sinn
Féin organisation in a position to intimidate any potential land
buyers or tenants of whom they did not approve, and the Congested
Districts Board unwilling to purchase land in the current political
climate. Lady Gregory was determined at all costs to keep the house
and adjoining lands for her grandson Richard, although her
daughter-in-law Margaret, to whom Coole actually belonged, was at
times disposed to sell the whole estate, house and all. A portion of the
land, without the house, was finally sold to the tenants' group in
October 1920. Shaw's 'Irish property', inherited from his sister and
maternal uncle, consisted at this time of seventeen pieces of property
in Carlow and a few in Wexford, from which ground rents were
earned.]

My dear Lady Gregory
    As far as I can see the only alternative to being carried to the
lake and invited to sign away the demesne lands at a derisory
price on pain of immediate drowning, is to return to London
and insist on a military occupation until normal dealing is
restored. There may be a way out open to mother wit; but I
cannot discover it.
    This Castle Government is, as I have often urged, nothing
but the forcible imposition of anarchy on the country. If the
people are taking advantage of it to get possession of the land by
hook or crook, small blame to them; but there is no guarantee
that a lawless redistribution will settle the land question any
better than the old lawful one in the long run. If your neigh-
bours can and will turn their cattle on to your demesne lands,
and the Government cannot prevent them, why, the cattle
must come; and you must come on the county for the

damage—or whatever else your legal remedy may be. Meanwhile the proprietors of the cattle will probably come to blows daily as to which are authentic Gort cattle, and which merely the strangers within your gates, also as to water, choice bits of pasture, and casualties in the private quarrels of the cattle themselves.

The would-be purchaser might also be open to demonstrations that you can give him no better title than you have yourself, and invite him to consider its value in the light of his liability to exactly the same treatment as you are receiving. Contracts made under duress are not binding.

I am writing very much at random, my own Irish property being town property of an airy and invulnerable kind (odds and ends of head rents); so you could hardly take a vainer opinion; but roughly it seems to me that in your place I should refuse to sell for less than enough to save the house and home enclosure, failing which I should let the cattle come, if they must, as trespassers. I should not dispute the general proposition that big reserves of land as park demesnes are doomed; and I should declare that if the County Council or any other body representing the Commune of Gort were to acquire the land for genuine public Irish use and profit by compulsory purchase I should not complain, but that to compel me to sell at a knock-out price, to a combination of land grabbers who might turn out to be worse employers and worse cultivators than I, would be only to change old landlords for new ones. I should urge that if my land were not safe no man's land would be safe, nor his house nor anything that is his, and that my park and Pat Murphy's potato patch had the same protection against being taken by any person that fancied them or any irresponsible combination of such persons, and that only the Irish nation had a right superior to mine — and who are yous, that calls yourself the Irish nation when you are only a pack of greedy grabbers that would turn a poor widow out of house and home and rob her little grandson etc etc etc etc etc; so shoot me or dhrownd me in the lake an' be dam to yez; for I'll stand be me homestead as Parnell tould me to, God be with him in glory. Anyhow, if the combination of *grande dame* and lone widda cannot prevail, what can?—I am writing great nonsense in the middle of my packing (we cross to Holyhead tonight); but I can think of nothing better; and even nonsense is sometimes suggestive.

Ever
G.B.S.

After the overwhelming victory of Sinn Féin candidates in southern Ireland in the 1918 General Election, the duly elected members refused to take up their seats in Westminster and established instead an independent parliament, Dáil Eireann. Though this was outlawed by the British in 1919, it continued to operate and to proclaim itself the true Republican government of the country, with an independent judicial system. The success of Sinn Féin, and of the guerrilla warfare waged by its military wing the Irish Republican Army, was such that by 1920 there were many parts of the country in which effectively the writ of British law did not run.

In the face of this situation, Sir Hamar Greenwood (formerly Grunebaum), Chief Secretary for Ireland (1920–22), reinforced the Royal Irish Constabulary in 1920 with numbers of undisciplined new recruits, many of them demobilised ex-soldiers, who from their mixed uniforms became known as the Black-and-Tans. Together with another force of Auxiliaries raised at the same time, they engaged in what amounted to a campaign of terrorism in reprisal for I.R.A. attacks. Although there was a great deal of press criticism of the Black-and-Tan outrages and the coalition government of Lloyd George, which continued in power until 1923, was under considerable political pressure over the situation in Ireland, Sir Hamar Greenwood continued to defend the police and military actions.

The guerilla war came very close to Lady Gregory at Coole, with attacks by the Black-and-Tans, shooting and looting in the local villages of Gort and Kiltartan. On 31st October 1920, she entered in her journal: 'Today I wrote to G.B.S., begging him to come over to Coole and examine into these Black and Tan horrors'.

SHAW TO LADY GREGORY
[TLS: Burgunder, Cornell]

10 Adelphi Terrace. [London]
[6th November 1920]

[Joseph Devlin, M.P. and head of the Ancient Order of Hibernians,
was an agitator for Home Rule. James Bryce, first Viscount Bryce,
jurist, diplomat, and Chief Secretary for Ireland under Campbell-
Bannerman, presided over a commission in September 1914 to consider alleged German atrocities. Winston Churchill, who was at this
time serving at the War Office and was to become Colonial Secretary
in 1921, took a hard line on Ireland, defending the policy of reprisals.
Shaw spent from 19th July to 21st September in Parknasilla, during
which time he was at work revising *Back to Methuselah* (which he had
completed on 27th May), preparing it for the printer.]

My dear Lady Gregory
    What would be the use? What need have we of witnesses?
The Daily News, The Manchester Guardian, The Times, and
all the anti-Coalition papers are publishing enough news of
burnings and slaughterings to make Timour the Tartar turn in
his grave. The Government replies that (a) they are all the work
of Sinn Feiners disguised in the uniforms they have stolen, and
(b) they are more than justified by the provocation given. The
incident of the woman at Kiltartan who was shot as unprotected
game with her child in her arms by a passing police sportsman
from a lorry has been in every paper here that I have seen; and
Sir H.G. has handsomely owned that it was an unfortunate
mistake, though *for what* he did not say. Meanwhile Asquith
thunders from every platform about the business, and is reported. Under these circumstances what earthly use is there in
adding one baby more to the record of the slaughter of the
innocents?
    The Meeting held in one of the Committee Rooms of the
House of Commons on the 25th October by the National Peace
Conference people was of the most ghastly futility. Plunkett
and Devlin spoke: so did I. But the others drivelled about
publishing information and rousing the conscience of England.
I am asked every day by virtuously indignant Liberals with
their eyes in the ends of the earth as usual, to join Anti-Reprisal
Societies and speak at Anti-Reprisal meetings. The Freeman's

Journal wants me to join in asking for an enquiry by the Bryce Committee which investigated the Belgian atrocities. All this hysteria is very British and very useless. In vain do I point out that the Prime Minister has given himself away by his submarine, floating mine, poison gas scare, and Churchill by his wild warnings against 'the fearful danger' of Ireland, because as everything they say of Ireland applies with tenfold force to France, America, and all the other Powers, we can appeal to the League of Nations and to the United States to protest against a new policy which menaces them just as much as us. As usual, I cannot get the Irish question out of the old grooves. An appeal signed by Plunkett, by you, and by half a dozen other eminent Irish persons (I offered to draft it) would make the Government sit up. But no: everybody prefers to go on screaming and clamouring for more telescopes to enable the English (entrusted, as Asquith says, by Providence with the duty of governessing Ireland) to see the sun at noon.

I have had a fearfully bad conscience with regard to you for months and months past. We spent a couple of months at Parknasilla, where I had in my desk your letter asking me to write something about Hugh Lane. But there were piles of other letters—a few of them equally sacred—and it was plain to me that unless I hardened my heart and set the completion of my great Methuselah pentalogy absolutely before everything, I should die leaving it unfinished. I gave up all my engagements in England; and when I left Kerry the book was complete and in the hands of the printer; but not a letter was answered.

What became of the screed I wrote [in 1912] about the Dublin National Gallery when that subscription was got up which had to be returned? That was very much what you wanted, I think.

I write in great haste, and address this to Coole, as it seems improbable that you are at Burrin now that the weather has turned to hideous fog and cold.

Ever
G.B.S.

SHAW TO LADY GREGORY
[TLS: Burgunder, Cornell]

10 Adelphi Terrace. London
[c. 20th March 1921]

[Sara Allgood, known to her friends as Sally, had been out of the Abbey company since 1915, though she had recently offered to return. The matinée referred to, for which Shaw had 'done his bit', was in all probability the Abbey Theatre Irish matinée, to be given at the Royal Court Theatre in London on 10th June, which Shaw finally was unable to attend. It is not clear what his contribution to it was, nor what was enclosed as 'documentary proof'. He had rehearsed Sara Allgood in the Stage Society production of *O'Flaherty V.C.* (19th-20th December 1920), and had noted an appointment in his engagement diary to see her on 11th March 1921. *Aristotle's Bellows*, Lady Gregory's latest play, had been produced at the Abbey on 17th March. An unsigned review of Lady Gregory's *Hugh Lane's Life and Achievement*, by A. Clutton Brock, art critic of *The Times*, appeared on 10th March in the *TLS*.]

My dear Lady Gregory

The enclosed from Sally Not In Our Alley is documentary proof that I have already done my bit for the matinée. As to the other things you suggest, I feel provoked to say that if the child needs so much nursing it had better die. Why should it survive when so many other children are being killed? The war and Sir Haman Grunebaum have destroyed my susceptibility to any calamity involving less than the death of ten million babies. When they discussed the best means of protecting St. Pauls against fire, Dean Inge's sole contribution to the debate was 'Let it burn'. I feel like that about the Abbey. Let it go smash. Then you will have to turn it into a Cinema house and make it comfortable. After that it can go back to the drama, redecorated, reseated, and even rebuilt.

Anyhow I am so utterly dead beat by six months continuous work without even a Sunday out that I am leaving London on the 2nd for a little tour in Wales or somewhere; and if the existence of the Abbey is incompatible with that, the Abbey shall perish. I think I should do you a good turn by demolishing it, though I should like to see Aristotle's Bellows very much.

If it were anyone else than you who had sworn to recapture

the Lane pictures, I should say that the feat is impossible. The review in the Times Literary Supplement saying that your case must be answered has elicited a bundle of letters declaring that it has been answered, and that there is no sort of doubt that Hugh fully intended the pictures to go to London, and was keeping the unwitnessed will in reserve only in case London should refuse them. This is an emaciated hypothesis; but it is good enough for acquisitive, victorious England. And it serves the Dublin corporation right. Besides, who cares for schools of Colorists nowadays. The only colors in vogue are black and tan. Even Charlotte has given up the idea of visiting Ireland at present: at least she has consented to Wales in spite of the blandishments of Horace Plunkett. But that is perhaps because I will not go, as I have to do a lecturing tour for the Labor Party in Scotland and the North. I have given up the Dublin people as hopeless. I might as well talk to the cockles on Sandymount Strand. They are not a bit in earnest about the national question, and never have been. It is something to talk about: that is all. Ask them to draft a Bill—! Yah!

Ever
G.B.S.

[Lady Gregory commented on this letter in her journal for 22nd March: '... a letter for me from G.B.S. refusing a lecture for our Theatre fund. He says he is overworked and I'm afraid it is true, but I wish some of his work could be given to Ireland'. In spite of this refusal, Shaw agreed subsequently to give a lecture in a series organised in London by J.B. Fagan in aid of the Abbey, on 27th May. Announced as 'The Spur of the Moment', an overliteral interpretation of Shaw's indication that he would speak impromptu, it in fact turned into a reading of the first two acts of the as-yet unpublished *Back to Methuselah*.]

LADY GREGORY: *JOURNALS*

[13th May 1921]

[*Back to Methuselah* would be given its first production by the Theatre Guild (the company that had produced *Heartbreak House*) at the Garrick Theatre, New York, in February and March 1922. Although

Shaw wrote the preface to *Immaturity* in the summer of 1921, the novel
was not finally published until 1930, when it appeared as the first
volume of Shaw's Collected Edition. Margaret Gregory was with a
group, driving home from a tennis-party on 16th May 1921, when the
car they were in was ambushed and her four companions, Capt.
C.A.M. Blake, District Inspector of the R.I.C., and his wife, Capt.
F.W.M. Cornwallis and Lt. R.B. McCeery, both of the 17th Lancers,
were all shot dead.]

... I came to Ayot St Lawrence. ... G.B.S. and Charlotte came
to meet me, he back from his Scotch lecturing, had immense
audiences. I asked what his moral purpose was in speaking to
the Scotch—what he was doing for them. He said he wasn't
doing them any good, that was the worst of it. He had gone to
lecture for the Fabian Society of Edinburgh, and when in
Scotland some time ago he had an audience of working men and
tried to help them; now he had a paying audience of many of the
well-to-do; but he must have set up that Fabian Society for ever
and ever.

He is pleased that *Heartbreak House* has had a good run [from
15th December 1920 to 9th February 1921] to a steady house in
America. After it had been accepted, the producer, a man with
a German name [Emmanuel Reicher], wrote to him, many
compliments, but saying he found it necessary to make several
cuts. G.B.S. sent a cable saying he was returning the £500 he
had been given in advance, as he would not allow this. The
answer was 'Producer sacked. Play proceeding', and no cuts
were made. He says you must either have a light play to go a
couple of hours or one that will take at least three hours and that
the audience will remember through their lifetime. *Methuselah*
is to be played in three nights and a matinée, and no one may
take a ticket for one performance only. ... A collected edition of
his works is coming out at £1.1 a volume, and he is writing
prefaces, giving his autobiography in that way, all that need
ever be told of him. Now that his mother and sister are dead
there is no one to be annoyed and he can tell the tale of his
father's drunkenness. I say it was his father's dreams when he
had been drinking which, speech failing at the same time would
not let him tell out, that are now being expressed by him! ...

In the evening I read *Aristotle's Bellows* to them. Both liked it.

He said it was a 'wonderful thing', 'homogeneous like a poem', and the language richer even than before—that if it is published with *Dragon* and *Jester* (which he remembers from my reading it two years ago) it will make a wonderful book. ...

6 [for 16] May. I read the Preface to *Methuselah* this morning —the 'nine months of gestation' in ? pages, and he read the last act tonight, a history of the race—a philosophy of its life— terrible in parts but leading to the freedom and life of the spirit at the last. He had tried to humanise his people, wrote a sort of domestic drama as a continuation of Eden ['The Domesticity of Franklyn Barnabas', later deleted], but Granville Barker said it was wrong, and he saw then that he must keep to this subject of the continuance of life. ...

The MSS of *Immaturity*, his first novel, never published, arrived today, all written in the most beautiful clear handwriting. He wrote five novels in all, without enthusiasm or much hope of their being taken. 'I bought sixpence worth of paper at a time, and wrote five pages a day, just to form a habit, but I was thought to be indolent, but I was sometimes so tired of it that when I came to the end of my five pages I would stop even in the middle of a line'.

17 May. This morning when I went down I said to G.B.S. 'I am happy to find that in spite of having travelled through the ages in your play I was still able to say my prayers'. He said 'There is bad news in the papers—but Margaret is not hurt', and told me of the shooting of Captain Blake and his wife and the two officers, and then I saw a telegram from Margaret for me 'Sole survivor of five murdered in ambushed motor'. It was a bad shock—the thought of the possibilities ... And then, though she is safe thank God, it is impossible to know how it will affect her outlook and the life of the children, and through them mine. I was quite broken up—went into the air for a while, and then when I came back, kind G.B.S. made coffee for me and spoke comfortably and wanted me to stay, but I thought I might be wanted at Coole and must get to London. Then he offered to motor me up, but I wouldn't let him waste his morning, but accepted the motor, and on my way sent a telegram asking Margaret if I should return. But in the afternoon an answer came 'No need, many thanks'.

SHAW: POEM FOR CATHERINE AND ANNE GREGORY

[AMS (on five postcards): Sotheby's, December 1979]

[16th October 1921]

[While gathering in apples from the orchard at Burren, Lady Gregory gave to her granddaughters, Anne and Catherine, one tree of Crofton apples for their own. They sent some of these to Shaw, who responded, as Lady Gregory noted in her journal: '19 October. G.B.S. wrote to the children, in return for the scarlet Croftons they sent him, some lines, and on such charming postcards, Reynolds' Angels, and Age of Innocence, Steen's Grace before meat, a girl's head by Greuze, De Hoogh's Dutch courtyard, with a child. They are delighted'. The poem was written on the back of the five picture postcards, reproductions of paintings in the London National Gallery. These cards were stolen from Sotheby's prior to their scheduled sale.]

I

Two ladies of Galway named Cath'rine and Anna
Whom some called acushla and some called alanna
On finding the gate of the fruit garden undone
Stole grandmamma's apples and sent them to London

II

And grandmamma said that the poor village
    schoolchildren
Were better behaved than the well-brought-up Coole
    children
And threatened them with the most merciless whippings
If ever again they laid hands on her pippins

III

In vain they explained that the man who was battening
On grandmother's apples would die without fattening
    She seized the piano
    And threw it at Anna
Then shrieking at Catherine 'Just let me catch you'
She walloped her hard with the drawingroom statue.

IV

'God save us, Herself is gone crazy' cried Marian
'Is this how a lady of title should carry on?'
'If you dare to address me like that', shouted Granny,
'Goodbye to your wages: you shant have a penny:
Go back to your pots and your pans and your canisters'
With that she threw Marian over the banisters.

V

'And now' declared Granny, 'I feel so much better
That I'll write Mr Shaw a most beautiful letter
And tell him how happy our lives are at Coole
Under Grandmamma Darling's beneficent rule'.

G.B.S.

LADY GREGORY: *JOURNALS*

20th January [1922]

[Following a lunch given by the British Government to honour
Molière's tercentenary, Shaw had spoken supporting the vote of
thanks for a lecture on Molière by the French Academician Maurice
Donnay, reported in the *Morning Post* and other papers on 19th
January. Edith Somerville, who was a cousin of Shaw's wife
Charlotte, was the surviving member of the writing partnership of
Somerville and Ross, whose great popular success had been *Some
Experiences of an Irish R.M.* The 'dreadful play' she had sent Shaw
was *A Horse! A Horse!*, a dramatised version of one of the Irish R.M.
stories, in which Flurry Knox was one of the principal characters.
Edith Somerville took Shaw's devastatingly critical reaction to her
play in good part, writing to thank him on 21st January [ALS: BL]: 'I
am *most sincerely* grateful to you and deeply recognise the value of all
that you say'.

At this stage, the Treaty of 1921 had been signed, establishing the
Irish Free State of twenty-six counties, excluding six counties of
Ulster, and power had been formally transferred to a provisional
government under the chairmanship of Michael Collins on 16th
January 1922. However, Éamon De Valera had refused to accept the
Treaty and had already seceded from the Dáil with a minority of

Republicans, a split which was to lead to the Civil War later in the year.]

I lunched at 10 Adelphi Terrace, so very pleasant. ...

G.B.S. full of the Molière lunch and meeting at which he had spoken. The lunch was given by 'The Government'—the Commissioner of Public Works, 'I suppose because Molière wrote "works" they thought he came into his Department'. There was a difficulty in getting anyone who could talk French to sit next the guest of the evening, so he was put there. ... He ... had made the witty speech about the four great men, Dante, Shakespeare, Goethe, Molière I had seen already reported. It was Paul Bourget who had said [in an article on Molière in *L'Illustration*, 14th January 1922] ... that these great men reflected the qualities of their nations, but he could only say that he had travelled in Italy and never met a Dante, and if there were Goethes in Germany they must have had influenza when he was there; and as to Shakespeare, look at our leading men and see which of them is like him. If they had worked at the Versailles treaty Dante would have approached it from his attitude of law giver; Shakespeare as an Englishman was a born anarchist; Molière alone would have given expression to the mind of the people. ...

E.S. had sent him 'a dreadful play' to criticise, and he had written her his opinion of it; that she ought to have given up that old opinion of the Irish upper classes that the peasant was ridiculous in poverty, in dishonesty, in dirt. I said it was the Gaelic League that had changed that, changed the table of values, made it ridiculous not to speak bad English but bad Irish, though they refrained from ridiculing the speaker; and they agreed. 'She had made Flurry Knox marry the niece, the young lady, and I wrote to her that he was nothing but a stableboy, and that if Molière made Scapin no better, anyhow he didn't marry him to Hyacinth'.

I asked when he would come back to Ireland but he said 'No, I'll not go. I would be treated as the common enemy'. I said De Valera had promised to join the others against a common enemy, so he might come to unite the two parties. He said 'I am growing fonder of England now, as Napoleon grew fonder of France than of Corsica because he had conquered it. One always loves the country one has conquered best, and I have conquered England; they hang on every word from my lips. There must be few English gentlemen left for this country, and they will have to come from Ireland, they have none of the old graces here'.

SHAW TO LADY GREGORY
[APCS: Burgunder, Cornell]

Ayot St Lawrence. Welwyn
12th February 1922

[Shaw's reluctant agreement to Lady Gregory's request for *The Man of Destiny* resulted in a production at the Abbey on 9th March, directed by Lennox Robinson, with P.J. Carolan playing Napoleon and Eileen Crowe the Strange Lady. It was performed as a double bill with George Shiels's three-act comedy, *Insurance Money*. The 'sanguinary news from Clones' in Co. Monaghan was of an IRA attack at the railway station on a party of Special Constabulary en route to Eniskillen, in which four constables had been killed, eight wounded and six apparently taken prisoner by the IRA, which suffered one death.]

Yes, if you think it wise. The play is an awkward length: however, you are accustomed to fill in with short plays at the Abbey. But merely excellent actors are no use whatever for Napoleon and the Strange Lady. They have to hold the stage for an hour; and unless they are stars of the strongest magic, the result is ghastly. The speech about the English always brings down the house *in England*. Nothing flatters men more than to treat them as irresistibly successful rascals. I doubt if the Irish will laugh with the right side of their mouths. And do you think, in view of the sanguinary news from Clones this morning, that comedy will be in tune? I should think twice, on all accounts, before meddling with that play. It has *never* been acted well enough to succeed.

G.B.S.

By the summer of 1922 the split between the Republicans led by De Valera and those who supported the Free State had become a bloody civil war. The Shaws holidayed in Rosslare from 7th to 19th August. On their way back to England through Dublin on the 19th they dined with Horace Plunkett at Kilteragh and met Michael Collins, who had recently succeeded Arthur Griffith as the head of the Free State government. Shaw was to recall the meeting with Collins years later in a letter to Lord Alfred Douglas (9th November 1940): 'His nerves were in rags: his hand kept slapping his revolver all the time he was talking pleasantly enough' [TLS: private collection of Lady Eccles]. Three days later, on 22nd August, Collins was shot in an ambush in Cork. Shaw wrote to his sister [John Lavery, *The Life of a Painter* (1940)]:

Dear Miss Collins

Dont let them make you miserable about it: how could a born soldier die better than at the victorious end of a good fight, falling to the shot of another Irishman—a damned fool, but all the same an Irishman who thought he was fighting for Ireland—'a Roman to a Roman'?

I met Michael for the first and last time on Saturday last, and am very glad I did. I rejoice in his memory, and will not be so disloyal to it as to snivel over his valiant death.

So tear up your mourning and hang up your brightest colors in his honor; and let us all praise God that he had not to die in a snuffy bed of a trumpery cough, weakened by age, and saddened by the disappointments that would have attended his work had he lived.

Sincerely
Bernard Shaw

The Anglo-Irish war had seen the burning of a number of Irish country houses, including Derry, the house in Co. Cork in which Charlotte Shaw had been born. In the winter of 1922–23, the Republicans attacked the houses of the supporters of the Free State including its Senators. In two successive night raids, on 29th and 30th January 1923, Kilteragh was destroyed, while Horace Plunkett, who had accepted nomination to the Senate, was away in America.

SHAW TO LADY GREGORY
[ALS: Burgunder, Cornell]

The Hotel Metropole. Minehead. Somerset
8th April 1923

[In Ireland Catholics of the name of Quinn commonly spell their name with two 'n's, Protestants with one. James Penrose had been a fellow-worker in C. Uniacke Townshend's land-agent's office during Shaw's employment there as a clerk 1871–76. Horace Plunkett had very recently had a prostate gland operation. The article Shaw refers to as 'How to Settle Ireland' was 'How to Restore Order in Ireland', which first appeared in the *New York American* on 5th to 7th March 1923.]

My dear Lady Gregory
   Do you know the address of John Quin (or has he two ns?)? James Penrose, who was in Townshend's office with me in the seventies, has a picture of Venus Rising from the Sea by the Irish painter James Barry, whose heroic pictures are known to people who attend the Society of Arts in the Adelphi. James's grandfather bought it from Barry to encourage him, and was 'read out' of the Quakers' meeting to which he belonged for possessing it. James, hard up like all Irish gentlemen, wants to sell it, and asks me how he should set about it. I have given him all the advice I can; but it suddenly occurs to me that as the picture is a rare sample of a rather extraordinary Irishman, it ought either to be in the Dublin National Gallery or in the collection of Quin, who might possibly bequeath it to his nation. Anyhow, I thought I would just ask you for Q's address, and give it to J.P.
   We are here on a vast slob of dreary mud which is inundated for a few hours daily by the Bristol Channel; and we propose to wander about in the old car until we go to Stratford for the first week in May, for the Shakespear Festival. As it is a wet Sunday I have time to write an unnecessary letter for the first time for months and months and months, and accordingly make Penrose, Barry and Venus an excuse for writing to you. And now I have no news for you, as you know everything that I know, probably, and more. Plunkett has got over his horrible operation. Yeats pressed me to join the Irish senate, and thereby incited me to write my article on How to Settle Ireland which I

sent to the Hearst Press as the only way of getting it into all the Irish papers, but without much success; for they all funked it more or less except the Irish Times. My remedy—to arm the whole Irish people and impose compulsory police service on all men of military age—only terrified them.

One advantage about the burning of the chateaux is that there will soon be no place to shelter us in Ireland but Coole, where, by the way, we should be much better and happier than here in Minehead. But I dare not approach you now, as they might burn even you for the sake of roasting me.

Ever
G.B.S.

LADY GREGORY: *JOURNALS*

19th May [1923]

I came down to Ayot by a train an hour too soon ... So I walked about the village, and then G.B.S. came in his little car. ... G.B.S. drove me home, and talked of his *Joan of Arc* play [commenced on 29th April]. He has not read Mark Twain [*Personal Recollections of Joan of Arc*], is afraid of being influenced by him. He has read a little of Anatole France [*Life of Joan of Arc*] and is reading the evidence at the trial [Jules Quicherat, *Procès de Jeanne d'Arc*, tr. T. Douglas Murray]; it was published some years ago. He does not idealise her as Mark does, and defends the Church, 'it didn't torture her'. I think there will be something good about the English soldiers. ...

20 May. ... G.B.S. read me the opening of his first act or scene of *Joan of Arc*. A fine and spirited opening, gay and yet getting much of the spiritual side of Joan. I asked about the end, the execution would be too tragic and he thinks so; he thinks of having a final scene of the rehabilitation, the canonisation of a Protestant, which he says is what she was and confessed to being in her examination. He had been working at the play without talking of it, but the other day [John] Drinkwater came to see him and remonstrate with him for having omitted to acknowledge his *Cromwell* [published 1922] which had 'A most laudatory dedication to me'. And he had said 'As you are

writing about historical characters I had better warn you that I
am writing a play on Joan of Arc'. 'So next day it was in the
papers, and I have had letters from every actress in the Kingdom asking for parts, and a distressed one from a Manager who
had commissioned [Lawrence] Binyon to write one on Joan.
But he does not seem to have begun it'. As we were going
upstairs he showed me a letter he had written in [*Times*] *Literary
Supplement* [17th May 1922] on 'Printed Plays' in which he says
'Some writers have a natural gift for writing dialogue and need
no training, and the first that come to mind in a literary sense
are Molière, Goldsmith, Chesterton and Lady Gregory'. Good
company to wind up the day with.

Today talking of Frank Harris and his faults 'If you ask him
to dinner and put him next a cocotte he will talk to her of
nothing but Jesus Christ, and if you put him beside a Duchess
he will talk to her as no one else would but to a cocotte. Yet he
never shows respect to meanness. George Moore on the other
hand, though his success is a triumph of industry, never does
homage to what is highest'. It is curious he says that the most
indecent writers just now should be three Irishmen, Harris,
Moore and Joyce. I think it is reaction from the Roman Catholic
teaching. ...

G.B.S. says he chose Joan of Arc because of Bernhardt and
others having played so many parts turning on sexual attraction
he wanted to give Joan as a heroine absolutely without that side.
And this he emphasises in the first scene, though keeping her
charm.

In all the revision of novels and business letters of these last
years he had felt as if his imagination had vanished, that he was
'done'. And now in the discovery that he writes as well as ever
he had grown young again, looks better than for years past,
though complaining of aches and pains from sawing wood,
which he has taken to for exercise. ...

21 May. ... Last night I asked if I might read a play to G.B.S.
... L[ennox] R[obinson] had written a note on it 'I rather like
this and think it might play amusingly, but I've read so many
bad plays in the last three days that my judgement may be
warped'. I thought it hopelessly bad but without saying
anything asked leave to read it. At the end G.B.S. burst out
'Piffle from the Sandymount sea front!' I showed him L.R.'s

note and he wrote under it 'Lock Lennox up at once. He has G.P.I (General Paralysis of the Insane) the thing is manifest piffle'! So I need give no opinion at all. A great relief. ...

24 May ... G.B.S. just before I left read me a new scene he had written in the morning, the relief of Orleans in a scene between Joan and Dunois and a boy. 'The wind' long waited for comes and is shewn to the audience by the waving of the pennon. I said if I had been writing it for Kiltartan I should have made the little boy sneeze.

SHAW TO LADY GREGORY

[ALS: Berg, NYPL]

Ayot St Lawrence. Welwyn
11th June 1923

[Shaw here refers to the American playbroking firm of Samuel French and the American Play Company, founded by Elisabeth Marbury, which represented him.]

I strenuously disapprove. French charges you £20.13.10, and gets all the work done by the American Play company or some other agency for £10.6.11. The A.P.C. would have done it for you for the same money 10% [circled]; so you have just made a present of £10–6-11 to Samuel French for nothing.

GBS

The Shaws went to Ireland on 17th July 1923 and spent from 19th July to 14th August at Glengarriff, 15th August to 18th September in Parknasilla, where, on 24th August, Shaw finished *Saint Joan*. On 31st July he wrote to the *Times*, scoffing at those who were afraid to come to Ireland because of the continuing unrest following on the ending of the Civil War in April, and comparing Irish holiday conditions favourably with those in England and Europe: 'there is not the smallest reason why Glengarriff and Parknasilla should not be crowded this year with refugees from the turbulent sister island and the revolutionary Continent, as well as by connoisseurs in extraordinarily beautiful scenery and in air which makes breathing a luxury'. But in spite of this encomium, the Shaws' holiday had got off to a bad start with a dock strike and was to conclude with Shaw's fall on the rocks at Parknasilla, in which he was quite seriously hurt. Although there were promises of a visit to Coole the following year, Shaw was in fact never to return to Ireland.

SHAW TO LADY GREGORY
[APCS: Berg, NYPL]

Eccles Hotel. Glengarriff. Co. Cork
8th August 1923

[Shaw had written to Yeats on 2nd July from Glengarriff to suggest agreed terms for what seems to have been a proposal for a production involving plays by both of them at the Neighborhood Playhouse, New York [ALS: NLI]. On 23rd August he wrote a postcard from Parknasilla, this time addressed to Merrion Square, repeating the substance of the earlier letter [APCS: NLI]. The first British production of *Back to Methuselah* by the Birmingham Repertory Theatre took place on 9th-13th October. Though Shaw took some of the rehearsals, the play was directed by H.K. Ayliff.]

Yes: here we are, with our main luggage strikebound at Fishguard, and Charlotte washing her stockings every day. Where is W.B. Yeats? I wrote to him on business (theatrical) to 73 Stephens Green, and can get no answer from him. I am afraid I shall have to go back from here or Parknasilla to rehearse Methuselah.

G.B.S.

SHAW TO LADY GREGORY
[APCS: Burgunder, Cornell]

10 Adelphi Terrace. [London]
23rd October 1923

Alas! I finished up at Parknasilla by slipping on the rocks and driving my camera through my ribs. Regulation surgery being quite useless, I had to get back as best I could to within reach of an osteopath [Elmer T. Pheils], who saw me through at Birmingham and set me to rights. I can now sneeze without horrid pangs. So Coole is off, unhappily, until next year. Charlotte looked forward eagerly to Ireland, but did not enjoy it a bit: in fact my accident saved her from going melancholy mad. I believe it did me good too.

G.B.S.

LADY GREGORY TO SHAW
[ALS: BL]

Abbey Theatre. Dublin
13th November 1923

[*John Bull's Other Island* was revived at the Abbey from 5th to 10th November. Many Republicans who had fought during the Civil War had been imprisoned: some 420 of them, in Mountjoy and Kilmainham jails, went on hunger strike. A letter protesting against the strike, and asking for concessions both from the Republican side and from the Government, appeared in the Irish papers on 13th November, signed by Lady Gregory, Lennox Robinson and James Stephens. Two of the hunger-strikers died later in November; the strike was then called off.]

Dear G.B.S.

Just a line to say that although we hadn't quite as good audiences as we ought (because of the Republican appeal to abstain from amusements) I never saw greater appreciation of 'John Bull'. I had been a little anxious—because of the complete change in political circumstance—but that made no difference in the delight in the play. Rather different sentences were applauded. Had some English grievances received with great sympathy—but no applause at all at [Matthew Haffigan's line] 'we'll cut the cable ourselves some day' which used to rouse the house. It was beautifully acted—our home-grown Broadbent [Barry Fitzgerald] a great success. Dublin quiet—but I am moved by the thought of the remaining hunger strikers. The authorities seem to think that all but a few, perhaps half a dozen—will give in—and that this residue must be allowed to die. They will certainly be the men with most courage, the ones one has most sympathy for. I think it is only opinion from the English side that will move our Government. I wish you could feel inclined to help. I go home on Wednesday. Love to you and Charlotte.

A Gregory

———————

Saint Joan was given its English première in London at the New Theatre on 26th March 1924, and was published on 25th June. Lady Gregory was in London on Lane pictures business and saw the Shaws briefly on 20th June, as she noted in her journal:

He was just going off to Constable to sign some of his books—was going to send me one but I begged for it at once that I might read it before the play (though he didn't want me to do so) and he found a copy upstairs and gave it to me and wrote my name. And gave me also stalls for the performance. Charlotte told me he had 'put in my sneeze' (that I had suggested at Ayot). I was quite pleased.

Lady Gregory was admiring both of the play—'a very fine piece of work even for him'—and of the performance (*Journals*, 24th June): 'Last night *St. Joan*. Wonderful and beautiful; but terrible in parts'. Yeats, much less enthusiastic, communicated his reaction in a letter to Lady Gregory, recorded in her journal on 15th July with her dissenting opinion:

Yeats in his note to me says 'I saw *St. Joan* last night and liked all the ecclesiastical part, thought it even noble, but hated Joan and the actress. Shaw is a dialectician and his genius leaves him when he leaves dialectics. I thought Joan half

Cockney slut and half nonconformist preacher. To speak with God and have neither simplicity nor dignity is incredible'. I don't agree with him at all. The Spirit was speaking through a country girl, not with her.

SHAW TO LADY GREGORY
[APCS: Burgunder, Cornell]

[Oban]
[1st September 1924]

[This was the first year the Shaws had taken their summer holiday in Scotland. Samuel Johnson visited the Scottish Highlands and the Hebrides with Boswell in autumn 1773, a visit described in his *A Journey to the Western Islands of Scotland.*]

Yes: we are repeating Dr Johnson's expedition, and have quite forgotten what sunshine and dry days are like. It rains and rains and rains and rains as if God's order to Cease Raining after the Flood had not reached the Highlands, or been defied there on principle. I wish you were here to talk to.

We shall not be back for some weeks yet.

You will hardly get round a Labor Committee by argument or sentiment; but if you could shew them the pictures—!

G.B.S.

SHAW TO LADY GREGORY
[APCS: Berg, NYPL]

10 Adelphi Terrace. London
3rd October 1924

[Ann Coppinger was an actress who performed frequently in Abbey Theatre productions.]

Is Ann Coppinger all right?

If so, tear this up and think no more of it. I have given Ann an appointment for Friday the 10th on the strength of her giving you as a reference; and as the audacities and mendacities of wandering women who want to get at me have destroyed all my faith in human nature I thought I would give you time to correct her if she has strained her credit with you.

When I say 'all right' I mean in reason, of course.

G.B.S.

SHAW TO LADY GREGORY
[APCS: Burgunder, Cornell]

10 Adelphi Terrace. London
22nd November 1924

[Lady Gregory did not take up Shaw's suggestion of performing *Back to Methuselah* instead of the unavailable *Saint Joan* at the Abbey. The complete five-play cycle, however, was to be seen in Dublin, produced by the Gate Theatre in 1930.]

Not possible. Sybil Thorndike is to take St. J. round the big cities.

Why on earth doesnt the Abbey do Methuselah? It is quite easy, and very popular; yet it produces an impression of tremendous enterprise and difficulty and exclusiveness.

G.B.S.

SHAW TO LADY GREGORY
[APCS: Berg, NYPL]

[Welwyn]
[Postmarked 28th April 1925]

[Sara Allgood, who had returned to the Abbey for a time, creating the part of Juno in Sean O'Casey's *Juno and the Paycock* in 1924, now had once again left the company. The Abbey was closing for a month on 2nd May, while the company performed in Cork. The two Shaw plays were not produced.]

Sarah Allgood wants to hang on at the Abbey with Mrs Warren's Profession and Getting Married. I can't quite see how, if it be worth her while to risk that, it is not also worth the Abbey's while instead of shutting up. Why is it shutting up? Can you put, me wise in any way?

GBS

SHAW TO LADY GREGORY

[TLS: Burgunder, Cornell]

Passfield Corner. Liphook. Hants
10th June 1925

[Sidney and Beatrice Webb were Shaw's closest associates in the Fabian Society. The Charles Macdona Company, a well-known touring company, performed almost entirely in the provinces, its repertoire consisting mainly of Shaw's plays. Macdona's Dublin production of *Saint Joan* opened on 22nd June at the Gaiety Theatre for a week's run. Sybil Thorndike and her husband Lewis Casson toured *Saint Joan* extensively in Britain and abroad with their own company in the years following the first London production.]

My dear Lady Gregory

I am staying here with the Sidney Webbs for a day or two for change of air. On the 13th May I spoke at a public meeting in my best form. A minute or two later, on rising to go home I found myself thunderstruck by some malignant affliction from the skies. I crawled to Adelphi Terrace and remained under the curse for exactly thirty days, when, to the hour and minute, I suddenly found myself well again. They called it influenza; but evidently it was a lunar phenomenon.

The Macdona company is taking St Joan to Dublin. Sybil Thorndike's husband, in a moment of aberration, let it slip through his fingers; and Dorothy Holmes Gore will create the part for Dublin. It would have ruined the Abbey, and ruined me (relatively): only a biggish house could stand the length of its cast and the price of its costumes and scenic fit-up. So thank your stars that you are delivered from temptation.

I have not your letter before me, only a report of it from London; so I may be omitting to answer things apart from St

Joan. Also I am writing to Coole though you may be in Dublin.
I shall see on Thursday evening, when I go up.

Ever
G.B.S.

LADY GREGORY: *JOURNALS*

30th June [1925]

[*The Intelligent Woman's Guide to Socialism and Capitalism*, which was
eventually to be published in 1928, had been inspired by a request to
Shaw from Charlotte's sister Mary Cholmondeley for a few of his ideas
on socialism to present to a Shropshire women's study circle. Lennox
Robinson's 'The Madonna of Slieve Dun', the ironic story of an Irish
country girl who imagines herself as the Virgin, had been published in
the first issue of the short-lived journal *To-Morrow* in August 1924,
provoking accusations of blasphemy.]

Ayot St Lawrence, in peace and luxury! ... G.B.S. is writing a
book on Socialism because Charlotte's sister had asked for some
instruction on it to convey to her class, and says he could have
written three plays in the time it has taken. Tonight the wireless
has been turned on, the first time I had heard it with a loud
speaker. I liked it no better than before, except when the music
was low sometimes—and the soldiers' song from Faust. But I
hated the voice giving news, and any ordinary news coming so
late may break one's peace.
  2 July. Back from Ayot yesterday. Talking of L[ennox]
R[obinson]'s story, G.B.S. said that when he was a boy he had
taken up and read a book given to one of the maids by a priest.
Its subject was the delight and profit it should be to young girls
to dwell and meditate on the delightful rapture of the Blessed
Virgin before the birth of Christ. I said 'During her pregnancy'
—'No, on what caused her pregnancy'.
  I spoke seriously to him about Hugh Lane, his codicil and his
last wishes and said 'I know you talk as you do to tease me'
(saying they never will be such asses as to give up the pictures)
'but now when the last fight comes on remember that your
sayings go round the world'. Charlotte said afterwards 'He
immensely admires the way you have held on to this fight. It is

not his way. He thought of going into politics at one time, and as
a beginning stood for the London County Council [in 1904],
but when he was beaten he threw up the idea. And the same way
about Ireland. He was most anxious to go on the Convention
and did all he could to get on. But when they would not put him
on it he gave up all interest in Irish politics. Now he is interested
in nothing but his work'. I told her how often I had quoted to
[W.G.] Fay at the Abbey when he was depressed 'Grip is a good
dog, but Hold Fast a better'.

SHAW TO LADY GREGORY
[ALS: Burgunder, Cornell]

Tongue Hotel. Sutherland N.B.
28th August 1925

[This was the second summer that the Shaws had holidayed in
Scotland rather than in Ireland. 'O, Caledonia! stern and wild' is a
quotation from Scott's 'Lay of the Last Minstrel'. On 11th June Yeats
had spoken in the Senate debate on divorce, attacking its proposed
prohibition in the Irish Free State as a measure oppressive to the
Protestant minority. His speech included a proud eulogy of the
Protestant Irish.]

My dear Lady Gregory
   Ireland is passing through a series of salutary disillusioning
humiliations; and the latest is having her nose put out of joint by
the north of Scotland.
   We are on the extreme verge of the northern mainland; and
we have been in Orkney and Shetland for ten days. The climate
is that of Kerry (alleged cause: the Gulf Stream) and the
mountains and moors, the lochs and bays, the granite and
heather, are a continual delight. The people are goodlooking,
civil, and free from obtrusive virtues and heroic traditions: in
short, quite likeable. Sell Coole and settle here: you will find all
the beauties of Ireland without the drawback of Irish inhabi-
tants.
   In Shetland, a zigzag strip of hillside between two oceans,
there are half a dozen Burrins to every mile of road. The
Shetland sheep is a quaint improvement on the Irish pig; and

the Shetland pony consoles one for the absence of Ireland's only dignified and intellectual animal, the donkey.

On Tuesday we move on to the west coast—Stafford Arms, Scourie, Sutherland, for a few days. We have been on the road since the 18th July; and I must soon get back to my work, which has *not* this time been accelerated by holidaying. If only Coole, and *you*, were here, we should make a perfect finish to our adventure with you.

Charlotte sends messages which I shall not repeat textually, as they verge on sentimentality.

I dare say nothing on my own account, as you will be furious at my seduction by Caledonia (not in the least stern and wild at this season in these latitudes) and betrayal of Erin.

I enclose a picture postcard—one that might be Kinvarra [Co. Galway].

Remember us favorably to W.B.Y. and his missus. I greatly like him in the Senate upholding the flag of modern civilization as the Protestant Boy who Carries the Drum.

Ever and ever

G.B.S.

LADY GREGORY: *JOURNALS*

28th [March 1926]

[Shaw was suffering from a fortnight's bout of influenza at this time. His contribution to the 13th edition of the *Encyclopaedia Britannica* (1926) was the entry on 'Socialism: Principles and Outlook'. Lady Gregory's article, published in the *Daily News* on 27th March, was 'How Great Plays are Born: the Coming of Mr O'Casey'. The book over which Shaw fell asleep was the Rt Hon. Sir James O'Connor's *History of Ireland 1798–1924*, (2 vols., London 1925). Sir Almroth Wright, an Irish-born bacteriologist, long associated with St Mary's Hospital, Paddington, was a personal friend of Shaw and a model for the central character in *The Doctor's Dilemma*. Sean O'Casey's *The Plough and the Stars*, which had caused highly emotional disturbances when performed at the Abbey in February, was now having a very successful London run at the Fortune Theatre.]

Margaret [Gregory] ... motored me to Ayot and left me there for the day. G.B.S. was sitting in the drawing-room looking very much pulled down—the maid had told me he was 'not quite so well today'. But he says he eats, sleeps, and there is nothing to complain of except the temperature going up at night, and that he cannot do any work and that frets him—the proofs of his book on Socialism are coming in and he had promised an article to the Encyclopaedia Britannica, 'it is work that other people's money depends on and that frets me'. But he was as bright and brilliant and sympathetic as usual—only I talked too much to let him say much, because he seemed so interested in everything, asked so much about the children ... and my article which he has read—and all Irish news, so that though Charlotte had said I was to take a book when he seemed tired, and sat there watching he never did. Then his doctor came and stayed to lunch and he talked all the time. And after lunch Charlotte said 'We must think what would be the most restful thing for him', and he said 'Get Lady Gregory to talk'. But the doctor then began professional talk, about aperient medicines, and I went into the other room, his working room, so simply furnished. And then Charlotte came to say the doctor was so hard to get rid of we must turn him out. But he went just then, and G.B.S. fell asleep over O'Connor's history of Ireland, and dozed till tea time, when Margaret ... came to tea and to fetch me. He waked up then and gave reminiscences. I told him I had now for the first time begun to like Dickens. He always did; hadn't ever seen him but was told by I forget who [the poet Richard Hengist Horne] that Dickens used to get immoderate fits of laughter and couldn't stop himself, and at a dinner party Mrs Dickens who had very fat arms and wore an immense number of glass bangles on them was on the other side of the table, and every now and then one of the bangles would go into her plate with a clatter, and off Dickens would go into a roar. ...

[18th April]. G.B.S. really on the mend. Charlotte reports twenty-four hours normal temperature. ...

28th [May]. I have a note from C. Shaw: 'Very good news! We went to London last week, saw Almroth Wright and he took G.B.S. straight away with him to his clinic. They have made a thorough examination and *nothing* wrong was found! It seems G.B.S. has cured himself as he said he would do. ... We have seen the *Plough and the Stars*. Wonderful! We were both worked up to a high pitch of excitement and admiration. O'Casey is a great man'.

SHAW TO LADY GREGORY
[ALS: Burgunder, Cornell]

10 Adelphi Terrace. [London]
22nd July 1926

[*The Glimpse of Reality*, the play about the 'ruffianly young Italian nobleman', originally known only as 'The Italian Play', was begun on 8th March 1909 but abandoned after some work on it later in the month. Shaw returned to the play in the following year, completing it at Parknasilla on 30th August 1910 just after his first visit to Coole. This may have led to his misrecollection of its place of composition, for he wrote 'Coole Park, Summer, 1909' on the Parknasilla section of the manuscript. Mary Grey was an actress who had appeared as Hesione Hushabye in her husband J.B. Fagan's original London production of *Heartbreak House*.]

My dear Lady Gregory

Do you remember my reading to you at Coole a little play I had written for Granville-Barker about a ruffianly young Italian nobleman disguised as a very old cackling whistling friar. I threw it aside as silly; but I am going to pad a volume of tomfooleries with it (it is not so bad as some of them); and a question has arisen as to the date of it. Do you happen to remember whether it belongs to the Augustus John visit or to another? I did not date the MS, and can find no clue.

The Labor Party is dining me publicly on Monday, my birthday, as a political demonstration. I have refused all other celebrations. Germany threatened a Shavian orgie. The British Government shews its sense of the occasion by refusing to allow my speech to be broadcast.

I am stoical about the Lane pictures, partly because I never believed they would give them up, and partly in malice, because it serves Dublin right for not securing them when it had the chance.

I have not time to finish this letter. Mary Grey came in in the middle of it, and left me only a few minutes to catch the late fee post. More when I hear from you.

Ever
G.B.S.

LADY GREGORY TO SHAW
[TLS: BL]

Coole Park. Gort
Saturday, 24th July 1926

[The passage in Montaigne that seems to come closest to the line Lady
Gregory quotes is in his essay, 'All Things Have their Day' (*Essays*,
II, Chapter 28): ' ... the only solace I find in old age [is] that it deadens
in me several desires by which life is disquieted—the care for the way
the world goes, the care for wealth, for fame, for knowledge, for
health, for myself'. On 22nd July Lady Gregory had noted in her
journal 'quite a good and very friendly letter from Lord Aberdeen in
The Times about the [Lane] pictures', and had written to thank him
for it on 23rd July.]

Dear G.B.S.

No, you cant have read that play in my hearing; if you had
done so there is no possible chance I should have forgotten it,
and I have no memory of it at all. Such a fine idea too, I should
love to hear it. I believe you must have written it before your
first visit here, in 1909 was it not, after the Blanco fight (for
which I at last forgive Lord Aberdeen after his good letter about
the pictures). I am equally aggrieved at not having heard that
play, which I am sure I should have loved, and not had the
chance of helping your memory.

I believe you will get this letter on your birthday after all.
Well, it brings you another load of good wishes; and congratu-
lations to the world in general for having you in strength and
vigour to help its sanity like the pike that is put in fish ponds to
chase the perch and keep them healthy. Someone—Montaigne
—?— says the advantage of old age is that 'it gives one a more
courageous and disdainful view of life' or some such words, but
I cant fancy you even on its threshold. And as to Charlotte, she
looked in her teens that last day at Ayot, as Marian would say 'as
if she had gone to the grinding young'. So God bless you both,
and even if you don't pity Dublin say a little prayer for me who
have carried on this fight through the years in which I should be
making my soul.

Always affectionately
A Gregory

SHAW TO LADY GREGORY
[APCS: Berg, NYPL]

Ayot St Lawrence. Welwyn
4th April 1927

['Mrs F.' was Hallie Flanagan, teacher, theatre scholar, and stage
director, who was researching in Europe for a book on comparative
styles of theatre production, under a Guggenheim Fellowship. The
move from Adelphi Terrace to Whitehall Court was undertaken by
the servants at the end of July 1927 after the Shaws had departed for a
holiday in Italy, spent at Stresa and environs.]

Why does Mrs F. want me to make an assignation in France? I
shant be there.

We shall get away to Malvern on the 11th to enable Charlotte
to shake off the rest of her flu; and that is about all.

We have a move on—leaving Adelphi Terrace in June for
Whitehall Court (service flat) as Charlotte is tired of having two
houses on her hands.

G.B.S.

SHAW TO LADY GREGORY
[APCS: Berg, NYPL]

Ayot St Lawrence. Welwyn
8th June 1927

Tell the creature to write to me when he arrives in London
and to say that he is your friend.

The book [*The Intelligent Woman's Guide*], frightfully con-
fused, and needing months of work on the proofs (it's in print)
contains 225,000 words, equal to 12½ plays. It has half killed
me, and will probably complete its fell work this year. We are in
the throes of moving from Adelphi Terrace to Whitehall Court,
or rather preparing to. Otherwise all well.

G.B.S.

LADY GREGORY: *JOURNALS*

[29th May 1928]

[*The Intelligent's Woman's Guide* was to be published on 1st June. The Dublin meeting to which Lady Gregory invited Shaw to speak was held under the auspices of the Friends of the National Collections of Ireland at the Theatre Royal on 17th June, to publicise once again the case for the return of the Lane pictures and to urge the building of a gallery to house the Municipal Gallery collection, since the lack of such a building was one of the arguments used against returning the Lane bequest.]

G.B.S. has sent me his new book, the *Intelligent Woman's Guide to Socialism*. That will be good reading. ...

30 May. ... I lay on the sofa reading G.B.S.'s book, first the last chapter, then the beginning—so clear, so simple, so convincing. I suppose that is why I was suddenly gripped with the idea that if he would come over and speak at the Dublin meeting it would make a triumph; and this so strongly that I came to my writing table and have written asking this of him. Perhaps tomorrow I may tear up the letter thinking it hopeless. No, I think I will send it, and say my prayers. ...

2 June. ... G.B.S.'s Socialism leads one on. I read last night more than was good for my eyes. Being a worker myself my withers are unwrung, but it would be hard to get the wasters into the traces.

A horse can only kick, can't voice his excuses. If the joy of work begun, work completed (I won't say anything of the hard dragging of the plough at noontide) were known all the world with any ounce of energy would hurry to take its share. And just now my back aches after some hours of going through these old diaries, striking out what is not worth reading or might give pain, and my eyes warn me that I must not spend too long with the *Intelligent Woman* bye and bye. I find it very hard to put down.

———————

Sean O'Casey, whose first plays at the Abbey, *The Shadow of a Gunman* and *Juno and the Paycock*, had done a great deal to

restore the theatre's fortunes, became a good friend of Lady
Gregory, who encouraged his early work. Since his move to
London in 1926, he had become friendly with the Shaws. In
March 1928 he submitted to the Abbey directors his play about
the First World War, *The Silver Tassie*. Lady Gregory, Lennox
Robinson and Yeats were all in agreement that the play needed,
at least, substantial revision before it could be produced, and
Lady Gregory returned the play to O'Casey with copies of the
criticisms of all three. The fourth director, Walter Starkie, who
was away at the time, subsequently dissented from the view of
the others, arguing that, in view of O'Casey's previous achievement, they should have produced the play and left the judgment to the audience. O'Casey reacted angrily, being particularly indignant over Yeats's critique of the play, though he did
not resent Lady Gregory's part in the rebuff. Withdrawing the
play from the Abbey, he went ahead with its publication, and
authorised publication of the correspondence between himself
and the directors in *The Observer* on 3rd June 1928. A bitter
press controversy followed.

Shaw took O'Casey's side in the dispute, expressing his view
in a letter of 19th June [ALS: Sotheby, 30th June 1982]:

My dear Sean
    What a hell of a play! I wonder how it will hit the public. Of
course the Abbey should have produced it—as Starkie
rightly says—whether it liked it or not. But the people who
knew your uncle when you were a child (so to speak) always
want to correct your exercises; and this was what disabled the
usually competent W.B.Y. and Lady Gregory.
    Still, it is surprising that they fired so very wide consider-
ing their marksmanship. A good realistic first act, like Juno,
an incongruously phantasmic second act, trailing off into a
vague and unreal sequel: could anything be wronger? What *I*
see is a deliberately unrealistic phantasmo-poetic first act,
intensifying in exactly the same mode into a climax of war
imagery in the second act, and then two acts of almost
unbearable realism bringing down all the Voodoo war poetry
with an ironic crash to earth in ruins. There is certainly no
falling-off or loss of grip: the hitting gets harder and harder
right through to the end.

Now if Yeats had said 'Its too savage: I cant stand it' he would have been in order. You really are a ruthless ironfisted blaster and blighter of your species; and in this play there is none righteous—no, not one. Your moral is always that the Irish ought not to exist; and you are suspected of opining, like Shakespear, that the human race ought not to exist—unless, indeed, you like them like that, which you can hardly expect Lady Gregory, with her kindness for Kiltartan, to do. Yeats himself, with all his extraordinary cleverness and subtlety, which comes out just when you give him up as a hopeless fool and (in this case) deserts him when you expect him to be equal to the occasion, is not a man of this world; and when you hurl an enormous smashing chunk of it at him he dodges it, small blame to him.

However, we can talk about it when we meet, which I understand is to be on Thursday next week. This is only to prepare you for my attitude. Until then, cheerio, Titan.

G.B.S.

———————

SHAW TO LADY GREGORY

[TLS: Mugar Library, Boston University]

Ayot St Lawrence. Welwyn
26th June 1928

[Lady Gregory's *Three Last Plays*, published in 1928, were *The Would-be Gentleman*, *Sancho's Master*, and *Dave*. Ernest Thesiger, one of Shaw's favourite actors, created the part of the Dauphin in the London production of *Saint Joan*. Manuel de Falla's operatic work *The Puppet Show of Master Pedro*, an adventure of Don Quixote in six scenes (libretto by J.B. Trend), was performed at the Court Theatre on 12th June.]

My dear Lady Gregory

In a desperate attempt to cope with last month's letters I discover, with a relief that I shall not disguise, that the meeting about the Gallery, at which I was to have spoken by your order, took place last Wednesday, and that evasions are now super-fluous. You must forgive as best you can.

I am not to be trusted in the matter of the Lane pictures. They represent a reaction which was inevitable and beneficial in the last half of the nineteenth century; but the benefit of it is now so thoroughly exhausted that the impulse they would give to painting in Ireland in the twentieth century would be a shove in the direction of the day before yesterday. When they were exhibited at the National Gallery here, having no longer the character and interest of incidents in a campaign, I did not like them. In Ireland they might be effective in starting an affec-tation, and an obsolete one at that, but not in inspiring genuine Irish genius. Consequently the very last reason I should give for the erection of a gallery ['in Dublin' is here inserted, not in Shaw's hand] (if I had never known Lane and never known you) would be to provide a home for those pictures. I am quite content that they should stay where they are.

Now to get up at a public meeting with you beside me on the platform and say that one of the best reasons for venturing on a new gallery is the improbability of the British Government giving the Lane pictures up as long as a scrap of interest attaches to them is not a thing to cross the seas for. You were better without me.

My personal sympathy with Hugh Lane leans rather towards the very justifiable fury in which, having cast his pearls before swine, he picked them up and threw them to the Bull, than towards his subsequent relenting.

Why did you and W.B.Y. treat O'Casey as a baby? Starkie was right: you should have done the play anyhow. Sean is now *hors concours*. It is literally a hell of a play; but it will clearly force its way on to the stage; and Yeats should have submitted to it as a calamity imposed on him by the Act of God if he could not welcome it as another Juno. Besides, he was extraordinarily wrong about it on the facts. The first act is not a bit realistic: it is deliberately fantastic chanted poetry. This is intensified to a climax in the second act. Then comes a ruthless return for the last two acts to the fiercest ironic realism. That is so like Yeats. Give him a job with which you feel sure he will play Bunthorne, and he will astonish you with his unique cleverness and sub-tlety. Give him one that any second rater could manage with credit, and as likely as not he will make an appalling mess of it. He has certainly fallen in up to the neck over O'C.

But this is not a very nice letter, is it? Consequently the very last sort of letter I want to send you; so I will stop before I become intolerable.

Ever
G.B.S.

Turn over. There is a
postscript on the back.

PS I quite forgot to say (O'Casey having interrupted) that of the Last Plays, which will, I hope, be followed by Positively the Last and The Very Last and A Few More, I of course liked Dave the best. Don Quixote cannot be put on the stage: its action cannot be represented there. Both Tree and (still) Thesiger tried to make me attempt it; but the [W.G.] Wills-[Henry] Irving and other versions as well as my professional sense forbade me. Manuel de Falla has set your puppet show scene to music. It has just been played at the Court Theatre. It is a bit of fun; but it isn't really Don Quixote.

PPS I am to see Yeats tomorrow evening, and Sean the day after; but I presume it is about the pictures that Y. is coming.

[On 3rd July, Shaw wrote to O'Casey, who was still negotiating conditions for a possible performance of *The Silver Tassie* at the Abbey [ALS at foot of TLS, O'Casey to Shaw: Sotheby, 30th June 1982]: 'I have just heard from Lady Gregory. I gather that she has been really on your side all through'.]

LADY GREGORY: *JOURNALS*

7th October [1929]

[*The Apple Cart*, first presented in English as the inaugural production of the Malvern Festival on 19th August, was now playing in London. Lady Gregory had just been to see C.B. Cochran's production of *The Silver Tassie* at the Apollo Theatre with Charles Laughton in the leading role. Lennox Robinson's play, *Give a Dog*, was published in

1928. John Dulanty, Irish commissioner for trade in Britain, was to become High Commissioner for Ireland in 1930 and, eventually, the first Ambassador of the Irish Republic to the United Kingdom.]

At Ayot, three wonderful days. G.B.S. and Charlotte called for me and motored me there. They had given me dinner at their own flat in London, and taken me on to *The Apple Cart*—could only get an upper box whence I saw and heard well, but they were cramped. The play went splendidly, finely staged—('that dress cost a hundred guineas' G.B.S. whispered and I said he must not say that aloud); wonderful 'back-chat'—give and take—the many vanquished in the end by the one, the King.

G.B.S. later, autographing some pamphlets for me, wrote on the programme 'Lady Gregory and I saw this play together and she liked it better than I did'. It is extremely clever, the tossing of the plates of conversation, the battledore and shuttlecock of talk. But my mind goes back to the *Tassie*—we ought not to have rejected it—we should have held out against L[ennox] R[obinson] that last evening of the season when the order to return it was given—it was rejected.

Charlotte told me L.R. had written G.B.S. an extraordinary letter, abusing him for what he had said in support of the *Tassie* and saying 'I enclose a really good play'—and this was that unhappy *Give a Dog* that they had I think been too vexed to read.

I liked sitting with him after dinner listening to the music from the wireless. And before I left he said he would like to give me one—for Coole! So *very* kind and I had been longing for music on those lonely evenings, had almost taken back the old gramophone from the maids! ...

... he had given one Talkie [Movietone News, 1928] to show how it should be done, and later he had been asked to do two more at £800 each, but had refused. Was he right? The vessel of ointment came to mind that could have been sold for so many coins to give to the poor. But G.B.S. has his own conscience and I dare not judge it—he is so wonderfully kind and does all on principle not impulse. So wonderfully kind—only he held out against writing an article for the *Spectator Supplement* that Dulanty wants for Patrick's Day. Evelyn Wrench, the Editor, had said 'There is no use printing it unless there is something of

Bernard Shaw, and there is no use writing to him for he won't answer'. However he let me write [to Dulanty] saying he gave me leave to ask him again when the time comes, and I am sure he will do it then. I want it because it would repay Dulanty for his energy about the Lane pictures.

SHAW TO LADY GREGORY
[ALS: Burgunder, Cornell]

Ayot St Lawrence. Welwyn
29th October 1929

[The photographs mentioned were presumably taken on Lady Gregory's visit to Ayot.]

Dear Lady Gregory
The portable wireless has just arrived, and is very satisfactory. Its description is Pye's Portable 5 value Receiver, No 25/C. The makers are Pye Radio, Ltd, Radio Works, Cambridge. The price in England is £23–10–0. I dont know what the I.F.S. import duties may add to that; so I enclose £25 (and 6^d exchange on London cheque). If you order from the garage it will be for the retailer to deliver to you in working order.

The photographs are not yet ready, as I have to use up a strip of three dozen negatives before I can get any of them printed.

With both our loves
G.B.S.

[Lady Gregory took delivery of her wireless on 12th November but, as she noted in her journal, 'It cost £30 (£5 duty in this) ... (I have not told this to G.B.S., he would rail at the heavy customs)'.]

SHAW TO LADY GREGORY
[ALS: Wellesley College Library]

Ayot St Lawrence. Welwyn
24th February 1930

[Lady Gregory had continued to press Shaw for a contribution to the St Patrick's Day issue of the *Spectator*, writing both to Shaw himself, and to Charlotte to remind Shaw. William H. Wise and Company were the publishers of the American 'Ayot St Lawrence Edition' of

Shaw's collected works, published 1930–32. Lady Gregory had been collecting together the copies of Shaw's pamphlets given to her over the years. Mary McSwiney, the sister of Terence McSwiney, the Mayor of Cork who had died on hunger strike in Brixton Prison in 1920, was, like Maud Gonne, an extreme Republican. In referring to the 'Bacon King', Shaw was alluding to a now discredited hypothesis presented by Gibbon in *Decline and Fall of the Roman Empire* that the historical figure underlying the legendary tale of St George, England's patron saint, was the tyrannical and predacious George of Cappadocia (d. AD 361), who supplied bacon to the military. Shaw's verse was an inversion of the well-known rhyme by Michael Moran written a century earlier:

> Saint Patrick was a gintleman,
> He came of decent people,
> In Dublin town he built a church,
> And upon't put a steeple ...

Shaw's version was not in fact printed in the special 'Ireland Today' issue of the *Spectator* published on 15th March 1930.]

My dear Lady Gregory

Tell Dulanty and the Spectator and St Patrick and all whom it may concern that I, being a distracted man trying to do just what you are doing, only against time specified in contract with Wise & Co. of America, will see them all sempiternally

before I will add one word of their silly stunt to my backbreaking burden. Who cares about St Patrick now? Is not the Irish State free? Are not contributions from Maud Gonne and Mary McSweeney to be had for the asking? They probably dont know that St Patrick wasnt an Irishman. I do.

And what business is it of the Spectator's anyhow? Let it look to its own wretched country and its own patron saint, the Bacon King.

Away with it. Shoo!!

I sympathize with you inexpressibly in your present afflicting job. I curse the day in which I ever undertook it. We should have exchanged: you collecting me and I you.

Ever
G.B.S.

[Accompanied by card headed 'With Bernard Shaw's compliments', dated 24th February 1930.]

I think [this] will be sufficiently convincing.
I am really far too busy to think of it.

GBS

See over for contribution.

St Patrick wasnt Irish born
Nor bred from decent people
Nor did he build a Dublin church
And on it put a steeple.

SHAW TO LADY GREGORY
[APCS: Berg, NYPL]

Buxton (we return to Ayot on Wednesday)
25th May 1930

[Shaw's 1885 short story 'The Miraculous Revenge' appeared, not in *Samhain*, the official organ of the Abbey Theatre, but in *The Shanachie* (No 1, Spring 1906), a Dublin literary journal published by Maunsel. Lady Gregory found a copy of the story for Shaw and sent it to him, as she wrote in her journal for 2nd June, 'rather proud of having brought it down at the first shot'. Charlotte, stricken with scarlatina, was incapacitated for several weeks, dangerously ill.]

I am collecting the very few short stories I have perpetrated to make a volume in my Collected Works. One of them I have lost. It was called The Miraculous Revenge; and I seem to recollect that it was reprinted in an Irish magazine with a barbarous name—Samhain or something like that, probably pronounced O'Shaughnessy—which was connected with Abbey Street. Could I buy, beg, borrow, steal, or otherwise obtain access to the number containing my story, if it really appeared there? Do you remember anything about it?

We came here at Easter for a week; but Charlotte fell ill and nearly died on me. However, she triumphed; and is ready for the journey home on Wednesday.

G.B.S.

SHAW TO LADY GREGORY
[APCS: Berg, NYPL]

Ayot St Lawrence. Welwyn
3rd June 1930

[Shaw was here returning the copy of *The Shanachie*, containing 'The Miraculous Revenge', which she had provided.]

Dear Lady Gregory

Many many thanks. I have just discovered another copy; so I need not send this one through the compositor's fingers.

Charlotte is now practically well.

Ever
G.B.S.

LADY GREGORY: *JOURNALS*

[12th November 1930]

[Charlotte Shaw had fractured her arm and her pelvis in a fall.]

As I write there is a post card on my writing table—a very frowning G.B.S. on it: I had written to give sympathy to Charlotte, who, the papers said, had fallen in the street and broken her leg in two places. He writes 'This picture will give you a notion of the effect of Charlotte's accident on me. She is black all down her left side, and is looking forward to being only blue presently. The two broken bones were only cracked. They are knitting up satisfactorily and will not leave her crippled in any way. She has not been in pain except when moving and she can now move much more than at first without hurting herself, so it might have been worse and will soon be better'. He is always so kind in illness—even outside his own 'milieu'. I always remember the hours he spent driving his car over the mountains in search of the doctor when Anne [Gregory] had been thrown when riding, and her arm put out.

SHAW TO LADY GREGORY
[APCS: HRC]

Ayot St Lawrence. Welwyn
28th June 1931

[St John Ervine had written to Shaw complaining that his fees were not being paid for performances of his plays at the Abbey. Shaw sent on Ervine's letter to Lady Gregory, having written to him on the same day [APCS: HRC]: 'Miss Patch [Shaw's secretary] tells me that there is nothing to complain of. They always pay. They put on Blanco Posnet for the week ending the 14th March, and paid on the 27th. No arrears. Possibly they treat me with special consideration. If they didnt I should tell the Society of Authors to blacklist them and ask for security before granting further authorisations. *On no account waive or undercut fees*. I'll write to Lady Gregory and let you know the result'.]

Dear Lady Gregory

I have written to Ervine to say that I have nothing to complain of; but I think I had better let you see his letter.

I am writing another play [*Too True to be Good*]; and I am going to Russia for a week to see for myself.

That is all the news as far as I am concerned. Have you any for me?

Ever
G.B.S.

INDEX